# Question Bank on Forestry

# Question Bank on Forestry

**Gopal Shukla**
**Nazir A. Pala**
**Vineeta**
**Sumit Chakravarty**

Department of Forestry
Uttar Banga Krishi Viswavidyala
Pundibari - 736165
Cooch Behar, West Bengal

***A Paperback Division of***
New India Publishing Agency
101, Vikas Surya Plaza, CU Block, LSC Market
Pitam Pura, New Delhi 110 034, India
Phone: + 91 (11)27 34 17 17 Fax: + 91(11) 27 34 16 16
Email: info@nipabooks.com
Web: www.nipabooks.com

Feedback at feedbacks@nipabooks.com



ISBN : 978-93-86546-37-1



Composed, Designed and Printed in India

উত্তরবঙ্গ কৃষি বিশ্ববিদ্যালয়
পুণ্ডিবাড়ী, কোচবিহার , পশ্চিমবঙ্গ-৭৩৬১৬৫
UTTAR BANGA KRISHI VISWAVIDYALAYA
P.O. PUNDIBARI, DIST. COOCH BEHAR, WEST BENGAL- 736165

ড: চিরন্তন চট্টোপাধ্যায়
উপাচার্য
Dr. Chirantan Chattopadhyay
M.Sc (Ag.)(BCKV), Ph.D. (IARI)
ICAR: ARS
FNAASc, FPSI, FPPAI, FISMPP, FISOR
FIMS, FSRMR
Vice-Chancellor

ফোন/Phone: 03582-270141/270013 (O)
ফ্যাক্স/Fax: 03582-270249
মো./Mob: +91-9434748016
ইমেল/E-mail: vcubkvv@gmail.com
ওয়েবসাইট/ Website: www.ubkv.ac.in

Ref. No. VC/UBKV- 1399

Date- 30 Jan 2017

# Foreword

Forests are the store houses of the biodiversity harbouring thousands of flora and fauna. They restore ecosystem regulation and provide number of tangible and intangible ecosystem services to mankind.

These diverse forest resources are diminishing day by day with the advancement of industrialization and other development activities. The forest resources of the country have been always looked as revenue generation sector and have the potential to provide employment to several rural communities. With increasing global warming and degradation of environmental conditions, the importance of the forests is being realized at local, regional, state, national as well as at international level. Forests are one of the main terrestrial GHG mitigation components and the only hope for several forest dependent communities needs to be conserved for future.

Forestry as an academic subject has also been getting promotion for introduction into mainstream subjects like agriculture, horticulture and other allied subjects. Forestry has been also one of the subjects for Indian Forest Service and other state level exams like ACF, Range Officer at administrative level. At University level, ARS, JRF, SRF, NET and banking sector forestry is being opted as the subject of interest by number of students.

The present book, "Question Bank on Forestry" is a compilation of the several subjects of forestry (Silviculture, Forestry Management, Biometry, Tree Improvement, Agroforestry, Biodiversity and Other allied subjects) and will be helpful in fulfilling the needs of IFS, JRF, SRF, ARS, NET and other interested graduates of Forestry.

I believe the book is having good informative collection and for this authors for all the hard work. congratulate the authors for all the hard work.

30 Jan 17

**Vice-Chancellor**

# Preface

The Forestry Education dates back to 18$^{th}$ Century when it was started by some institutes in Europe. In India Forestry Education was introduced at the University level by starting M. Sc. (Forestry) in 1976 at Solan. Now at present due to population growth, industrialization and urbanization more and more trained man power in forestry sector is required. In the era of climate change the importance of "Forestry Science" is increasing day by day as because forest is the cheap option to combat climate change and offer clean environment. Importance of forestry is increasing day by day to produce forestry professionals with forestry education and to meet challenges of high forest productivity. Forest is a commodity which if managed scientifically can be a major source for protection of environment as well as will be helpful to sustain livelihood of the dependent communities. To fulfill and achieve these goals and demands we need a trained and professional man power in forestry sector. This book entitled "Question Bank on Forestry" has been constructed to fulfill the dream of younger minds. Book comprises of the multiple choice type questions, true & false and fills in the blanks for JRF/SRF/NET/ARS and other competitive examination. The questions from each and every subject of forestry are constructed with full care and avoid the complication so that students understand the subject in an easy manner. The book have separate chapters highlighting the forestry history, law, silviculture, forest management, biodiversity, agroforestry, forest seed, nursery management, comprehensive list of forestry and ICAR institutes and other event related to forestry.

Authors

# Contents

# 1

# Agroforestry

1. The tree species suitable for Agroforestry in hot and arid climate is
   a. *Prosopis cineraria* b. *Albizia lebbeck*
   c. *Salix alba* d. *Eucalyptus globulus*

2. *Acacia Senegal* is suitable for Agroforestry in
   a. Hill soils b. Alluvial soils
   c. Laterite soils d. Desert soils

3. Find the odd man out with reference to suitability of the species to a particular site factor?
   a. *Prosopis chilensis* b. *Acacia tortilis*
   c *Acacia nilotica* d. *Juglans regia*

4. A non-leguminous nitrogen fixing tree species is
   a. *Leucaena leucocephala* b. *Casuarina equisetifolia*
   c. *Albizia lebbeck* d. *Acacia nilotica*

5. The following species like *Eucalyptus* hybrid, *Prosopis chilensis*, *Gliricidia maculata* and *Cassia siamea* are suitable for Agroforestry system because of
   a. The species are generally not grazed b. Deciduous in nature
   c. Nitrogen fixing d. All of these

6. *Casuarina equisetifolia* is preferred for Agroforestry because it is
   a. Atmospheric nitrogen fixer in the soil b. The bole is upright and straight
   c. None of these d. Both a&b

7. In some parts of India, *Eucalyptus* hybrid, *Populus deltoids*, *Leucaena leucocephala* and *Casuarina equisetifolia* became popular because these species could be harvested within a period of eight years.
   a. The statement is correct
   b. The statement is partially correct as harvest period is higher than mentioned
   c. The statement is partially incorrect as all the species mentioned are not popular
   d. The statement is incorrect

8. Agrisilvicultural system classification of Agroforestry is based on
   a. Nature of components
   b. Arrangement of components
   c. Functional basis
   d. Ecological basis

9. The Agroforestry system that is based mainly on temporal arrangement of components is
   a. Home gardens
   b. Shifting cultivation
   c. Tea gardens
   d. None of these

10. Deforestation refers to
    a. Planting of trees
    b. Cultivation of crops
    c. Disappearance of forests
    d. Depletion of forests

11. Which of the following is not a feature of shifting cultivation?
    a. Parts of the forest are cut and burnt in rotation
    b. Seeds are sown in the ashes
    c. Plots cleared are cultivated for a few years and then left follow
    d. Single crop is grown on these plots

12. Local name for Sweden Agriculture in India is
    a. Milpa
    b. Lading
    c. Kumri
    d. Chena

13. In which part of world Sweden agriculture is practiced?
    a. Asia, Africa and S. America
    b. Asia, S. America and Thailand
    c. Asia, Africa and China
    d. Asia, S. America and Europe

14. What was not a factor in discouragement of shifting agriculture?
    a. Land so used could not grow timber
    b. It made it harder for government to calculate taxes
    c. Many local communities were displaced
    d. There was danger of flames spreading

15. ICRAF came into existence in which year
    a. 1975
    b. 1985
    c. 1977
    d. 1980

16. Taungya system was introduced in South Africa in the year
    a. 1925
    b. 1908
    c. 1887
    d. 1808

17. First advance study centre on Agroforestry for post-graduate education was established in year
    - a. 1990
    - b. 1992
    - c. 1993
    - d. 1994

18. When forest plantations are established along with agriculture crops by employing contract labour such plantations are called as
    - a. Village taungya
    - b. Leased taungya
    - c. Departmental taungya
    - d. Both (a) and (b) are true

19. Ratio of height and width in shelter belts should be roughly
    - a. 1:15
    - b. 1:10
    - c. 1:20
    - d. 1:5

20. Minimum length of a shelter belt should be about how many times its height in m.?
    - a. 20
    - b. 15
    - c. 25
    - d. 30

21. A wind break of 20 m height will give protection from
    - a. 100-500 m
    - b. 200- 800 m
    - c. up to 1 km
    - d. up to 2 km

22. Most dominating agroforestry system in humid tropics is
    - a. Silvipasture
    - b. Silvihorticulture
    - c. Homegardens
    - d. Hortipasture

23. To allow more light inside the agroforestry system the rows of trees should be planted in which direction
    - a. East- west
    - b. North-south
    - c. South-west
    - d. North-west

24. Which among the following is a key feature of Diagnosis and Design?
    - a. Flexibility
    - b. Productivity
    - c. Sustainability
    - d. Adoptability

25. Which among the following is true while designing agroforestry system?
    - a. Design and evaluation precedes diagnostic stage
    - b. Planning stage precedes design and evaluation stage
    - c. Planning stage precedes prediagnostic stage
    - d. Design and evaluation precedes planning stage

26. Criteria of good agroforestry design are
    a. Productivity and sustainability
    b. Sustainability and adoptability
    c. Productivity and adoptability
    d. Productivity, adoptability and sustainability
27. Which among the following is a systematic design for laying out agroforestry trials?
    a. 'Y' design
    b. Beehive design
    c. Fan design
    d. Nearest neighbor
28. Which among the following doesn't match with rest of the choices?
    a. Homegardens
    b. Agrisilvipasture
    c. Multitier agroforestry system
    d. Homestead gardens
29. Headquarter of ICRAF is located in which country
    a. Australia
    b. Kenya
    c. New Zealand
    d. India
30. Headquarter of NARCF is located in which city of India
    a. Solan
    b. Ludhiana
    c. Jhansi
    d. Dehra Dun
31. Suitable tree species for Agroforestry are
    a. NFT
    b. MPTS
    c. a and b
    d. None of the above
32. Major causes of soil erosion is
    a. Deforestation
    b. Mining
    c. a and b
    d. None of the above
33. Which among the following is a major cause of deforestation?
    a. Shifting cultivation
    b. Agriculture
    c. Dam construction
    d. All of them
34. Oldest agroforestry system of the world is
    a. Block plantation
    b. Taungya system
    c. Shifting cultivation
    d. a and c both
35. Taungya system was first started at
    a. Burma
    b. South Africa
    c India
    d. None of the above

36. Who introduced Taungya system in India?
    a. Brandis
    b. Swaminathan
    c. Tipu Sultan
    d. Maclland

37. How many types of Taungya systems exist?
    a. 1
    b. 2
    c. 3
    d. 4

38. Most successful Taungya system is
    a. Department
    b. Village
    c. Leased
    d. a and b both

39. Taungya system was introduced in India in the year
    a.1925
    b. 1908
    c. 1896
    d. 1808

40. In which state Taungya system was first introduced in India
    a. West Bengal
    b. Sikkim
    c. Uttar Pradesh
    d. Kerala

41. In which year Taungya system was adopted in Kerala
    a. 1925
    b. 1908
    c. 1920
    d. 1808

42. In which year Taungya system was adopted in Uttar Pradesh
    a. 1925
    b. 1911
    c. 1923
    d. 1931

43. In which year Taungya system was adopted in Madhya Pradesh
    a. 1925
    b. 1921
    c. 1900
    d. 1931

44. Taungya system is famous for
    a. Teak Plantation
    b. Sal Plantation
    c. a and b both
    d. Coconut Plantation

45. Shifting cultivation is mostly practiced in which region
    a. North East Region
    b. Eastern Region
    c. Western Region
    d. Southern Region

46. Agroforestry work was started during which five year plan
    a. First five year
    b. Third five year
    c. Six five year
    d. Seventh five year

47. Basis of arranging component in Home garden is
    a. Height  b. Diameter
    c. Maturity  d. None of the above

48. According to Nair (1987) agroforestry system is classified into….. number of types?
    a. 2  b. 4
    c. 5  d. 3

49. Land without crops in called
    a. Taungya  b. Fallow land
    c. a & b  d. None of the above

50. Objective of improved fallow species in shifting cultivation is
    a. Sustain the crop yield  b. Recover depleted soil nutrients
    c. Increase forest cover  d. None of the above

51. Institute responsible for agroforestry research in India
    a. ICFRE & FRI  b. ICAR & NRCAF
    c. a and b  d. None of the above

52. How many broad agroecological regions are in India?
    a. 10  b. 8
    c. 5  d. 9

53. How many agroclimatic regions are there in India?
    a. 15  b. 11
    c. 12  d. 13

54. Which agroforestry system is practiced without capital input?
    a. Taungya  b. Shifting cultivation
    c. Silvipostoral system  d. Aquaforestry

55. Shifting cultivation is also known as
    a. Jhum  b. Taungya
    c. a and b  d. None of the above

56. Present day fallow period is shorter due to
    a. Adequate rainfall  b. Accurate land shortage
    c. a & b  d. None of the above

57. Suitable plant species for improved fallow cultivation is
   a. NFT
   b. MPTs
   c. TBOs
   d. a & b

58. In which year Taungya system was started in Burma
   a. 1850
   b. 1887
   c. 1860
   d. 1840

59. In southern part of India Taungya system is known as
   a. Jhum
   b. Kumari
   c. Podu
   d. a & b

60. Modified form of shifting cultivation is
   a. Agrosilviculture
   b. Taungya
   c. Improved fallow
   d. None of the above

61. In which area first Taungya plantation was raised in India
   a. North Bengal
   b. Assam
   c. Odisha
   d. Kerala

62. Size of village Taungya is normally
   a. 1 ha
   b. 0.5 ha
   c. 0.8 to 1.7 ha
   d. 1.5 ha

63. Main aim of Taungya system was
   a. Regeneration of teak plantation
   b. Regeneration of Sal plantation
   c. Food production
   d. a & b

64. Main function of multi species tree garden is
   a. Fuel production
   b. Fruit production
   c. Wood and Fodder production
   d. a & c

65. Alley cropping is also known as
   a. Intercropping
   b. Hedgerow intercropping
   c. Mixed cropping
   d. None of the above

66. Main aim of alley cropping system is
   a. Sustain crop yield
   b. Improvement of soil & microcli mate
   c. Reducing soil erosion
   d. all of them

67. Hedgerow should be planted in which direction
   a. North-South b. South-West
   c. East-West d. North-East

68. In hedgerow system spacing between R x R is (m)
   a. 4 x 8 b. 6 x 8
   c. 5 x 8 d. 3 x 8

69. In hedgerow system spacing between P x P is (m)
   a. 0.4 x 2 b. 0.6 x 2
   c. 0.25 x 2 d. 0.3 x 2.5

70. In hedgerow system closer spacing is used in which region
   a. Hill b. Humid
   c. Tropical d. Arid

71.In hedgerow system wider spacing is used in which region
   a. Arid b. Sub humid & semi arid
   c. Sub tropical d. Temperate

72. Several row of trees established at right angles to prevailing wind is known as
   a. Wind breaks b. Alley cropping
   c. Shelter belt d. a and c

73. Main aim of shelter belt is
   a. Protect crop from insect & Pest b. Reduce rainfall
   c. Reduce wind velocity d. None of the above

74. Ideal shape for shelter belt is
   a. Rectangular b. Triangular
   c. Both a and b d. None of the above

75. Suitable position of tall tree in shelter belt is
   a. Centre b. Outer side
   c. Both a and b d. Corner

76. Ratio for height and spacing in shelter belt is
   a. 1: 10 b. 1: 12
   c. 1: 20 d. 2: 10

77. Length of shelter belt should be
   a. 10 times of tree height b. 25 times of tree height
   c. 15 times of tree height d. 5 times of tree height

78. Ideal width of shelter belt in India is
   a. 5 m
   b. 20 m
   c. 50 m
   d. 40 m

79. Which species is not suitable in single row shelter belt?
   a. Eucalyptus
   b. Dalbergia
   c. Gamar
   d. Arjuna

80. Strip of trees and or shrubs planted to protect field is
   a. Wind breaks
   b. Shelter belts
   c. Both a and b
   d. None of the above

81. Height of wind break depends upon
   a. Size of tree
   b. Size of sheltered area
   c. Both a and b
   d. None of the above

82. Wind breaks reduce the open wind speed up to
   a. 25 times of tree height
   b. 35 times of tree height
   c. 45 times of tree height
   d. 15 times of tree height

83. Ideal length for wind breaks is
   a. 22 times of tree height
   b. 12 times of tree height
   c. 15 times of tree height
   d. 10 times of tree height

84. Number of rows in wind breaks depends upon
   a. Value & availability of land
   b. Productivity of land
   c. Ownership right of land
   d. None of the above

85. Single row wind break is good for which type of land
   a. High value land
   b. Degraded land
   c. Sloppy land
   d. Both a and b

86. Why eucalyptus species is not suitable for single row wind breaks?
   a. Due to high water requirement
   b. Due to self pruning
   c. Due to open crown
   d. all of them

87. Wind breaks should be planted in which direction
   a. East-West
   b. North-South
   c. Only East
   d. Only West

88. When woody plant is combined with pasture the system is called
   a. Silvopastoral
   b. Silvo-Agro-Pastoral
   c. Agropastrol
   d. Both a and b

89. Silvopastoral system is mostly practiced in which area
   a. Cold
   b. Dry
   c. Rainy
   d. None of the above

90. Silvopastoral system is classified into....... number of types
   a. 3
   b. 4
   c. 5
   d. 2

91. Protein bank is the example of which type of agroforestry system
   a. Silvopastoral
   b. Agropastoral
   c. Hortipastoral
   d. Pastoral

92. Living fence of fodder trees & hedge comes under which agroforestry system
   a. Alley cropping
   b. Silvopastoral
   c. Hortipastoral
   d. Block plantation

93. Tree and shrubs in pasture is referred as
   a. Agroforestry
   b. Fodder production
   c. Silvopastoral
   d. None of the above

94. How many types of agrosilvopastrol systems are practiced?
   a. 2
   b. 4
   c. 3
   d. 1

95. Home garden falls under which type of agroforestry system
   a. Agrosilvopastoral
   b. Silvopastoral
   c. Both a and b
   d. Wood hedgerows

96. Most preferred agroforestry system of humid tropics is
   a. Home garden
   b. Hedge row
   c. Shifting cultivation
   d. Aquaforestry

97. Suitable agroforestry system for high rainfall area is
   a. Shifting cultivation
   b. Shelter belt
   c. Home garden
   d. None of the above

98. Main crop of home garden is
   a. Fruit trees
   b. Vegetables
   c. Lemon
   d. Both a & b

99. Types of components arranged in home garden are
   a. 3
   b. 2
   c. 4
   d. 5

100. Spatial arrangement is the main feature of which agroforestry system

a. Improved fellow
b. Shifting cultivation
c. Taungya
d. Home garden

101. In India, generally the size of home garden is

a. 0.2 to 0.5 ha
b. 0.5 ha
c. 0.2 ha
d. 0.2 to 0.4 ha

102. Primary objective of home garden is

a Wood production
b. Food production
c. Fodder production
d. Soil protection

103. How many strata are there in home gardens?

a. 3 to 4
b. 2 to 4
c. 1 to 4
d. Both a & b

104. Which agroforestry system supports higher diversity?

a. Home garden
b. Taungya
c. Shifting cultivation
d. None of the above

105. Which type of arrangement is followed in dense mixed stand?

a. Spatial arrangement
b. Temporal arrangement
c. Both a and b
d. None of the above

106. Type of agroforestry system suitable for small land holding?

a. Tree for soil conservation
b. Alley cropping
c. Multistorey cropping
d. All of them

107. Which agroforestry system is having two-in-one objective?

a. Hedgerow intercropping
b. Forage-cum-mulch alley crop ping
c. Intercropping
d. Both a and b

108. States of India having arid land among the following is?

a. Raj & GUJ
b. Punjab& HR
c. MH, KR & AP
d. All of them

109. Which state is having highest area under arid condition?

a. Rajasthan
b. Haryana
c. Punjab
d. Gujarat

110. Characteristic feature required for arid agroforestry species is ?
   a. Deep root system & Wax coating on leaf
   b. Only deep root system
   c. Covered stomata on leaves
   d. Both a & c

111. Best time for tree planting for agroforestry in arid zone is
   a. Beginning of rain
   b. Beginning of winter
   c. After rain
   d. None of the above

112. Major problem in arid zone agroforestry is
   a. Unavailability of moisture
   b. Soil fertility
   c. Both a & b
   d. None of the above

113. On the basis of structure, agroforestry systems are classified into how many types
   a. 2
   b. 4
   c. 3
   d. 1

114. Based on the nature of component, agroforestry systems are classified into how many types
   a. 4
   b. 5
   c. 6
   d. 2

115. First university to start PG programme in Agroforestry was
   a. YSPHF, Solan`
   b. Gujarat Agricultural University
   c. GB Pant Agricultural University
   d. CCS Agricultural University

116. All India Co-ordinated Research Project on Agroforestry was started in which year
   a. 1983
   b. 1963
   c. 1993
   d. 1973

117. Most complicated and sophisticated farming system in Asia is
   a. Taungya
   b. Hanunoo
   c. Improved fallow
   d. Both a & b

118. Which tree species is suitable for shifting sand-dunes in arid area?
   a. Eucalyptus
   b. Prosopis
   c. Mango
   d. Neem

119. Which is suitable agriculture crop for arid area?
   a. Pearl-millet
   b. Cowpea
   c. Both a and b
   d. None of the above

120. Which is suitable horticultural plant for arid area?
   a. *Zizyphus mauritiana* b. Mango
   c. Papaya d. None of the above

121. Preferred agroforestry system for wetland is
   a. Aquaforestry b. Hortipastrol
   c. Both a & b d. Silvopastoral

122. Wetland can be classified into how many types?
   a. Moist land b. Water-logged lands
   c. Immerged lands d. All of them

123. Type of measure taken to improve the condition of wetland is?
   a. Ditching b. Terracing
   c. Contour d. Both a & b

124. Most prominent agroforestry system for Hill region is
   a. Silvi-Horticulture b. Agri-Horticultue
   c. Aquaforestry d. Both a and b

125. Block planting of tree is known as
   a. Forest b. Agroforestry
   c. Wind breaks d. Woodlot

126. Which farming system is sequestering highest carbon?
   a. Agriculture b. Agroforestry
   c. Wind breaks d. Forest

127. Farm forestry should be practiced in which type of land
   a. Farmers land b. Community land
   c. Government land d. None of the above

128. Which type of species should be selected for farm forestry?
   a. Short rotation b. Medium rotation
   c. Both a & b d. None of the above

129. Community forestry should be practiced in which type of land
   a. Waste land b. Community/Public land
   c. Both a and b d. Road side land

130. Main aim of community forestry is
   a. Production of Fuel wood b. Production of fodder
   c. Both a and b d. Production of timber

131. Types of pruning practices applied in agroforestry are

a. 2 b. 3

c. 1 d. 4

132. Which type of tree is used in agroforestry system?

a MPTs b. NFTs

c. Both a and b d. Only a

133. Based on management agroforestry systems are managed under?

a. Tree Management c. Agriculture Management

c. Soil Management d. a and b both

134. Which one is the most prominent silvicultural tool for manipulation of tree growth in agroforestry system?

a. Thinning and pruning b. Only thinning

c. Only pruning d. None of the above

135. Which design is used to study tree/crop interface?

a. 'Y' design b. Parallel rows

c. Concentric rows d. All of them

136. Which research organization developed D & D?

a. NRCAF b. ICRAF

c. ICFRE d. ICAR

137. Method of removing all the branches below a prescribed point on the stem is known as

a. Selective pruning b. Variable-lift pruning

c. Fixed-lift pruning d. None of these

138. Taungya system is a

a. Agricultural system b. Silvipastoral system

c. Agrosilvopastoral system d. All of these

139. Eucalyptus is a

a. Fodder trees b. Timber trees

c. Leguminous trees d. Fruit trees

140. A macro diagnosis and design is completed in

a. 1 month b. 2 months

c. 3 months d. 4 months

141. In Madhya Pradesh babul is used only for
   a. Fuel
   b. Fodder
   c. Timber
   d. Multipurpose

142. Growing of trees with crop is called
   a. Agrisilviculture
   b. Silvopasture system
   c. Agri horticulture
   d. Agri-silvi pasture system

143. In Andhra Pradesh and Orissa state, shifting cultivation is called
   a. Jhum
   b. Podu
   c. Nill cultivation
   d. Alley cropping

144. For cooking 1 kg of food how much quantity of fuel wood is required
   a. 1 kg
   b. 1.2 kg
   c. 1.5 kg
   d. 1.7kg

145. Taungya system is followed in area having rainfall
   a. 100-1200m
   b. 1200-1500m
   c. 1500-2000m
   d. 1800-2000m

146. In village taungya, people cultivate the crops for
   a. 1-2 year
   b. 2-3 years
   c. 3-4 years
   d. 4-5 Years

147. In conventional shifting cultivation cycle involving 2-4 years of cropping with how much years of fallow cycle
   a. 5
   b. 10
   c. 15
   d. 20

148. Trees for fuel wood should have
   a. High calorific value
   b. Moderate calorific value
   c. Low caloric value
   d. High calorific value and specific gravity

149. In agrihorticulture system, fruit trees should be pruned
   a. Once in year
   b. Once in two years
   c. Once in five years
   d. Regularly

150. How much per cent of the total living biomass of the trees is in roots?
   a. 10-20
   b. 15-20
   c. 20-25
   d. 25-30

151. How many specialists are there in a typical Diagnosis and Design team?
   a. 1-5 b. 2-4
   c. 3-6 d. 5-10

152. A micro D & D team usually completes their work in
   a. 1 month b. 2 months
   c. 3 months d. 4 months

153. This is not the criteria of good agroforestry design
   a. Productivity b. Flexibility
   c. Sustainability d. Adoptability

154. This is not a key feature of D & D.
   a. Flexibility b. Speed
   c. Repetition d. Productivity

155 In village taungya the land allotted to each family to raise the crop & tree is about
   a. 5 to 10 ha b. 0.6 to 1.2 ha
   c. 0.7 to 1.4 ha d. 0.8 to 1.7 ha

156. National Agroforestry Policy was released in year
   a. 2015 b. 2014
   c. 2013 d. 2011

157. The term Social forestry is introduced by
   a. Robert black b. Tansely
   c. Westoby d. Brandis

## Mark the statement as true or false

i. *Leucaena leucocephala* is a multi-purpose tree species.

ii. The basic components of an agroforestry system are woody perennials, herbaceous plants and animals.

iii. The structure of an agroforestry system can be defined in term of its component only.

iv. Shelterbelts and windbreaks are agrosilvopastoral agroforestry system.

v. The 1st Taungya plantations were raised in 1896 at Axom (erstwhile Assam).

vi. Trees and shrubs on pasture is a silvipastoral agroforestry system.

vii. Home gardens are common agroforestry system in humid tropics.

viii. Boundary planting of trees on edges of plots and fields is based on temporal arrangement of components.

ix. Tea or coffee under shade trees is coincident type of temporal arrangement of components.

x. *Prosopis cineraria* and *Acacia nilotica* are suitable for low pH soils.

xi. Fallow period vary from region to region.

xii. Shifting cultivation is called 'Podu' in Andhra Pradesh and Odisha.

xiii. Taungya is Burmese word.

xiv In sloppy land hedge should be planted in East-West direction also.

xv. Temporal arrangement is the main feature of hedge row intercropping.

## Fill in the blank

1. What is the full form of ICRAF ------------------------------
2. Components of agroforestry are----------, ---------, --------
3. Total geographical area of India is --------------------
4. A major cause of soil erosion is ----------------------
5. ------------ is collective name for land use system involving trees combined with crops/or animals on the same unit of land.
6. An agroforestry system always has --------- or more -------------.
7. Agroforestry normally involves two or more species of------------------ plants at least one of which is always ----------------
8. Agroforestry is more ----------------- as compared to macro- crop farms.
9. There are ------------ agro climatic regions of India.
10. According to Nair (1987) agroforestry system can be classified on the basis of ------------,------------, ------------,-------------
11. On the basis of structure agroforestry system are grouped into two categories, they are ---------------&-----------
12. In improved fallow species in shifting season to --------- years.
13. The objective of improved fallow species in shifting cultivation is to--------------- depleted soil nutrients.
14. Shifting cultivation is practiced extensively in the ---------- hill region.
15. The main feature of the improved fallow system of agroforestry is that trees and shrubs are not grown with ----- on the same plot at the same time.
16. The Taungya is a Burmese word coined in Burma in the year -----
17. The Taungya system was introduction into India by -------- in 1980.
18. The first Taungya plantation were raised in 1896 in -----------

19. Components of agroforestry are ................., ................., .................
20. Classification of agroforestry system on structural basis are --------------, ------------
21. Growing of tree with crops is called ---------system.
22. System of production of crop under which plots of land are cleaned using dao or axe and fire cultivated for a short period called .......................
23. Shifting cultivation is practiced extensively in the ..................... hill region of the country.
24. Shifting cultivation is also called .............. in north eastern hill region.
25. Shifting cultivation is also called ................... in Andhra Pradesh.
26. Taungya system was introduced into India by ............ in 1890.
27. The first taungya plantation was raised in 1896 in .........
28. In southern India, taungya system of cultivation is called .....................
29. Taungya system is practiced in area with an assured annual rainfall of over...........mm
30. In taungya system 'taung' means hill and 'ya' mean ...............
31. In village taungya, each family has about 8 to 1.7 ha of land to raised trees and cultivate crops for ............to .........year.
32. Taungya system is not 3 types viz.,......... ........... .........
33. .................... is the system of agroforestry in which various kinds of tree species are grown mixed.
34. Alley cropping is also known as ............. inter cropping.
35. The primary purpose of alley cropping is to maintaining or increase crop ...........
36. Ideally hedge row intercropping should be positioned in............ direction.
37. In alley cropping, the spacing used in field is usually.............to.........m between tree rows.
38. In alley cropping the spacing used in field is usually ......... to ........... mts between trees within rows.
39. On sloping land hedge rows should always be placed on the .............
40. The system in which various multipurpose fuel wood/firewood species are inter planted on or arranged agricultural land called...........
41. In shelter belt, there are several............. established at right angles to the prevailing wind.

42. The purpose of shelter belt is to reduce the .......... of prevailing wind.
43. Shelter belt have a typical............ shape.
44. In shelter belt, tall trees are raised in the ......... of the shelter belt.
45. Ideal tree density in shelter belt is approximately ...............
46. Shelter belt up to............ m width are considered ideal under Indian condition.
47. In shelter belt, the ratio of height and width should be roughly......
48. The minimum length of a shelter belt should be about......... times its height.
49. The minimum length of a shelter belt should be about 25 times its .........
50. ............ are strips of trees and/or shrubs planted to protect fields, homes, canals from wind ....................
51. On level ground a wind breaks will reduce the speed of wind for about.............. times the tree height.
52. A wind break of 20 m tall will give some protection from 100 m on the upward side to .......m on the downwind side.
53. .......... row wind break should be used only where land is valuable.
54. Wind breaks of .............. to ............. rows are more effective for most farm situation
55. In shelter/wind breaks .............. growing species should be planted in the centre rows and smaller bushy species in the ................ rows
56. In general, tree with.......... vertical growth is ideal for wind breaks.
57. The production of woody plants combined with pasture is referred to as a .................
58 In protein bank rich trees are planted on or around farm land and range land.
59 Home garden is found extensively in ...........rainfall area.
60. Home gardens are characterized by high species diversity and usually.......... vertical canopy strata.
61. System in which honey bees are planted on the boundary, mixed with agriculture crop is called..............
62. In ............. system various trees and shrubs preferred by fish are planted on the boundary and around fish ponds
63. .............. agroforestry system is between commercial and subsistence scale of production and management.
64. ........... agroforestry system, where use of land is directed towards satisfying basic needs and is managed mostly by the owner/occupant and his family.

65. Freshly cut wood contains about............ % moisture.
66. For cooking 1 kg of food............... kg wood is required.
67. Wood lots are .......... planting of trees.
68. ................. is defined as the elimination of branches in order to obtain trees with clean bole.
69. The elimination of branches by physical and biotic agencies of the environment is called..................... pruning.
70. Removal of branches from the selected portions of the tree by mechanical means is referred as ................ pruning.
71. Coppice shoot are those that arise from.......... buds near the base of a woody plant.
72. Flexibility, speed and repetition are the key feature of ..............
73. An agroforestry research programme normally begins with a ............ D&D exercise covering an entire ecological zone within a country.
74. The D&D team comprises ............ to .............. specialist.
75. A macro D&D is usually completed in about............ months.

**Answer Key**

| | | | | | | | | | |
|---|---|---|---|---|---|---|---|---|---|
| 1 | A | 2 | C | 3 | D | 4 | B | 5 | D |
| 6 | D | 7 | A | 8 | A | 9 | B | 10 | D |
| 11 | B | 12 | C | 13 | C | 14 | D | 15 | C |
| 16 | C | 17 | B | 18 | C | 19 | A | 20 | C |
| 21 | A | 22 | C | 23 | A | 24 | A | 25 | D |
| 26 | D | 27 | A | 28 | B | 29 | B | 30 | C |
| 31 | C | 32 | C | 33 | D | 34 | D | 35 | A |
| 36 | A | 37 | C | 38 | B | 39 | B | 40 | A |
| 41 | C | 42 | C | 43 | A | 44 | C | 45 | A |
| 46 | D | 47 | A | 48 | C | 49 | B | 50 | B |
| 51 | C | 52 | C | 53 | A | 54 | B | 55 | A |
| 56 | B | 57 | D | 58 | B | 59 | C | 60 | C |
| 61 | A | 62 | D | 63 | A | 64 | D | 65 | B |
| 66 | D | 67 | C | 68 | A | 69 | C | 70 | D |
| 71 | B | 72 | C | 73 | C | 74 | B | 75 | A |
| 76 | A | 77 | B | 78 | C | 79 | A | 80 | C |
| 81 | B | 82 | A | 83 | B | 84 | A | 85 | A |
| 86 | D | 87 | A | 88 | A | 89 | B | 90 | A |
| 91 | A | 92 | B | 93 | C | 94 | B | 95 | A |
| 96 | A | 97 | C | 98 | B | 99 | C | 100 | D |
| 101 | A | 102 | B | 103 | D | 104 | A | 105 | C |
| 106 | D | 107 | B | 108 | D | 109 | A | 110 | D |
| 111 | A | 112 | C | 113 | A | 114 | A | 115 | A |
| 116 | A | 117 | B | 118 | B | 119 | C | 120 | A |
| 121 | A | 122 | A | 123 | D | 124 | D | 125 | D |
| 126 | B | 127 | A | 128 | C | 129 | B | 130 | C |
| 131 | D | 132 | C | 133 | D | 134 | A | 135 | D |
| 136 | B | 137 | C | 138 | C | 139 | C | 140 | C |
| 141 | D | 142 | A | 143 | B | 144 | D | 145 | D |
| 146 | C | 147 | A | 148 | A | 149 | D | 150 | B |
| 151 | D | 152 | C | 153 | B | 154 | D | 155 | D |
| 156 | B | 157 | C | | | | | | |

## Mark the statement as true or false

i. True
ii. True
iii. False
iv. True
v. False
vi. True
vii. True
viii. True
ix. False
x. True
xi. True
xii. True
xiii. True
xiv. False
xv. False

## Fill in the Blanks

1. International center for Research in Agroforestry
2. Crop, tree, animal
3. 329 m ha
4. Deforestation
5. Agroforestry
6. Two, output
7. woody ,perennials
8. complex
9. 15
10. Structural, functional, socio eco nomic & ecological
11. Nature of components, arrangement of components
12. One, several
13. Recover
14. North Eastern
15. Crop
16. 1850
17. Brandis
18. North Bengal
19. Tree, Crop, Animal
20. Nature of components, Arrange ment of components
21. Agrisilviculture
22. (Shifting cultivation)
23. (North East)
24. (Jhum)
25. (Podu)
26. (Brandis)
27. (North Bengal).
28. (Kumari)
29. (1200-1500 mm.)
30. (Cultivation)
31. (3 to 4)
32. (departmental, leased and village taungya.)
33. (multispecies tree gardens)
34. (hedge row)
35. (yield)
36. (east-west)
37. (4-8m)
38. (25cm to 2)

39. (contour)
40. (Agroforestry fuel wood production)
41. (rows of trees)
42. (right angels)
43. (velocity)
44. (triangular)
45. (Centre)
46. (50-60%)
47. (50)
48. (1:10)
49. (25)
50. (height)
51. (wind breaks)
52. (25)
53. (500)
54. (single)
55. (3 to 5)
56. (Tall, outsides)
57. (Narrow)
58. (Silvopastural system)
59. (Protein)
60. (High)
61. (3-4)
62. (apiculture with trees)
63. (Aqua forestry)
64. (Intermediate)
65. (Subsistence)
66. (23-25%)
67. (1.2 kg)
68. (block)
69. (pruning)
70. (natural)
71. (artificial)
72. (dormant)
73. (D&D)
74. (macro)
75. (5 to 10)
76. (3)

# 2

# Silviculture and Silviculture System

1. Clear felling system of forest management is
   a. Diffused regeneration system
   b. Accessory system
   c. Concentrated regeneration
   d. both b&c are true

2. Clear felling system was for the first time introduced in 19th century on commercial scale. The system was introduced by
   a. Heinrich Von Cotta
   b. Henry Von Cotta
   c Troup
   d. D. Brandis

3. In Shelter wood system, during seeding felling in deodar (*Cedrus deodara.* the number of seed bearer to be kept per hectare are
   a. 12- 18
   b. 45 – 50
   c. 25 – 30
   d. 35 – 45

4. Floating periodic block was first introduced in
   a. Germany
   b. France
   c. United Kingdom
   d. India

5. Karl Gayer developed which silvicultural system
   a. Group system
   b. Shelterwood strip system
   c. Irregular shelterwood system
   d. Wedge system

6. Dauerwald system of managing forest was first used by which of the following
   a. Alfred Moller in year 1920
   b. Alfred Moller in year 1900
   c. Harting in year 1920
   d. Harting in year 1900.

7. Light intensity at which amount of $CO_2$ taken up in photosynthesis exactly equals the amount concurrently given off in respiration is known as
   a. $CO_2$ compensation point
   b. $CO_2$ saturation point
   c. Light compensation point
   d. Light saturation point

8. Turgor-pressure gradient theory for movement of sugars in plant system was proposed by
   a. Shiroya
   b. Canny
   c. Roberts
   d. Munch

9. In genus Juniperus the shoot growth is
   a. indeterminate
   b. determinate
   c. both fixed and free growth
   d. None of these

10. Which of the following is having dioecious flowering
   a. *Betula*
   b. *Quercus*
   c. *Robinia*
   d. *Populus*

11. Intensity of light in southern aspect is ____________ time's higher then northern aspects.
   a. 0.5 – 0.9
   b. 2.4 – 3.0
   c. 1.6 – 2.3
   d. 2.8 – 3.2

12. The term 'forest succession' was first used by
   a. Clements
   b. Richard peters
   c. Dawson
   d. Thoreau

13. In hills secondary succession starts with which species
   a. *Woodfordia fruticosa*
   b. *Cedrus deodara*
   c. *Macaranga*
   d. *Acrocarpus fraxinifolius*

14. Which of the species is climatic climax in North Indian Tropical Moist Deciduous forests
   a. Teak
   b. *Terminalia*
   c. Sal
   d. *Hardwickia*

15. Which of the following species is a edaphic climax in Himalayan moist temperate forest (Type 12/E1). due to presence of limestone
   a. *Cedrus deodara*
   b. *Cupressus*
   c. *Alnus*
   d. *Pinus roxburghii*

16. Which of the following species is a biotic climax
   a. *Cedrus deodara*
   b. *Pinus rox burghii*
   c. *Toona ciliata*
   d. *Picea smithiana*

17. When forest are classified into forest types on the basis of growth form and seasonal changes in vegetation such basis is called as
   a. Structure
   b. Function
   c. Floristic
   d. Physiognomy

18. Northern tropical wet evergreen forest are found in which of the following state
   a. West Bengal
   b. Himachal Pradesh
   c. Uttrakhand
   d. Uttar Pradesh

19. Forest growing at or near the sea shore is known as
    a. Swamp forest
    b. Littoral forest
    c. Riparian forest
    d. Fringing forest

20. Scientific name of 'Kharsu oak' is
    a. *Quercus incana*
    b. *Quercus leucotricophora*
    c. *Quercus dilatata*
    d. *Quercus semecarpifolia*

21. Dry Alpine scrub forest is found in which State
    a. West Bengal
    b. Sikkim
    c. Arunachal Pradesh
    d. None of these

22. A forest area which is under one silvicultural system and one set of working plan prescription is known as
    a. Coupe
    b. Working circle
    c. Compartment
    d. Block

23. A species which is of relatively little silvicultural importance in a forest is known as
    a. Auxiliary species
    b. Accessory species
    c. Principal species
    d. None of these.

24. A forest area which had been provided limited degree of protection under chapter IV of Indian Forest Act, 1927 is called as
    a. Reserved forest
    b. Protected forest
    c. National park
    d. Social forest

25. Which of the following is a shade bearer species?
    a. *Mesua ferrea*
    b. *Xylia xylocarpa*
    c. *Rhododendron*
    d. *Cedrus deodara*

26. Dominated tree are those trees which have a height of
    a. 5/8$^{th}$ of the tallest trees
    b. ½ of the tallest trees
    c. 3/4$^{th}$ of the tallest trees
    d. 5/6$^{th}$ of the tallest trees

27. A forest is called as dense when the canopy density is
    a. 0.5 – 0.75
    b. 0.75 – 0.8
    c. 1.0
    d. 0.75 – 1.0

28. In Indo-gangetic plains of India with increase in one degree latitude the temperature variation will be
    a. Increase of 0.55$^0$C
    b. Decrease of 0.55$^0$C
    c. Increase of 1$^0$C
    d. Decrease of 1$^0$C.

29. Frost occurring in night when the sky is clear is known as
    a. Advective frost
    b. Pool frost
    c. Radiation frost
    d. Convection frost

30. Types of frost existing normally are
    a. 4
    b. 5
    c. 3
    d. 2

31. Which of the following species is frost hardy
    a. *Tectona grandis*
    b. *Boswellia serrata*
    c. *Garuga pinnata*
    d. *Hardwickia binnata*

32. Frost resistance of a plant is as a result of
    a. Large sized cell
    b. More osmotic concentration
    c. Less water binding colloids
    d. None of these

33. High nitrogen application will
    a. Reduce frost hardiness
    b. Increase frost hardiness
    c. No effect on frost hardiness
    d. Both can happen

34. Resistance of plants to heat will
    a. Decrease with low water content and high sugar
    b. Increase with low water content and high sugar
    c. Decrease with high water and high sugar
    d. Increase with low water and low sugar

35. A rainy day is a day when a minimum amount of rainfall is
    a. 2.0 mm
    b. 2.5 mm
    c. 3.0 mm
    d. 3.5 mm

36. A month is referred to as dry month when rainfall is
    a. > 50 mm
    b. < 50 mm
    c. <100 mm
    d. >100 mm

37. Intensity of light on southern aspect is
    a. 2.0 – 2.5 times higher then northern aspect
    b. 1.6 – 2.3 times higher then northern aspect
    c. 2.0 – 2.5 times higher then western aspect
    d. 1.6 – 2.3 times higher then western aspect

38. Process of laterization will lead to which of the following processes
    a. Leaching of Iron
    b. Accumulation of Iron
    c. Leaching of aluminium
    d. Both a & b. are true.

39. In Parbatti valley of Himachal Pradesh chir pine occurs at higher altitude then deodar due to
    a. Lime stone
    b. Climate
    c. Quartzite
    d. Laterites

40. Secondary immature soil which is derived from soil material of older origin is known as
    a. Aeolian soil
    b. Alluvial soil
    c. Sedentary soil
    d. Colluvial soil

41. Which of the following ratio (clay: silt: sand) will give rise to a course-textured soil
    a. 2:3:3
    b. 1:3:4
    c. 4:2:2
    d. 4:3:1

42. Capillary water is amount of water which is retained around the soil particle and capillary pores in the soil at forces between
    a. pF 2.0 – 3.5
    b. pF 3.5 – 5.5
    c. pF 2.7 – 4.5
    d. pF 1 – 2.6

43. Increase in pH of soil will leads to decreased availability of
    a. Calcium
    b. Magnesium
    c. Molybdenum
    d. Iron

44. Availability of nitrogen to plants is correlated with C/N ratio. In which ratio nitrogen will become immobilised
    a. 17:1
    b. 17:15
    c. 33:1
    d. 33:15

45. *Hoplocerambyx spinicornis* is an insect of which species
    a. Teak
    b. Deodar
    c. Sal
    d. Toon

46. A fast growing species gives a minimum yield of......... per hectare per annum rotation
    a. 15m$^3$
    b. 20 m$^3$
    c. 10 m$^3$
    d. 5m$^3$

47. Which of the following is not included in tending operations?
    a. Soil working
    b. Cleaning
    c. Weeding
    d. Pruning

48. Which of the following is Glover's formula for mechanical thinning; where D is spacing of trees in feet and d is diameter of trees in inches?
    a. D=1.5d
    b. D = 2d
    c. D = d
    d. D = 2.5 d

49. In which of the following species "German thinning" is applied
    a. Teak
    b. Deodar
    c. Sal
    d. None of these

50. Selection thinning will be applied to which of the following crops
    a. Even-aged crops
    b. Uneven-aged crop
    c. Even-aged irregular crop
    d. Uneven-aged irregular crop

51. In which of the following species dormancy is due to immature embryo
    a. *Swietenia mahagoni*
    b. *Zizyphus jujube*
    c. *Ginkgo biloba*
    d. *Plantanus* spp.

52. Which of the following can be tested for viability through cutting test?
    a. *Eucalyptus*
    b. *Populus*
    c. *Fraxinus*
    d. *Toona*

53. Which of the following species has orthodox seed?
    a. *Acacia*
    b. *Pinus*
    c. *Cassia*
    d. *All of them*

54. Rudimentary embryo dormancy occurs in which of the following species
    a. Gingko biloba
    b. Ilex opaca
    c. *Fraxinus* spp.
    d. All of them

55. Which of the following species has double dormancy?
    a. *Dalbergia latifolia*
    b. *Fraxinus excelsior*
    c. *Trewia nudiflora*
    d. *Pinus silvestris*

56. In which of the following situations double trench soil working techniques will be employed
    a. Salt impregnated soil
    b. Stony and sloppy soil
    c. Low and ill distributed rainfall zone
    d. Clayey soil

57. Which of the following silvicultural system is also called as system of "successive regeneration felling?
   a. Alternative strip system
   b. Clear strip system
   c. Shelter wood system
   d. Dauerwald system

58. How many months do it takes from first appearance to ripening of cones of Cedrus deodara
   a. 12-13 months
   b. 10 -11 months
   c. 14-15 months
   d. 15-16 months

59. Which of the following species has hypogeous germination?
   a. *Cedrus deodara*
   b. *Pinus roxburghii*
   c. *Populus ciliata*
   d. *Artocarpus hirsuta*

60. Which of the following species do not have parthenocarpic fruits?
   a. *Acer*
   b. *Ulmus*
   c. *Betula*
   d. *Populus*

61. National Commission on Agriculture proposed ____ no. classes of forest
   a. 4
   b. 3
   c. 5
   d. 6

62. In Maurya period head of the forest department was called as
   a. Vanapalas
   b. Kupyadhyaksha
   c. Nawabs
   d. Jagirdars

63. In British period the first ever forestry commission was established in the year
   a. 1800
   b. 1887
   c. 1890
   d. 1850

64. Central Board of Forestry was constituted in which year
   a. 1950
   b. 1975
   c. 1948
   d. 1952

65. Linking the protected areas to maintain the genetic continuity through corridors were suggested in which National Forest Policy
   a. 1894
   b. 1952
   c. 1966
   d. 1988

66. Forest conservation act came into being in the year
   a. 1988
   b. 1980
   c. 1998
   d. 1981

67. Peculiar feature of forestry enterprise is
    a. Income and capital are separate
    b. Income and capital are not distinct
    c. Both a &b are true
    d. Both a &b are false

68. National Commission on Agriculture was constituted in the year
    a. 1970
    b. 1976
    c. 1973
    d. 1972

69. Which amendment to the constitution brought forest and wildlife on the concurrent list in seventh schedule.
    a. $24^{th}$ amendment
    b. $42^{nd}$ amendment
    c. $38^{th}$ amendment
    d. $40^{th}$ amendment

70. Which of the following is not included in tending operations?
    a. Soil working
    b. Cleaning
    c. Weeding
    d. Pruning

71. In which of the following species "German thinning" is applied
    a. Teak
    b. Deodar
    c. Sal
    d. none of these

72. Selection thinning is applied to which of the following crops
    a. Even-aged crops
    b. Uneven-aged crop
    c. Even-aged irregular crop
    d. Uneven-aged irregular crop

73. Which of the following is a cut worm
    a. *Agrotis ipsilon*
    b. *Apogonia*
    c. *Melolontha*
    d. *Granida*

74. Which of the following species causes damping-off diseases in nursery
    a. *Rhizoctonia solani*
    b. *Botryodiplodia theobromae*
    c. *Uncinula* spp.
    d. All of them

75. Temperature at equator is highest because
    a. Ray of the sun strike the earth vertically
    b. Ray of the sun strike the earth horizontally
    c. Ray of the sun strike the earth oblique
    d. None of the above

76. Temperature at equator decreases from north to south because
    a. Ray of the sun strike the earth vertically
    b. Ray of the sun strike the earth horizontally
    c. Ray of the sun strike the earth oblique
    d. None of the above

77. with the rise of 270 m attitude in hills, the fall in temperature is normally
    a. 1.0 $^0$C
    b. below 1.0 $^0$C
    c. 1.5 $^0$C
    d. 0.5 $^0$C

78. Major forest groups according to Champion and Seth, 1968 are ...... in number
    a. 5
    b. 6
    c. 17
    d. 13

79. Type 1A/$C_1$represent .............. forest type
    a. Giant evergreen forest
    b. Evergreen forest
    c. Northern evergreen forest
    d. None of them

80. Enzyme activity is stopped at what temperature
    a. below 1 $^0$C
    b. above 50 $^0$C
    c. 45 $^0$C
    d. a and b both

81. The branch of forestry which deals with the establishment, development, care and reproduction of stands of timber is known as
    a. Silivics
    b. Silviculture
    c. Both a and b
    d. Only b

82. The forest without human disturbance is known as
    a. Reserve forest
    b. Virgin Forest
    c. Protected forest
    d. None of them

84. The planned no of years between the formation of crops and its final felling is known as
    a. Rotation
    b. Felling
    c. Harvesting time
    a. None of them

85. The process of renewal of forest crop by natural or artificial means is
    a. Establishment
    b. Regeneration
    c. Germination
    a. None of them

86. The species introduced outside from its native area is known as
   a. Exotic b. Local
   c. Indigenous a. None of them

87. On the basis of life span plant can be classified into ____ types
   a. 4 b. 3
   c. 5 a. 2

88. Plant having green and tender and height is usually not more than one metre is known as
   a. Herb b. Shrub
   c. Liana a. None of them

89. Woody climber is also known as
   a. Climber b. Creepers
   c. Vine a. Lianas

90. A perennial woody plant having branches from its base is known as
   a. Tree b. Shrub
   c. Herb a. Lianas

91. The height of *Pseudosuga taxifolia* tree in British Colombia has been found up to
   a. 127.1 m b. 117.1 m
   c. 137.1 m d. 107.1 m

92. In India maximum height of tree recorded is
   a. 65 m b. 75 m
   c. 85 m d. 55 m

93. Deodar tree having maximum girth in India was reported from
   a. Himachal Pradesh b. Uttarakhand
   c. West Bengal d. Madhya Pradesh

94. Sub group 4A represent
   a. Littoral forest b. Alpine forest
   c. Mangrove forest d. Both a and c

95. Which category of tree produces softwood timber?
   a. Board leaf b. Conifer
   c. a and b both d. None of them

96. Which category of tree produces hardwood timber
    a. Conifers b. Board leaf
    c. Both a & b d. None of them

97. The size of crown depend upon which factor
    a. Crown Development b. Crown Length
    c. Crwon Weidth d. All of them

98. Which type of tree is known as deciduous
    a. Leafless for sometime during the year b. Leafless whole year
    c. All of them d. None of them

99. Which plant show both deciduous and evergreen character
    a. *Santalum album* b. Chir Pine
    c. Coconut d. Noe of them

100. plant which grows in moist site is
    a. Hygrophyte b. Mesophyte
    c. Zerophyte d. None of them

101. The decrease in diameter of the stem of a tree from the base to upward is known as
    a. Stem b. Taper
    c. Bole d. all of them

102. Tropical rainforest occurs in area where annual rainfall is usually more than --mm
    a. 2000 b. 2500
    c. 1500 d. all of them

103. A plant that can subsist in dry situation is
    a. Xerophyte b. Hygrophyte
    c. Hydrophyte d. All of them

104. Total biomass per hectare in the rainforest is about -------- tones/ha.
    a. 1200 b. 000
    c. 1100 d. 900

105. A large area in India is occupied by ......... tropical forest.
    a. Deciduous b. Evergreen
    c. Semi Deciduous d. Semi Evergreen

106. The average rainfall in tropical deciduous forest varies from ---------- to ---------mm.

a. 750 to 2500
b. 500 to 2500
c. 750 to 1500
d. 500 to 2000

107. The vegetation comprising of evergreen, salt tolerant trees and not grow very tall.

a. Alpine
b. Littorial
c. Mangrove
d. All of them

108. The word "forest" is derived from Latin word-------------.

a. Foris
b. Fos
c. None of the above
d. Both of them

109. An area occupied by different kind of trees, shrubs herbs, and grasses and maintained as such is known as

a. Forest
b. Grassland
c. Agroforestry
d. a and b both

110. Even aged forest is also called ----------Forest

a. Inregular
b. Regular
c. Mixed
d. a and b both

111. True even aged forest can be only ________Forest

a. Man made
b. Natural
c. Departmental
d. None of them

112. When trees vary widely in age group in forest, it is.

a. Even
b. Uneven
c. Regular
d. All of them

113. The regeneration of forest obtained from seeds is known as

a. Medium Class Forest
b. High Forest
c. None of them
d. a and b both

114. When the regeneration is obtained naturally, the forest are called as

a. Natural Forest
b. Artifical Forest
c. Plantation Forest
d. a and b both

115. When regeneration is obtained artificially, the forest is known as

a. Natural Forest
b. Artificial Forest
c. Plantation Forest
d. Man made Forest

116. ---------------- forests are composed almost entirely of one species, usually to the extent of not less than 50 percent.

a. Mixed Forest
b. Artificial Forest
c. Pure Forest
d. All of them

117. The practice of forestry with the object of developing and maintaining high scenic value is

a. Recreational
b. Community
c. Form
d. All of them

118. The practice of forestry to maximize production per unit area is

a. Intensive Forestry
b. Mechanized Forestry
c. Form Forestry
d. None of them

119. Percent of the forest owned by the government in the country is.

a. 100
b. 95
c. 93
d. 97

120. The extent to which the gross volume of soil is unoccupied by solid particle is

a. Pore space
b. Soil profile
c. Soil porosity
d. a and c both

121. Which among the following represents the environment of forest?

a. Site
b. Ecosystem
c. Plant
d. a and c both

122. The best indicator of site quality for a given period is

a. CAI
b. MAI
c. None of them
d. a and b both

123. Site quality classes are determined on the basis of .

a. Height
b. Mid Height
c. Top Height
d. All of them

124. In plants light is essential for -------------- activity.

a. Photosynthesis
b. Respiration
c. Transpiration
d. Both a and c

125. The percent of light utilized by plant in chemical reaction is.

a. 0.5
b. 1.0
c. 1.5
d. 2.0

126. Category of plants able to develop chlorophyll in absence or under reduced light conditions is

a. Algae
b. Higher plant
c. Both a and b
d. None of the above

127. Best possible range of temperature for growth lies between ---------- to --------- $^{0}$C.

a. 20-25
b. 20-30
c. 25-35
d. 25-30

128. Coagulation in protoplasm resulting in death of plants occur at temperature above

a. 75$^{0}$C
b. 50$^{0}$C
c. 65$^{0}$C
d. 55$^{0}$C

129. *Acacia catechu* is frost ---------- species.

a. Resistance
b. Suscptiable
c. a and b both
d. None of them

130. *Tectona grandis* is frost --------------species.

a. Resistance
b. Suscptiable
c. Tender
d. None of them

131. The humic sesquioxide cemented material forming the pan in the V horizon of iron podosols is

a. Ortstein
b. Silican pan
c. Kankar pan
d. Clay pan

132. Which species among the following is a drought hardy?

a. Popular
b. *Acacia nilotica*
c. *Terminalia*
d. All of them

133. The decomposed organic matter is called

a. Humus
b. FYM
c. Vermicompost
d. All of them

134. Leaf litter and other plant residue contain about ---to --- % carbon.

a. 5 to 10
b. 2 to 5
c. 4 to 8
d. None of them

135. Height of a place from mean sea level is known as

a. Altitude | b. Latitude
c. Longitude | d. All of them

136. ---------------- represent a symbiotic relationship in which some fungi are associated with roots of higher plants

a. VAM | b. Mycorrhiza
c. Tricoderma | d. All of them

137. The plants which grow on the trunk and branches of other plant for the purpose of support in known as

a. Epiphyte | b. Hydrophytes
c. a and d only | d. Parasites

138. Steady increase in the temperature of Earth's surface and the lower atmosphere is referred as

a. Climate change | b. Global warming
c. None of them | d. Both of them

139. A belt of trees and /or shrubs maintained for the purpose of shelter from the wind, sun, snow drift etc. is known as

a. Wind break | b. Block plantation
c. Shelter belt | d. Boundary plantation

140. The part of the bole which is free from branches is known as

a. Pole | b. Stem
c. Log | d. All of them

141. A situation where a stem has more than one leader is known as

a. Taper | b. Buttress
c. Frocking | d. All of them

142. An outgrowth from the base of the tree connecting it with the roots is known as

a. Frocking | b. Buttress
c. Fluting | d. None of them

143. When a stem shows irregular involutions and swelling, it is called as

a. Frocking | b. Buttress
c. Fluting | d. None of them

144. A large number of species grow well in which type of soil?
   a. Well drained soil
   b. Red soil
   c. Black soil
   d. None of them

145. When the roots grow from any part of the plant body other than radiate they are called as
   a. Arial Root
   b. Tilt Root
   c. Prop Root
   d. All of them

146. Plants growing in marshy places develop special kinds of roots called as
   a. Arial Root
   b. Tilt Root
   c. Prop Root
   d. Pneumatophores

147. The period from germination to the stage, the young trees develop few leaves is
   a. Pole
   b. Sapling
   c. Seedling
   d. All of them

148. The period from recruit stage up to a height of 1m of the young plant is called as
   a. Pole
   b. Sapling
   c. Seedling
   d. All of them

149. Growth in volume is the product of diameter and -------------.
   a. Length
   b. Height
   c. Width
   d. All of them

150. Annual growth rings of the tree are generally used for determination of
   a. Quality of wood
   b. Value of wood
   c. Age of tree
   d. None of them

151. The stage of trees characterized by very little or almost no growth is
   a. Initial Stage
   b. Mid Stage
   c. Maturity stage
   d. Pole stage

152. When the stand is formed by single species it is called
   a. Mixed stand
   b. Coppice stand
   c. Pure stand
   d. All of them

153. Density refers to relative -------------- of trees in a unit area
   a. Size
   b. Diameter
   c. Height
   d. Number

154. A crown free to grow at the tip not competitive with its neighbours is known as

a. Suppressed tree
b. Dominant tree
c. Co-dominant tree
d. Tallest tree

155. A crown which is over topped and /or shaded by other trees is called

a. Suppressed
b. Dominant
c. Co-dominant
d. None of the above

156. Succession, subsequent to a disturbance, which destroys existing biotic community either partially or totally is called

a. Primary
b. Biotic succession
c. Secondary Succession
d. a and c Both

157. Secondary succession is more ----------- than primary succession

a. Progressive
b. Regressive
c. a and b Both
d. None of the above

158. Which succession involves the predominance of green plants in the initial stages?

a. Progressive
b. Regressive
c. Primary
d. Secondary

159. The different stages in xerarch are known as

a. Xeroseres
b. Xerarch seres
c. a and b both
d. None of the above

160. The replacement of one community by another due to modification of the environment by community themselves is

a. Autogenic succession
b. Heterogenic succession
c. Allogenic succession
d. a and c both

161. Which succession involves the replacement of one community by another due to force other than the effects of communities on the environment?

a. Autogenic succession
b. Progressive succession
c. Allogenic succession
d. Regressive succession

162. The succession initiated in extremely dry condition is known as

a. Hydrarch succession
b. Xerarch succession
c. a and b both
d. None of them

163. The succession which takes place on site after the destruction of the whole or part of the original vegetation is

a. Primary succession
b. Secondary succession
c. Xero succession
d. a and b both

164. Which one is the right sequence of the succession stages?

a. Primary, Secondary, Progressive and Regressive
b. Regressive, Secondary, Progressive and Primary
c. Primary, Progressive, Secondary, Regressive
d. None of the above

165. The species which grow in the area for the first time are called

a. Pioneer Species
b. Introductory Species
c. Native Species
d. All of them

166. Stage of vegetation said to be in equilibrium with environment and remain stable indefinitely by reproduction, itself efficiently is

a. Succession
b. Climax
c. a and b both
d. None of the above

167. The combination of climatic, edaphic, physiographic and biotic factors are known as

a. Environment
b. Climate
c. Locality factor
d. Site quality

168. Wet forests include forests occurring in area having mean annual rainfall of

a. 1500 mm
b. 1700 mm
c. 2000 mm
d. 2500 mm

169. Which type of forest are found in mean annual rainfall of 2500 mm

a. Wet forest
b. Dry forest
c. Alpine forest
d. Mixed forest

170. Moist and semi moist forests occurs in areas having mean annual rainfall of

a. 1000 to 1200 mm
b. 800 to 1600 mm
c. 1200-3000 mm
d. None of them

171. The various operations carried out in the forest crop at different stages of growth for improving the healthy environment for their development is termed as

a. Thinning
b. Cleaning
c. Tending
d. Pruning

172. The tending operation carried out in a crop which has not crossed the sapling stage is

a. Thinning b. Cleaning

c. Weeding d. Pruning

173. Cleaning is done mainly to reduce the competition for

a. Moisture b. Irrigation

c. Fertilizer d. All of them

174. The most common method of cleaning for removal of inferior growth with some sharp implements is

a. Spade b. Axe

c. Ho d. All of them

175. Intensive cleaning in not recommended in

a. High rainfall area b. Dry area

c. Open area d. Moderate rainfall area

176. Which type of cleaning is recommended for light demander species?

a. Moderate cleaning b. No cleaning

c. Heavy cleaning d. None of them

177. Felling made in an immature stand for the purpose of improving the growth and forms of the trees is

a. Final felling b. Improved felling

c. a and b both d. None of them

178. The forest composed of almost entirely of one species usually to the extent of not less than 80 % is

a. Low forest b. Poor forest

c. Pure forest d. All of them

179. Thinning helps in ------------- the rotation age

a. Maintaining b. Maximizing

c. Reducing d. Fixing

180. Reduction in number of trees in thinning, increases the -------------of the reaming trees

a. Diameter b. Height

c. Size d. Health

181. Which practice among the following helps in acceleration of diameter increment?

a. Environment
b. Cleaning
c. Thinning
d. Weeding

182. The practices of thinning may also improve the

a. Colour of wood
b. Value of wood
c. Strength of wood
d. Quality of wood

183. The basic principle involved in thinning is to ------------ the number of stem/ha

a. Reduce
b. Increase
c. a and b both
d. None of the above

184. Which thinning is usually applied in young crops/young plantations before the crown differentiation taken place

a. Crown Thinning
b. Selection thinning
c. Mechanical thinning
d. French thinning

185. Removal of wolf trees form natural stand or plantations along with thinning is known as

a. Cutting
b. Wolfing
c. Fluting
d. All of them

186. Which thinning is also known as low thinning or German thinning or thinning from the below

a. Mechanical
b. French
c. Free
d. Ordinary

187. Mechanical thinning is also known as

a. Thinning from the below
b. Stick thinning
c. a and b both
d. none of the above

188. In ordinary thinning, the trees are removed from which crown classes

a. Lower
b. Upper
c. Middle
d. None of the above

189. Which thinning is most suites for light demander species

a. Free
b. Ordinary
c. Crown
d. Selection

190. Ordinary thinning is simple in execution and ....................is required for selection of trees

a. Technical Skill
b. Scientific Skill
c. Ordinary skill
d. All of them

191. The thinning useful in forests infested with climbers and risk of crown fire?

a. Elite thinning
b. Crown Thinning
c. Mechanical thinning
d. Ordinary Thinning

192. The unit of Silviculture is

a. Forest
b. Stand
c. Tree
d. None of them

193. In which type of thinning the less promising ones being removed in the interest of the best individuals

a. Mechanical Thinning
b. Selection Thinning
c. Ordinary Thinning
d. Crown Thinning

194. Free thinning is the modification of

a. Crown Thinning
b. Selection Thinning
c. Advance Thinning
d. Elite Thinning

195. Crown thinning is also known as

a. French Thinning
b. Advance Thinning
c. German Thinning
d. None of the above

196. The origin of crown thinning is

a. German
b. India
c. France
d. Japan

197. In which type of species crown thinning is best suited

a. Light shade tolerant
b. Light demander
c. Heavy shade tolerant
d. Moderately shade tolerant

198. Which thinning is suited for areas where there is no demand for small size timber?

a. Crown
b. Advance
c. Elite
d. Free

199. Crown thinning provides better environmental condition for growth and development of retained

a. Suppressed tree
b. Dominant trees
c. Co-dominant tree
d. Dead tree

200. Free thinning is also called
    a. Crown thinning
    b. Mechanical Thinning
    c. Elite thinning
    d. Advance thinning

201. In which thinning method, elites are first selected in number appropriate to the size/age of the crops with special reference to their stem form and to their even spacing
    a. Free thinning
    b. Selection thinning
    c. Advance Thinning
    d. All of them

202. Which thinning is applied before the competition among individual trees has started
    a. Crown thinning
    b. Mechanical thinning
    c. Free thinning
    d. Advance thinning

203. Which thinning practice is applied in irregular crops
    a. Advance thinning
    b. Mechanical thinning
    c. Selection thinning
    d. Elite thinning

204. Which factor among the following can affect thinning practice?
    a. Age
    b. Nature of species
    c. Site quality
    d. All of them

205. Shade bearing species usually respond better to ______thinning
    a. Crown
    b. Elite
    c. Selection
    d. Free

206. Effect produced by early and heavily thinning on stem is
    a. Bushy
    b. Branchy
    c. Poor shape
    d. b and c both

207. Craib & O'Conner developed which type of thinning
    a. Free
    b. Mechanical
    c. Selection
    d. Advance

208. Who developed free thinning?
    a. Heck's
    b. Gehrhardt
    c. a and b both
    d. None of the above

209. Gehrhardt developed which type of thinning
    a. Crown
    b. Elite
    c. Maximum
    d. Selection

210. Advance thinning is also known as
a. Heck's thinning
b. Craib & O'Conner thinning
c. Craib thinning
d. O'Conner thinning

211. Advance thinning was developed for which crop
a. Wattle plantation
b. *Pine Plantation*
c. *Chir Plantation*
d. a and b both

212. The main aim of root pruning is
a. Healthy seedling
b. Good quality planting stock
c. Well developed root system
d. All of them

213. Advance thinning was first developed in which country
a. India
b. South Africa
c. New Zealand
d. Kenya

214. Removal of less valuable tree from a crop with the interest of better growth of more valuable individual is known as
a. Improved felling
b. Cleaning
c. Thinning
d. Tending

215. The elimination of branches by physical and biotic agencies of the environment is called
a. Pruning
b. Manual pruning
c. Natural pruning
d. Thinning

216. The elimination of branches in order to obtain trees with clean bole is termed as
a. Tending
b. Cutting
c. Thinning
d. Pruning

217. What type of pruning is helpful for developing clear bole tree in shorter rotation?
a. Natural
b. Artificial
c. Mechanical
d. all of them

218. The silvicultural system in which the regeneration is normally of seedling origin either natural or artificial and when rotation is generally long?
a. High forest system
b. Natural forest
c. Plantation forest
d. a and b both

219. Silvicutural system in which regeneration felling are for the time being concentrated or part of the felling series
a. System of regeneration
b. System of concentrated regeneration
c. a and b both
d. None of them

220. Silviculture systems in which the mature crop is removed in one operation is known as

a. Final harvesting
b. Clear felling system
c. Strip felling system
d. b and c both

221. The removal of the last seed or shelter trees after regeneration has been affected under a shelter wood system is

a. Final harvesting
b. Final clearing
c. Final felling
d. b and c both

222. Silviculture systems which result in irregular or two storied high forest is

a. Accessory system
b. Alluxery system
c. a and b both
d. None of them

223. In which state of India Teak and Sal are grow together as naturally?

a. Chhattisgarh
b. Madhya Pradesh
c. Andhra Pradesh
d. Tamil Nadu

224. Pinus kesiya is managed under which system

a. Accessory system
b. *Clear strip system*
c. *Coppice system*
d. b and c both

224. Which among the following is drought hardy?

a. Acacia
b. Prosopis
c. Zizyphus
d. All of them

225. Coppicing ability of tree shows

a. Increase with age
b. No relationship with age
c. Decrease with age
d. Initially increase then constant

226. Which of the following statements does not fit in to the concept of clonal forestry?

a. Reduce biodiversity
b. Costly proposition
c. Avoid the process of genetic the year recombination
d. Process of natural selection

227. Who introduced Eucalyptus in India?

a. Brandis
b. Akbar
c. Tipu Sultan
d. a and b both

228. *Cedrus deodara* is the species of which region of India?
 a. Eastern Himalaya  b. Darjeeling Himalaya
 c. Western Himalaya  d. All of them

229. When and where was eucalyptus introduced in India for first time
 a. 1790, Nandhi hills  b. 1790, Nilgiri hills
 c. 1860, Malabar  d. 1920, Kodaikanal

230. Sandal is
 a. Partial root parasite  b. Total parasite
 c. Stem parasite  d. All of them

## Filling the blanks

1. The removal of less valuable trees in a crop with the interest of better growth of more valuable individual in called---------------
2. Improved felling is usually carried out in mixed forest beyond the ---------------- stage.
3. Improvement felling is usually prescribed in forests which are in --------------correlation.
4. Removal of branches from the selected portions of the trees by mechanical mean's is referred as ------------------- pruning.
5. The simplest method of obtaining natural pruning is to develop and maintain ----------------- stocking in the main crop.
6. In artificial pruning, the use of ------------- has been found useful than bladed instruments.
7. In young plantation, artificial pruning should be carried out up to -------------to ------------of the total height of the tree.
8. The object of pruning is to obtain ------------ free timber.
9. Which type of tree is known as evergreen
10. A normal forest is an ideal forest with regard to growing stock, age class distribution and -----------------.
11. Social Forestry is the practice of Forestry which aims at meeting the requirement of ---------- and ------------ population.
12. The practice of forestry on land outside the conventional forest area for the benefit of local population has been called -------------.
13. The practices of forestry in all its aspect on farms or village lands generally integrated with other farm operations.
14. The most primitive member of plant kingdom is perhaps ------------

15. ---------------- and ----------- are exuded by trees a result of wound or injury to the bark of wood.
16. Rotation is counted period in years from ------------ to -------------.
17. A large part of solar radiation reflected is called -----------.
18. *Dalbergia sissoo* is a ------------ drought handy species.
19. *Tecctona grandis* is a drought ----------- species.
20. Texture of soil refers to ------------ particles.
21. The availability of water in soil for plant growth decrease with decrease in ..........
22. The decomposed organic matter is called -----------.
23. Humus is regarded as the ------------ of soil.
24. Rainfall is more on ------------ side of the hill than on ---------- side. ---------------
25. ..................stage starts with germination and extends upto a period till the plant reaches upto a height of one meter.
26. The science which deals with interrelationships of the organisms with environment is called------------.
27. The word ecology is derived from the Greek --------------
28. ----------------refers to the replacement of one set of biotic community or biota by another set of different nature.
29. Several activities such as overgrazing, srapping, shifting cultivation, industrial pollution etc. may cause ..................... type of succession
30. Pioneer stage refers to the primary stage when the bare site is occupied by the .....................
31. The series of stages in the succession are called ...............
32. Migration means mass.............. of plants or animals from one place to another.
33. ................ Climax is a stage in succession of forest just preceding the climax community.
34. ................. structure means stratification in forest dimensions especially height and ....................
35. ----------------- is unwanted plant.
36. *Lantana camera* can be successfully control by ------- ---------
37. In cleaning -------------- species are usually removed.
38. Thinning principles have been developed on the basis of natural development of the ----------------

39. Density has a direct influence upon the ----------.
40. In method where trees are cut in line or row throughout the area called ----------thinning.
41. -------------------- Thinning trees from upper crown classes are removed in order to favour the growth and development of most promising trees of the same class.
42 In -------------- thinning, the object is to promote the growth of trees which show sign of success in the competition and promise a good value as a future crop.
43. ------------- thinning is especially suited for area where there is denser of site deterioration due to removal of trees of lower crown classes.
44. ---------------- thinning requires greater skill in execution.
45. Free thinning is a modification of crown thinning and is also called.................
46. ----------------- is the number of trees corresponding to a given standard average diameter.
47. For a given site quality the optimum number of trees per unit area is found to be inversely proportional is the sequence of the height of the stand is called -----------------
48. Light demanders tree species are less tolerant to ---------- than shade bearers.
49. Light demander species usually respond better to ---------- thinning.
50. On------------ site heavy thinning is not recommended.
51. On steep slope, drier area and poor site --------- thinning should not be done.
52. Good sites may support ------------- number of trees than poor sites.
53. ------------ is defined as the planned interval in years which elapsed between successive thinning in the same crop.
54. Thinning cycles are shorter during ---------------- period of growth.
55. Thinning cycle is -------------- during middle aged to mature.
56. Thinning intensities are described as light or heavy according to ------------ of trees that are removed.
57. Which type of Silviculture system is good for producing fuel and small timber.
58. Which operation is responsible for shape and size of tree
59. The time elapses which between successive main felling on the same area is called ......................

60. Silvicultural system in which the crop originates mainly from coppice and where rotation of the coppice is short- .........
61. Necessitated change sometimes from one silvicultural system to another is usually referred as –
62. The part of forest set aside to be regenerated in a particular period is --------
63. Group system of silvicultural system is applicable in................
64. Silvicultural system in which felling step is located in the middle of the cutting section is ------------------
65. Silvicultural system applicable in Salix spp is ----------------
66. In aesthetic consideration which silvicultural system is considered as most suitable-
67. Silvicultural system applicable to Sal and Deodar forest is –
68. Tropical rain forest is managed under -------------- Silvicultural System
69. Silvicultural system mostly applicable to frost prone area is -----------
70. System is considered suitable for light demanding species is.
71. Species with long seed intervals are mostly managed under -----------
72. Uniform system is also known as -----------
73. Crop obtained under alternate strip system is -----------

## Fill in the blanks

1. Improved felling
2. Sapling
3. Poor
4. Artifical
5. Dense
6. Hand saw
7. One half to three fifth
8. Knot
9. Leaf appear for whole year
10. Diameter
11. Rural and Urban
12. Community forestry
13. Farm forestry
14. Alage
15. Gum and resins
16. Regeneration to Harvesting
17. Albodo
18. Moderate
19. Sensitive
20. Arrangement of primary
21. Temperature
22. Humus
23. Upper layer
24. Outer and leeward
25. Seedling
26. Ecology
27. Ekios
28. Plant
29. Induced
30. Species

31. Seres
32. Movement
33. Climatic
34. Stand
35. Weed
36. Biological methods
37. Unwanted
38. Crown
39. Growth
40. Mechanical
41. In crown
42. Crown
43. Crown
44. Crown
45. Single stem Silviculture
46. Stand density index
47. $N/H^2$ relationship
48. Crowding
49. Ordinarily
50. Poor
51. Heavy
52. Large
53. Thinning cycle
54. Early
55. Larger
56. Number
57. Coppice System
58. Silvicultural System
59. Felling cycle
60. Coppice system
61. Conversion
62. Periodic block
63. Deodar and Khair
64. Wedge system
65. Pollard system
66. Selection system
67. Selection system
68. Indian irregular shelter wood
69. Shelter wood coppice system
70. Clear felling system
71. Selection system
72. Compartment system and shelter wood compartmen system
73. Even aged

## Answer Key

| | | | | | | | | | |
|---|---|---|---|---|---|---|---|---|---|
| 1. | C | 2. | A | 3. | B | 4. | B | 5. | A |
| 6. | A | 7. | C | 8. | D | 9. | A | 10. | D |
| 11. | C | 12. | D | 13. | A | 14. | C | 15. | B |
| 16. | B | 17. | D | 18. | A | 19. | B | 20. | D |
| 21. | D | 22. | B | 23. | A | 24. | B | 25. | D |
| 26. | C | 27. | B | 28. | B | 29. | C | 30. | C |
| 31. | D | 32. | B | 33. | A | 34. | B | 35. | B |
| 36. | B | 37. | B | 38. | B | 39. | C | 40. | D |
| 41. | B | 42. | C | 43. | D | 44. | A | 45. | C |
| 46. | C | 47. | A | 48. | A | 49. | C | 50. | D |
| 51. | C | 52. | C | 53. | D | 54. | D | 55. | B |
| 56. | A | 57. | A | 58. | D | 59. | C | 60. | D |
| 61. | B | 62. | B | 63. | A | 64. | C | 65. | D |
| 66. | B | 67. | B | 68. | A | 69. | B | 70. | A |
| 71. | A | 72. | a | 73. | A | 74. | A | 75. | A |
| 76. | C | 77. | A | 78. | A | 79. | A | 80. | D |
| 81. | D | 82. | B | 83. | B | 84. | A | 85. | B |
| 86. | A | 87. | B | 88. | A | 89. | A | 90. | B |
| 91. | A | 92. | B | 93. | A | 94. | A | 95. | B |
| 96. | B | 97. | A | 98. | A | 99. | A | 100. | A |
| 101. | B | 102. | B | 103. | B | 104. | B | 105. | A |
| 106. | A | 107. | C | 108. | A | 109. | A | 110. | B |
| 111. | A | 112. | B | 113. | B | 114. | A | 115. | D |
| 116. | C | 117. | A | 118. | A | 119. | B | 120. | C |
| 121. | A | 122. | B | 123. | C | 124. | A | 125. | B |
| 126. | A | 127. | D | 128. | B | 129. | A | 130. | C |
| 131. | A | 132. | B | 133. | A | 134. | B | 135. | A |
| 136. | B | 137. | D | 138. | D | 139. | C | 140. | B |
| 141. | C | 142. | B | 143. | C | 144. | A | 145. | A |
| 146. | D | 147. | C | 148. | B | 149. | B | 150. | C |
| 151. | C | 152. | C | 153. | D | 154. | B | 155. | A |
| 156. | C | 157. | A | 158. | D | 159. | A | 160. | C |
| 161. | D | 162. | C | 163. | B | 164. | A | 165. | A |
| 166. | B | 167 | C | 168 | D | 169 | A | 170 | C |
| 171 | C | 172 | C | 173 | A | 174 | D | 175 | B |
| 176 | C | 177 | B | 178 | C | 179 | C | 180 | A |

| | | | | | | | | | |
|---|---|---|---|---|---|---|---|---|---|
| 181 | C | 182 | D | 183 | A | 184 | B | 185 | D |
| 186 | D | 187 | B | 188 | A | 189 | B | 190 | C |
| 191 | D | 192 | B | 193 | D | 194 | A | 195 | A |
| 196 | C | 197 | D | 198 | A | 199 | B | 200 | C |
| 201 | A | 202 | D | 203 | C | 204 | D | 205 | A |
| 206 | D | 207 | D | 208 | A | 209 | C | 210 | C |
| 211 | D | 212 | D | 213 | B | 214 | A | 215 | C |
| 216 | D | 217 | B | 218 | A | 219 | B | 220 | B |
| 221 | C | 222 | A | 223 | A | 224 | B | 225 | C |
| 226 | D | 227 | C | 228 | D | 229 | A | 230 | A |

# 3

# Forest Nursery, Seed Technology & Tree Improvement

1. Which of the following is a cut worm
   - a. *Agrotis ipsilon*
   - b. *Apogonia*
   - c. *Melolontha*
   - d. *Granida*

2. Which of the following species causes damping-off diseases in forest nurseries
   - a. *Rhizoctonia solani*
   - b. *Botryodiplodia theobromae*
   - c. *Uncinula spp.*
   - d. All of these

3. Type of beds prepared in forest nursery are?
   - a. 2
   - b. 3
   - c. 4
   - d. 5

4. Raised bed in nursery are required for region having?
   - a. Dry area
   - b. Wet land
   - c. High rain fall area
   - d. None of the above

5. Sunken beds are prepared for which region
   - a. Dry area
   - b. Wet land
   - c. High rain fall area
   - d. None of the above

6. On thc basis of irrigation how many type of nurseries are made
   - a. 2
   - b. 3
   - c. 4
   - d. None of the above

7. The size of nursery varies from ......... to ............ % of the total area of the plantation
   - a. 0.4 to 0.8
   - b. 0.1 to 0.6
   - c. 0.2 to 0.4
   - d. 0.5 to 2.5

8. Standard size of nursery bed is
   - a. 10 x 1.5 m
   - b. 11.2 x 1.2 m
   - c. 12.2 x 1.2 m
   - d. 12.5 to 2.5 m

9. Levelled type of beds are preferred for the area having
   a. Dry area b. Wet land
   c. High rain fall area d. Normal rain fall area

10. Which among the following is seed sowing method?
   a. Dibbling b. Broadcast
   c. Drill sowing d. All of them

11. The species having dormancy due to immature embryo is
   a. *Swietenia mahagoni* b. *Zizyphus jujube*
   c. *Ginkgo biloba* d. *Plantanus spp.*

12. Which of the following can be tested for viability through cutting test?
   a. *Eucalyptus* b. *Populus*
   c. *Fraxinus* d. *Toona*

13. Which of the following species has orthodox seed?
   a. *Acacia* b. *Pinus*
   c. *Cassia* d. All of them

14. Rudimentary embryo dormancy occurs in which of the following species
   a. *Gingko biloba* b. *Ilex opaca*
   c. *Fraxinus spp.* d. All of them

15. Which of the following species has double dormancy?
   a. *Dalbergia latifolia* b. *Fraxinus excelsior*
   c. *Trewia nudiflora* d. *Pinus silvestris*

16. Identification of seed production areas, collection of seed from elite trees and seed testing of collected seeds is
   a. Tree Improvement b. Forest genetics
   c. Tree breeding d. a and c both

17. Which variation is easily exploited for tree improvement programme?
   a. Additive variance b. Non-additive variance
   c. Provenance variance d. a and b both

18. Interaction of specific alleles at gene loci is
   a. Variance b. Epistasis
   c. Gene d. None of them

19. Geographic variation is also known as
    a. Local Variance
    b. Regional variance
    c. Provenance variation
    d. a and b both

20. The genetic variation in a species arises because of
    a. Mutation and gene migration
    b. Selection
    c. Genetic drift
    d. All of them

21. The number of seeds/kg used in calculating sowing rate and determine the size of the seed is
    a. Germination test
    b. Purity analysis
    c. Seed testing
    d. Seed weight

22. A complex mechanism that operates the chance of fluctuations in allele frequencies within a population is called as
    a. Genetic variance
    b. Selection
    c. Genetic drift
    d. Gene

23. Specifically designed programme for the crossing of parent trees is known as
    a. Hybridization
    b. Selection
    c. Mating design
    d. a and c both

24. Design in which one parent is known for given progeny is
    a. Incomplete design
    b. Incomplete pedigree design
    c. Complete pedigree design
    d. a and c both

25. Design in which both the parents are known to breeder is
    a. Incomplete design
    b. Incomplete pedigree design
    c. Complete pedigree design
    d. All of them

26. Multitrait selection that combines information on all traits of interest into a single index is
    a. Selection index
    b. Selective index
    c. Index for selection
    d. a and b both

27. Immune response of plants for pathogen infection is known as
    a. Hypo-sensitivity
    b. Sensitivity
    c. Hypersensitivity
    d. a and b both

28. Resistance offered by one or few dominant genes against the particular pathogen is

    a. Oligogenic resistance
    b. Polygeneic resistance
    c. a is correct & b is wrong
    d. b is correct & a is wrong

29. Resistance offered by many genes for general protection is

    a. Oligogenic resistance
    b. Polygeneic resistance
    c. a is correct & b is wrong
    d. b is correct & a is wrong

30. Ability of the host plant to withstand the pathogen attack is

    a. Tolerance
    b. Resistance
    c. Neither tolerance & neither resistance
    d. a and b both

31. The situation in which a vegetative propagule does not assume tree form but continues to grow like a branch is known as

    a. Plagiotropic growth
    b. Orthotropic growth
    c. a is correct & b is wrong
    d. B is correct & A is wrong

32. PDZ stands for

    a. Pollen distance zone
    b. Pollen distance zone
    c. Pollen dilution zone
    d. All of them

33. The width of PDZ in upwind side for wind pollinated trees is

    a. 300m
    b. 100m
    c. 150m
    d. 200m

34. Functional unit of inheritance is

    a. Pollen
    b. Loci
    c. Gene
    d. a and c both

35. Each of the alternate forms for a given gene is called

    a. Pollen
    b. loci
    c. Gene
    d. Allele

36. The numbers of set of chromosomes a tree has is termed as

    a. Ploidy
    b. Loci
    c. Gene
    d. Allele

37. Polyploidy is more common in

    a. Hardwood
    b. Heartwood
    c. Sapwood
    d. Softwood

38. The best known Polyploidy conifers is
    a. *Pinus roxiburgii* b. *Sequia sempervirens*
    c. *Pinus wallichiana* d. All of them

39. Red wood tree is
    a. Polyploidy b. Hexaploid
    c. Tetraploid d. All of them

40. The most successful species for afforestation of sand dunes is
    a. *Acacia tortilis* b. *Prosopis chilensis*
    c. *P. juliflora* d. a and b both

41. The forces in nature working to increase variation are
    a. Provenance b. Geographic source
    c. Geographic race d. All of them

42. The concept of ecotype was suggested by
    a. Turreson, 1912 b. Turreson, 1902
    c. Turreson, 1922 d. Turreson, 1920

43. Population of individuals that has become adapted to a specific environment in which it has been planted is
    a. Land race b. Local variety
    c. Selected variety d. a and b both

44. Average performance of the progeny of an individual when it is mated to a number of other individuals in the population is known ad
    a. Combining ability b. General combining ability
    c. a is correct & b is wrong d. a is wrong & b is correct

45. Ratio of total genetic variation in a population to the phenotypic variation is
    a. Narrow sense heritability ($h^2$) b. Broad sense heritability ($H^2$.
    c. a is correct & b is wrong d. a is wrong & b is correct

46. Selection of parent tree based upon the performance of their progeny is
    a. Germination test b. Progeny test
    c. Performance test d. All of them

47. Method of multitrait selection that involves setting minimum valued for each trail of interest is termed as
    a. Independent culling b. Simple Culling
    c. Dependent culling d. a and c both

48. The selection procedure that involves many cycles of selection and breeding is known as

a. Current selection
b. Recurrent selection
c. Selection
d. All of them

49. A tree that has been selected for grading because of desirable phenotypic qualities is

a. Candidate tree
b. Plus tree
c. Selected tree
d. a and b both

50. Ratio of total additive genetic variation to total variation is called

a. Narrow sense heritability
b. Broad sense heritability
c. a and b both
d. None of them

51. A tree that has been recommended for production or breeding orchard is called

a. Plus tree
b. Superior tree
c. Candidate tree
d. a and b both

52. The tree against which the selected trees are graded is known as

a. Comparison tree
b. Check tree
c. Candidate tree
d. a and b both

53. Area where seeds are mass produced to obtain the greatest genetic gain and inexpensively as possible

a. Seed orchard
b. Seedling orchard
c. Orchard
d. Plantation area

54. Resistance in which the insect is not attracted to or is repelled from feeding and ovipositing on a tree

a. Resistance
b. Non resistance
c. Non performing
d. b and c both

55. Resistance in which the insect is killed, injured or prevented from completing its normal life cycle after feeding on a tree can be termed as

a. Antibiosis
b. Anti biotic
c. Aero biotic
d. a and b both

56. Ultimate source of variation is

a. Mutation
b. Environment
c. Genetic erosion
d. None of them

57. Cumulative effect of alleles at all gene loci for a particular trait is
    a. None additive variance
    b. Additive variance
    c. Only variance
    d. a and b both

58. Polycross design is also known as
    a. Pollen mix design
    b. Mix design
    c. Poly design
    d. Pollen design

59. Complex mechanism that operates through chance fluctuations in allele frequencies with in a population is
    a. Genetic erosion
    b. Genetic differentiation
    c. Genetic drift
    d. All of them

60. Group of plants of similar genotype that occupy a specific ecological niche is
    a. Ecotone
    b. Ecotype
    c. a and b
    d. Only a

61. Selected tree that has proven to be genetically superior by means of progeny testing is
    a. Elite tree
    b. Plus tree
    c. Candidate tree
    d. None of them

62. The tree from which the vegetative propagules have been taken for vegetative propagation is known as
    a. Donor
    b. Ortet
    c. Only a
    d. a and b both

63. Swelling above the point of grafting and scion overgrowth of the root stock caused by blockage of phloem is commonly referred as
    a. Saddle overgrowth
    b. Sudden growth
    c. Over growth
    d. All of them

64. The practice of applying a layer of dead vegetable materials to assist soil productivity is called
    a. Mulching
    b. Protection cover
    c. Covering
    d. All of them

64. Which among the following is used for viability testing?
    a. TZ Test
    b. X-ray test
    c. Embryo test
    d. All of them

65. Plagiotropic growth is common in genera
    a. *Abies* b. *Picea*
    c. *Aurocaria* d. All of them

66. Central America and Mexico coniferous resource cooperative popularly known as
    a. CAMCORE b. CACORE
    c. CMCORE d. All of them

67. The most common and destructive disease in the nursery is
    a. Damping off b. Root rot
    c. Shoot rot d. All of them

68. Damping off is caused by which fungi
    a. *Pythium* b. *Rhizoctonia*
    c. *Fusarium* d. All of them

69. Damping off is caused by which type of fungi
    a. Soil borne b. Root borne
    c. Seed borne d. Air borne

70. Damping off in Neem is caused by
    a. *Pythium* b. *Rhizoctonia solani*
    c. *Fusarium oxysporum* d. All of them

71. Leaf blight of teak is due to
    a. *Pythium* b. *Rhizoctonia solani*
    c. *Fusarium oxysporum* d. *Ravenalia clemensiae*

72. Leaf rust of *Albiza* is caused by
    a. *Pythium* b. *Rhizoctonia solani*
    c. *Fusarium oxysporum* d. All of them

73. Powdery mildew of *Sissoo* is caused by
    a. *Phylloctonia dalbergia* b. *Rhizoctonia solani*
    c. *Fusarium oxysporum* d. All of them

74. An operation under which forked are multiple stems are reduced to a single stem to improve the form of the planted tree
    a. Singling b. Mulching
    c. Staking d. All of them

75. The species not resistant to termite attack is
    a. Ailanthus b. Sal
    c. Teak d. Deodar

76. The species most resistant to decay is
    a. Bamboo Sp. b. *Mangifera indica*
    c. a and b both d. *Acacia nilotica*

## A. Fill up the following blanks with appropriate words

1. The content of other than seeds such as straw, soil particles, small stones and seeds of other species is called............................
2. The loss of the weight of a sample when it is dried is known as................
3. A specified quantity of seed, physically identifiable in respect of which an international analysis certificate may be issued is called................
4. The blowers are used for..................
5. The reagent used for biochemical test for determining seed viability is..............................
6. The food material contained in ...................... that nourishes the embryo during its development.
7. A large proportion of seed used in forest regeneration is obtained from........................
8. The condition of a viable seed which presents it from germinating when supplied with suitable environmental condition is called..................
9. The disruption of seed coat by chemical treatment in a strong acid to increase their permeability to water and gases is called....................
10. Rainfall at ................ is the most limited factor that affect the fruit setting and seed production.
11. The reduction in ....................... considerably slows down the metabolic process which intern retard respiration process.
12. A group of genetically identical plants desired a sexuality from a single mother tree is called........................
13. ................. ensures the supply of reproductive material for scientific trials and introduction of species in exotic areas.
14. The genetically superior seeds for afforestation programme can be produced in ..................
15. The colour change in fruits is a suitable criteria for judging the.................
16. The propagators or protectors of their own kind are known as.........

17. ............ denotes the defective floral structure such as short style and long filament and long styles and short filaments.
18. The full name of ICIA is ............................
19. The safe moisture content in storage is.............................
20. The genetically superior reach for a forestation programme can be produced in .........................
21. To meet the continuous short and long term supply of reproductive material for planting is called.................
22. ................ is the supply of seeds for establishment of gene banks, botanical gardens, expansion of arboretums, seed herbaria.
23. ..................... is a mature floral ovary which may contain one or more seeds and includes accessory floral parts.
24. ................... refers to a condition in viable seed which prevents it from germinating when supplied with the factors which are adequate for germination.
25. .................. is defined as one which can germinate under favorable conditions, providing any dormancy may be present is removed.
26. The method through which the genetic and physical characteristics of the seeds could be improved is called.................
27. ...................... is the practice of burying seeds in moist medium, in alternate layers to overcome dormancy which keeps seeds in a cold and most environment.
28. ...................... denotes those seed properties which determine the potential of rapid uniform emergence and development of normal seedlings under a side range of field condition.
29. .............. plays an important role in blossoming fruit setting and seed formulation.
30. ................ at the time of flowering is the most limiting factor that affects the fruit setting and seeds production.
31. In deciduous forest................. plays an important role in pollinate.
32. Excess supply of ............. and ................ may result in fast vegetative growth poor flowering and fruit bearing.
33. The seeds produced by over matured and immature trees are..............
34. The plants raised by................. means flower early as compared to the seedling plants raised by seeds.
35. ....................is the cause of self unfruitfulness in which the pollens of some varieties are in capable of fertilizing the flowers of other varieties or of the same varieties.

36. High temperature is injurious to ............ in which blossom drip occur in summer due to low atmospheric humidity.
37. The process and development of fruit and seeds will not be normal, the young fruits turn yellow, shrivel and fall off, if there is not adequate supply of................
38. When seeds for............... can be sown immediately after collection, no storage of seed in required.
39. The seeds which can be dried down to a low moisture content of around 5% and can be stored at low temperature for long period of time are called.........................
40. The seeds which can not survive drying below a high moisture content (20-50%. and cannot be stored for long time is called................
41. If seeds are stored in .................... heating occurs which is caused by the respiration of seeds.
42. When seeds are stored in................. the seeds survive for longer period in storage without loss in germination capacity.
43. A reduction in moisture content considerably slows down the............ Process which intern retards the respiration process.
44. If the seeds are stored at lower temperature the rate of respiration will be............. thus higher will be the lifespan of seeds.
45. Fully ripped seeds return viability longer than seeds collected when immature because of formation of ........................ in matured seeds which conserve viability.
46. Seeds damaged mechanically during extraction and cleaning rapidly loose its..................
47. The fungicidal and insecticidal treatments should not be used during................as it can be harmful to the seeds.
48. The low moisture content, high temperature and high $O_2$ pressure provide optimum storage conditions for most of the............ seeds.
49. A number of changes occur in cell tissue with ageing of the seeds, these changes are called..................
50. When a tree species seeds abundantly in year it is said to be....................
51. .................... refers to the area where the mother trees of the seeds are growing.
52. The techniques used for vegetative propagation of a clone for mass production is called..............
53. The outstanding individuals of a particular species selected and reserved for improvement................ of the species by selection who breeding is called........................

54. .................. is a plantation of genetically superior tress, isolated in order to minimize pollination from financially inferior individuals.
55. A crop of vigorous, healthy and ideal growth that has been selected and reserved for seed collection for raising seed orchards or plantation is called..............
56. The orchards which are raised by grafting clones in the form of bud of plus trees is called...................
57. The orchards which are raised from the seeds of plus trees is called...............
58. The specific gravity of the seeds/fruits decreases as the moisture content of the seeds fruits................. with maturity.
59. The method of seed extraction from fleshy fruits is called...................
60. ................. can be used to separate out impurities having different specific gravity than that of the seeds.
61. The methods lowering down of the seed moisture known as...............
62. The objective of seed certification is to ensure.............and of the seed to the purchasers.
63. ...............is a legally sanctioned system for quality control of seed multiplication and production which consists of different committee members.
64. The .................. of standing seed crops is an essential step in varying conformity of seed crops to prescribed certification stand orders.

## B. Write True/False for the following statements

1. The object of sampling is to determine the percentage composition by weight of a sample being tested.

   (True/False)
2. Hard seeds are those which remain hard at the end of the test period because they have not absorbed water.

   (True/False)
3. The submitted samples should be used in the lab on which the various tests are performed.

   (True/False)
4. The methods prescribed for the determination of moisture content are designed to reduce the oxidation, decomposition or loss of other volatile substances.

   (True/False)
5. The longevity of the seed can be defined as one which can germinate under favorable conditions providing any dormancy that may be present is removed.

   (True/False)

6. Excess supply of nutrients and water may result in fast vegetative growth poor flowering and fruit bearing.

(True/False)

7. The seeds produced by over matured and immature trees are infertile.

(True/False)

8. Bigger the size of crown bigger the production of seed

(True/False)

9. The seedling plants raised by seeds flower early as compared to the plants raised by vegetative means.

(True/False)

10. Some kind of trees produce abundant bloom but fail to set fruits this failure may be due to excess moisture and nutrient supply.

(True/False)

11. Incompatibility is the cause of self fruitfulness in which pollens of some varieties are capable of fertilizing the flowers of same varieties.

(True/False)

12. High temperature is injurious to pollination in which blossom drop occurs in summer due to low atmospheric humidity.

(True/False)

13. If ample food is not available at the time of fruit setting, the young fruit Yellow, shrivel and fall off.

(True/False)

14. When seeds for afforestation can be sown immediately after collection no storage of seed is required.

(True/False)

15. The seeds which can be dried down to a low moisture content of around 5% and can be stored for long period is called recalcitrant seeds.

(True/False)

16. The seeds which can not survive drying below a high moisture content (20-50%) and can not be stored for long time is called orthodox seeds.

(True/False)

17. The seeds should not be stored in high moisture content because heating occurs due to respiration of seeds.

(True/False)

18. The seeds should be stored in low moisture content to survive for longer period in storage without loss in germination capacity.

(True/False)

19. The loss of viability precedes more rapidly under un favorable storage conditions than in case of fresh vigorous seeds.
(True/False)
20. The seed lot which loses its germination capacity may be subjected to genetic drift.
(True/False)
21. An increase in moisture content considerably slows down the metabolic process which intern retards the respiration process.
(True/False)
22. Oily seeds can not tolerate drying to some what lower moisture content than non-oily seeds.
(True/False)
23. If the seeds are stored at higher temperature, lower in the rate of respiration, thus higher the life span of seeds.. (True/False)
24. Ultra violet light is harmful to the seeds. (True/False)
25. Fully ripped seeds retain viability longer than seeds collected when immature. (True/False)
26. Fully ripped seeds retain viability longer than seeds collected when immature due to formation of more biochemical compounds in matured seeds with consequent viability.
(True/False)
27. Seeds damaged mechanically during extraction and cleaning, rapidly increases its viability. (True/False)
28. Dry seeds suffer less damage than moist seeds. (True/False)
29. The attack of insect, pest and fungi in the most rapid on the forest floor.
(True/False)
30. Fungicidal and insecticidal treatments should not be used during storage unit can be harmful to the seeds. (True/False)
31. Seeds with high initial viability and germinative capacity have a lower longevity in storage.
(True/False)
32. The optimum storage conditions for most recalcitrant seeds are low moisture content/ low temperature. (True/False)
33. The optimum storage condition for most orthodox seed are high moisture content, high temperature and $O_2$ preserve.
(True/False)

34. Provenance refers to meet the requirement of seed in artificial reparation of forest and afforestation of special site.

(True/False)

35. The seeds should be collected from vigorous wolf trees.

(True/False)

36. The seeds should be collected from middle aged to mature trees because the seeds from young and over mature trees have low viability.

(True/False)

37. The collection of seeds should be avoided from isolated trees.

(True/False)

38. The method of seed collection from fallen fruits or seeds is cheap and does not require skilled labour.

(True/False)

39. A group of genetically identical plants desired a sexually from a single mother tree is called plus tree.

(True/False)

40. Interior trees should be removed from the seed stand to improve the genetic quality of the seed.

(True/False)

41. Thinning may not be carried out to provide better spacing to the trees for flowering and fruiting.

(True/False)

42. Removal of under growth of trees from the seed stand is very important to facilitate seed production and collection.

(True/False)

43. The fertilizers should be applied to the seed stand to improve seed production and seed quality.

(True/False)

44. The insecticide and fungicide should be applied to protect flowering and fruiting from insect, pest and disease

(True/False)

45. The seed orchards raised by grafting clones in the form of bud of plus trees is called seedling seed orchards.

(True/False)

46. The seed orchards which are raised form the seedling obtained from the seeds of the plus trees is clonal colonel seed orchards.

(True/False)

47. The seed orchards should be located within the natural geographical zone of the species.

(True/False)

48. The climate and soil should be highly productive for high seed production for selecting location of seed orchards.

(True/False)

49. The site for the location of seed orchards should be protected from wind, fire and animals.

(True/False)

50. The specific gravity of the fruits decreases as the moisture content of the fruits/seeds decreases with maturity.

(True/False)

51. The method of seed extraction from fleshy fruits is called de-winging.

(True/False)

52. Grading methods can be used to separate out impurities having different specific gravity than that of the seeds.

(True/False)

53. The objective of seed certification is to ensure genuineness and quality of the seed to the purchasers.

(True/False)

54. Seed certification is a legally sanctioned system for quality control of seed multiplication and production which consists of different committee members.

(True/False)

## Answer Key

| | | | | | | | | | |
|---|---|---|---|---|---|---|---|---|---|
| 1. | A | 2. | A | 3. | B | 4. | A | 5. | A |
| 6. | A | 7. | D | 8. | C | 9. | D | 10. | D |
| 11. | c | 12. | C | 13. | D | 14. | D | 15. | B |
| 16. | A | 17. | A | 18. | B | 19. | C | 20. | D |
| 21. | D | 22. | C | 23. | C | 24. | B | 25. | C |
| 26. | A | 27. | C | 28. | A | 29. | B | 30. | A |
| 31. | A | 32. | A | 33. | D | 34. | C | 35. | D |
| 36. | A | 37. | A | 38. | D | 39. | B | 40. | D |
| 41. | D | 42. | C | 43. | A | 44. | C | 45. | B |
| 46. | B | 47. | A | 48. | B | 49. | A | 50. | A |
| 51. | A | 52. | D | 53. | A | 54. | B | 55. | A |
| 56. | A | 57. | B | 58. | A | 59. | C | 60. | B |
| 61. | A | 62. | D | 63. | A | 64. | A | 65. | D |
| 66. | A | 67. | A | 68. | D | 69. | A | 70. | C |
| 71. | D | 72. | B | 73. | A | 74. | A | 75. | |
| 76. | D | . | | | | | | | |

## A. Fill up the following blanks with appropriate words

1. Inert Material
2. Moisture content
3. Seed lot
4. Purity of seeds
5. Tetrazolium chloride or Bromide
6. Endosperm
7. Natural stand
8. Dormancy
9. Scarification
10. Flowering
11. Moisture content
12. Clone
13. Evaluation
14. Seed orchards
15. Seed maturity
16. Seed
17. Heterostyly
18. International Crop Improvement Association
19. 4-8%
20. Seed orchard
21. Utilization
22. Conservation
23. Fruit
24. Dormancy
25. Viable seeds
26. Seed Technology
27. Stratification
28. Vigor

29. Temperature
30. Rainfall
31. Wind
32. Nutrient supply and water
33. Infertile
34. Vegetative
35. Incompatibility
36. Pollination
37. Food material/nutrients
38. Afforestation
39. Orthodox seeds
40. Recalcitrant seeds
41. High moisture content
42. Low moisture content
43. Metabolic process
44. Lower
45. Biochemical compounds
46. Viability
47. Storage
48. Orthodox seeds
49. Recalcitrant seeds
49. Physical changes
50. Good seed year
51. Provenance
52. Grafting
53. Plus trees
54. Seed orchards
55. Seed stand
56. Clonal seed orchards
57. Seedling seed orchards
58. Decreases
59. Depulping
60. Floatation
61. Seed drying
62. Genuineness and quality
63. Seed certification
64. Field inspection

## Answer for True/False

1. False
2. True
3. False
4. True
5. False
6. True
7. True
8. True
9. False
10. False
11. False
12. True
13. True
14. True
15. False
16. False
17. True
18. True
19. True
20. True
21. False
22. False
23. False
24. True
25. True
26. True

27. False
28. False
29. True
30. True
31. False
32. False
33. False
34. False
35. False
36. True
37. True
38. True
39. False
40. True
41. False
42. True
43. True
44. True
45. False
46. False
47. True
48. True
49. True
50. Truc
51. False
52. False
53. True
54. True

4

# NTFPs and Wood Technology

1. In batten board the thickness of the strips of wood in the core should be

   a. 2.5 cm  b. 7.5 cm
   c. 2.5 mm  d. 7.5 mm

2. Which of the following is not a particle board?

   a. Chip board  b. Flake board
   c. Shaving board  d. Wall board

3. Which of the following is not a water soluble wood preservative

   a. Zinc-chloride  b. Mercuric chloride
   c. Cuprinol  d. Zinc-meta-arsenite

4. Modern paper making started in India in year

   a. 1850  b. 1830
   c. 1930  d. 1950

5. In which of the following process of pulping sodium sulphide is used

   a. Soda process  b. Sulphate process
   c. Sulphite process  d. All of the them

6. Which among the following is not the principal effect of beating process in paper making?

   a. Decrease in fibre length  b. Formation of fibrils
   c. Retardation of drainage  d. Decrease in fibre flexibility.

7. Which of the following is an edible bamboo species?

   a. *Bambusa balcooa*  b. *Dendrocalamus asper*
   c. *Dendrocalamus strictus*  d. *Bambusa tulda*

8. Palmrosa oil is extracted from which species

   a. *Aquilaria agallocha*  b. *Vetivera zizanioides*
   c. *Eucalyptus globules*  d. *Cymbopogon martini*

9. Which of the following species is a source of leaf tannin

   a. *Carissa spinarum*  b. *Gmelina arborea*
   c. *Bixa orellana*  d. All of them

10. 'Gum Kino' is obtained from which species
    a. *Acacia modesta*
    b. *Pterocarpus marsupium*
    c. *Butea monosperma*
    d. *Moringa pterygosperma*
11. Which of the following species produces 'white dammar?'
    a. *Canarium strictum*
    b. *Vateria indica*
    c. *Shorea robusta*
    d. *Hopea odorata*
12. The edge of the tooth in the saw blade which faces the cutting direction is
    a. Faces back
    b. Kerf
    c. Set
    d. All of them
13. The edge of the tooth in the saw blade which faces the cutting direction is
    a. Back
    b. Kerf
    c. Space
    d. Set
14. The entire opening between the two adjacent teeth is known as
    a. Back face
    b. Gullet
    c. Space
    d. Set
15. The angle between the face of a tooth and the line passing through the points of teeth is known as
    a. Gauge
    b. Gullet
    c. Set
    d. Pitch
16. The angle between the face of a tooth and the line passing through the points of teeth is known as
    a. Gauge
    b. Space
    c. Set
    d. Pitch
17. The thickness of the blade is known as
    a. Set
    b. Space
    c. Gullet
    d. Gauge
18. The width of the saw cut is known as
    a. Kerf
    b. Space
    c. Gullet
    d. None of the above
19. For practical requirement the length of the saw for 30 cm diameter of stem should be
    a. 120-130 cm
    b. 130-150 cm
    c. 140-150 cm
    d. 180-200 cm

20. For practical requirement the length of the saw for 30 cm diameter of stem should be
    a. 120-130 cm
    b. 130-150 cm
    c. 140-150 cm
    d. 180-200 cm

21. For practical requirement the length of the saw for 80-100 cm diameter of stem should be
    a. 110-130 cm
    b. 180-200 cm
    c. 160-175 cm
    d. 150-200 cm

22. Boom is a
    a. Dutch word
    b. Spanish word
    c. German word
    d. None of the above

23. What is the meaning of Boom?
    a. Group of logs
    b. Floating obstruction
    c. Raft
    d. All of them

24. A quantity of wood firmly bound together is termed as
    a. Group of log
    b. Wet slides
    c. Raft
    d. All of them

25. Wet sliders are used for which purpose
    a. Extraction of timber
    b. Harvesting of log
    c. Raft
    d. Floating

26. Forest depots are usually of
    a. Intermediate depot
    b. Temporary nature
    c. Permanent nature
    d. None of them

27. Intermediate depots inside or outside the forest is known as
    a. Forest depot
    b. Sale depot
    c. Storage depot
    d. Transit depot

28. The amount of produce is fixed for sale, while the exact quantity of such produce is known or not is termed as
    a. Payment on outturn
    b. Fixed tariff
    c. Lump sum sale
    d. All of them

29. The light coloured outer portion of a tree log consisting of the youngest growth ring is called
    a. Dead tissue  b. Sapwood
    c. Heartwood  d. All of them

30. Conduction of sap and food storage takes place in
    a. Heartwood  b. Sapwood
    c. a and b both  d. b is correct and a is wrong

31. Wood preservation on scientific and modern basis was introduced in India by
    a. Sir Ralph Pearson  b. Brandis
    c. S. Kaineson  d. a and c both

32. In which year wood preservation was started
    a. 1905  b. 1907
    c. 1906  d. 1908

33. The credit of development of wood preservative technique goes to
    a. S. Kaineson  b. Sir Ralph Pearson
    c. a and b both  d. a is correct and b is wrong

34. The development of which wood preservative bought international recognition on wood preservative in India
    a. CSAU  b. ASCU
    c. SACU  d. None of the above

35. The chief characteristics of ideal wood preservative are
    a. High toxicity  b. High permanency
    c. High penetrability  d. All of the above

36. Creosote is ---------- type of wood preservative
    a. Oil type  b. Water type
    c. b is correct and a is wrong  d. a is correct and b is wrong

37. Which one is the extremely toxic to wood destroying fungi is
    a. Copper sulphate  b. Zinc chloride
    c. Mercuric chloride  d. All of them

38. In case of full cell process cylinder filled with preservative is subjected to an antiseptic pressure of
    a. 3.50 to 12.30 $Kg/cm^2$  b. 4.50 to 12.30 $Kg/cm^2$
    c. 3.50 to 10.30 $Kg/cm^2$  d. 4.50 to 11.30 $Kg/cm^2$

39. Glued wood construction built of veneers in such manner that the grain of each veneer is at right angle to that of adjacent veneer is called
    a. Face to face construction b. Cross band construction
    c. Plywood d. a and b both

40. The outer piles in a plywood panel are called
    a. Face and back b. Back and face
    c. Only back d. Only face

41. The maximum length of logs used for peeling in plywood is
    a. 250-275 cm b. 155-280 cm
    c. 225-280 cm d. 280-325 cm

42. Process of harvesting, converting and disposing of forest produce and other resources of forest is known as
    a. Forest Utilization b. Forest Marketing
    c. Forest Management d. None of them

43. Portion of branch that is embedded in wood is
    a. Knot b. Joint
    c. Loose knot d. a and c both

44. Percentage of timber wasted during conversion is?
    a. 45 b. 50
    c. 55 d. 40

45. Which one is recommended logging branch in India?
    a. Dr. Huber b. Mr. Koreleff
    c. Dr. A. Huber d. Dr. Huber and Mr. A. Koroleff

46. Logging branch started in India during which five year plan?
    a. $1^{st}$ plan b. $2^{nd}$ plan
    c. $3^{rd}$ plan d. None of the above

47. In which year logging branch came into existence?
    a. June 1957 b. June 1967
    c. July 1957 d. June 1967

48. In which institute of India logging branch started first?
    a. ICFRE, Dehra Dun b. FRI, Dehra Dun
    c. TFRI, Jabalpur d. a and b both

49. Which type of saw is generally used for cutting tree?
    a. Crosscut saw b. Bow saw
    c. Pruning saw d. All of them

50. Bow saw is also known as
    a. Crosscut saw b. One man saw
    c. Pruning saw d. None of them

51. Preferred use of Bow saw is
    a. Cutting of log b. Cutting of tree
    c. Felling of small timber d. All of them

52. Measuring stick is used for which purpose?
    a. Measuring of log length b. Measuring of tree height
    c. a and b both d. None of them

53. Which month is usually good for felling in mountain area?
    a. March b. April
    c. October d. May

54. Which is most convenient season for felling of tree?
    a. Summer b. Rainy
    c. Winter d. Spring

55. Why we avoid summer season for felling of tree?
    a. High Temperature b. Splitting of wood
    c. Quick fire d. Rapid drying

56. The convenient height of stump during cutting is
    a. 15-20 cm b. 10-25 cm
    c. 05-20 cm d. 05-25 cm

57. Root felling is usually used in which species?
    a. Sandal b. Khair
    c. Walnut d. All of them

58. Which is the cheapest way of timber transport?
    a. Road b. Rail
    c. Water d. All of them

59. Floating type transport is used for which type of wood?
    a. Hardwood b. Softwood
    c. Winter wood d. All of them

60. Light coloured outer portion of tree is known as?
   a. Sapwood b. Resin wood
   c. Heart wood d. All of them

61. Which among is a type of timber storage depot?
   a. Forest depot b. Transit depot
   c. Sale depot d. All of them

62. Deep coloured inner portion of wood is called?
   a. Dead wood b. Heart wood
   c. Sapwood d. All of them

63. Function of sapwood is
   a. Transportation of water b. Food storage
   c. Conduction of sap d. b and c both

64. Heart wood consists of?
   a. Dead tissue b. Living tissue
   c. a is correct and b is wrong d. a is wrong and b is correct

65. Function of heartwood is
   a. Storage of food b. Mechanical support to stem and crown
   c. a and b both d. None of them

66. Which among the following is not having true heartwood?
   a. Ebonies b. Chir pine
   c. Salix d. All of them

67. The plant having reddish coloured heartwood is?
   a. Shisham b. Khair
   c. Sal d. Jamun

68. Longer durability of heartwood depends upon
   a. Deposition of gum b. Resins and oils
   c. Only resin d. a and b both

69. Gum, Resin and oils deposition in heartwood act as
   a. Preservative b. Synthetic preservative
   c. Natural preservative d. b and c both

70. Why heartwood is susceptible to fungal attack?
    a. Carbohydrate and starch deposition b. Oil deposition
    c. Gum deposition d. Resin deposition

71. Bark having diagnostic features is helpful in
    a. Protection of tree b. Identification of tree
    c. Valuation of tree d. All of them

72. The season favouring the growth or trees in temperate region is?
    a. Spring b. Summer
    c. Rainy d. a and b both

73. Rapid growth in the beginning of season in a form of thin wall is called as
    a. Early or spring wood b. Late of summer wood
    c. Heart wood d. Hard wood

74. Size of ring in fast grown timber species is……mm.
    a. 0-15 b. 5-10
    c. 5-25 d. 5-15

75. Which type of timber is having narrow rings?
    a. Fast growing timber b. Slow growing timber
    c. Medium growing timber d. None of the above

76. Growth ring is responsible to show wood formation
    a. Seasonally b. Monthly
    c. Yearly d. Half yearly

77. Growth ring is more prominent in shape and size from which region
    a. Tropical b. Temperate
    c. Humid d. Sub-tropical

78. Counting of annual ring in spring and autumn depend upon
    a. Arrangement of vessels b. Arrangement and even distribution of vessels
    c. Arrangement of Pores d. Only distribution of vessels

79. Autumn season wood is having …….. type of structure?
    a. Open structure b. Wide structure
    c. Thin structure d. Dense structure

80. In which type of wood vessels conduct liquid sap?
    a. Narrow leaves b. Broad leaves
    c. Niddle type leaves d. All of them

81. Find out the light weight species timber
    a. *Bombax ceiba* b. *Abies pindrow*
    c. *Cryptomeria japonioca* d. a and b both

82. Silver fir and semul comes under which category of wood
    a. Heavy b. Very heavy
    c. Light d. Very light

83. Which is moderately heavy timber species?
    a. Siris b. Deodar
    c. Walnut d. All of them

84. Which is heavy timber species?
    a. Teak b. Mulberry
    c. Arjuna d. a and b both

85. Sal, Babul, Sissoo and Dhau come under which category of timber species
    a. Very heavy b. Heavy
    c. Extremely heavy d. All of them

86. Find out the name of extremely heavy wood
    a. Oaks b. Rohan
    c. Teak d. All of them

87. How many types of grains are found in wood?
    a. 4 b. 5
    c. 6 d. 3

88. Which type of grain is most suitable?
    a. Interlocular b. Spiral
    c. Irregular d. All of them

89. How many types of texture is formed in wood?
    a. 5 b. 3
    c. 4 d. 6

90. Which texture of wood take polish easily?
    a. Fine textured b. Coarse textured
    c. Even textured d. Uneven textured

91. Which type of wood is more decorative?
    a. Even textured b. Coarse textured
    c. Fine textured d. Uneven textured

92. Narrow, Spindle shaped elongated cells with closed end is known as
    a. Fibre b. Tissue
    c. Grain d. All of them

93. Fibre provides mechanical strength and rigidity to which type of species?
    a. Softwood b. Niddle type leaves
    c. Broad leaves d. a and c both

94. Wood having tracheids is known as
    a. Hardwood b. Ply wood
    c. Heart Wood d. Softwood

95. The knots which are inseparable during sawing are called as
    a. Dead or tight knot b. Live or tight knot
    c. Live or loose knot d. Dead or losse knot

96. Ring porous wood is rare in which country?
    a. India b. Pakistan
    c. Australia d. USA

97. Which one is the ring porous timber wood?
    a. Teak b. Sal
    c. Tun d. a and b Both

98. Indian dicotyledonous comes under which category of wood?
    a. Ring porous wood b. Diffuse porous wood
    c. a is correct & b is wrong d. b is correct & a is wrong

99. Formation of diffuse porous wood is due to which reason?
    a. Extending rainy season b. Extended growing season
    c. Reduction of rainy season d. Increasing pollution

100. Mostly tyloses are present in which type of wood?
    a. Sapwood b. Hardwood
    c. Heartwood d. All of them

101. In sapwood tyloses are.................. present
    a. Always b. Occasionally
    c. Frequently d. None of them

102. Tyloses are indicator of which character in wood?
a. Mechanical strength
b. Shininess of wood
c. Durability of wood
d. All of them

103. Why tyloses are responsible for wood durability?
a. Increasing air movement
b. Impede the air and moisture movement
c. Increasing food storage
d. All of them

104. In which species gum and resin ducts are irregular?
a. Sal
b. Teak
c. Tun
d. a and b both

105. At what stage of tree age, branch wood is more in comparison to stem wood?
a. Early age
b. Middle age
c. Maturity
d. Harvesting

106. Regular and even distribution of gum and canal duct are common is which species
a. Gurjan
b. Pine
c. Spruce
d. all of them

107. In which type of wood parenchyma is absent?
a.Broad leaves
b. Coniferous
c. Dead wood
d. a and b both

108. Pith flakes are developed due to which reasons?
a. Fungal attack
b. Fast growth
c. Insect attack
d. a and c both

109. Resin canals and gum ducts are.........features of coniferous wood
a. Rare
b. Some time
c. Common
d. frequent

110. Pine and Spruce have which type of resin canal and gum ducts
a. Vertical
b. Horizontal
c. Clock wise
d. a and b both

111. How much % of wood is contributed by branch?
a. 20-25
b. 5-7
c. 8-10
d. 15-20

112. Ripple mark character usually helps in?
   a. Identification b. Quality
   c. Value d. a and c both

113. Decorative and silver grain effect in wood is due to?
   a. Tylosis appear b. Wood ray appearance
   c. Tracheids d. all of them

114. Which type of timber or wood is having clean shape and superior in nature?
   a. Uneven wood b. Softwood
   c. Even aged wood d. a and c both

115. Colour of wood is due to?
   a. Chemical b. Site factor
   c Food d. All of them

116. Discoloration of wood is due to?
   a. Insect attack b. Fungal attack
   c. Site Quality d. Injury

117. Natural colour of wood shows............. value of wood
   a. Nature of wood b. Soundness of wood
   c. Condition of wood d. b and c both

118. Decorative nature of wood depends upon?
   a. Lusture b. Sheer
   c. Light d. a and b both

119. Odour of wood is due to?
   a. Tannins & fatty acid b. Gum & fatty acid
   c. Tannins & gum d. All of them

120. Odour is very high in?
   a. Old wood b. Preserved wood
   c. Freshly cut wood d. a and c both

121. In which type of wood odour is very high?
   a. Ply wood b. Hard wood
   c. Sap wood d. Heart wood

122. Floatability of wood depends upon?
   a. Weight b. Specific gravity
   c. Colour of wood d. None of the above

123. Percentage of moisture present in dry wood is?
a. 10-20 b. 15-25
c. 8-15 d. Above 25

124. Which wood is harder in nature?
a. Fast grown b. Slow grown broad leaves
c. Slow grown coniferous d. b and c both

125. Which process increases the flexibility of wood?
a. Steaming b. Polishing
c. Preservation d. a and b both

126. Separation of fibre along the grain of standing or freshly felled tree is known as
a. Cross grain b. Knot
c. a and b both d. Shake

127. Which factor helps to improve elasticity?
a. Dryness b. Specific gravity
c. Moisture content d. a and b both

128. Fissibility is more important character for?
a. Ply wood b. Fuel wood
c. Heart wood d. Soft wood

129. Costus oil is extracted from?
a. *Saussure lappa* b. *Valeriana wallichii*
c. *Pandamus tectorius* d. All of them

130. Costus oil is obtained by distillation of?
a. Flower b. Root
c. Bark d. Wood

131. Valerian oil is obtained from the plant
a. *Acacia fornesiana* b. *Bursera delpechiana*
c. *Valeriana wallichii* d. a and c both

132. Valerian oil is extracted by stem distillation of the dry
a. Rhizome b. Runner
c. Sucker d. All of them

133. Keora oil is a

a. Root oil
b. Flower oil
c. Leaf oil
d. Wood oil

134. Keora oil is obtained from flower of

a. *Panadamus tectorius*
b. *Saussure lappa*
c. a is correct & b is wrong
d. a and b both are correct

135. Perfumery product attar of Keora is obtained from

a. Flower of Keora
b. Flower Saussure
c. Root of Keora
d. a and c both

136. Cassie perfume of commerce is obtained from

a. *Acacia nilotica*
b. *A. fornesiana*
c. *A. catechu*
d. All of them

137. *Bursera delpechiana* oil is known as

a. Linoloe oil
b. Citrus oil
c. Root oil
d. All of them

138. Which part of *Bursera delpechiana* yields linaloe oil?

a. Heart wood
b. Berries
c. Sapwood
d. a and b both

139. The chief constitute of oil obtained from *Citrus limonia* is?

a. Citrus
b. Citrol
c. Citral
d. All of them

140. Which tree yields a valuable edible fat known as Kokum butter?

a. *Garcinia indica*
b. *Pongamia pinnata*
c. *Shorea robusta*
d. a and c both

141. Chailmugra oil is obtained from which tree?

a. *Shorea robusta*
b. *Pongamia pinnata*
c. *Hydnocarpus kurzii*
d. None of them

142. Chailmugra oil is used?

a. Fever
b. Headache
c. Allergy
d. Leprosy

143. The seed oil from *Madhuca indica* is known as?

a. Mahua milk
b. Mahua sap
c. Mahua butter
d. All of them

144. Which is the wax yield tree?
   a. *Sapium sebiferum* b. *Melia azadarach*
   c. *Sapium bacata* d. a and b both

145. Japan wax candles are made from seeds of?
   a. *Rhus succedanea* b. *Melia azadarach*
   c. *Azardichata indica* d. a and b both

146. Avarum bark is obtained from which plant?
   a. *Casia auriculata* b. *Casia fistula*
   c. *Acacia nilotica* d. a and b both

147. Avarum bark contains______ % of tannin?
   a. 13 b. 33
   c. 23 d. 25

148. Bark of Sal contains________ % of tannin?
   a. 5-15 b. 5-10
   c. 1-5 d. 3-9

149. Light brown colour leather is produced from bark of?
   a. *Terminalia arjuna* b. *Shorea robusta*
   c. *Acacia nilotica* d. a and c both

150. The most important myrobalnis is produced from fruit of?
   a. *Terminalia arjuna* b. *T. belerica*
   c. *Acacia nilotica* d. a and c both

151. Santaline dye is obtained from?
   a. *Pterocarpus santalinus* b. *Pterocarpus marsupium*
   c. a is correct and b is wrong d. a is wrong and b is correct

152. Santaline dye is obtained from which part of wood?
   a. Heardwood b. Sapwood
   c. Softwood d. Heartwood

153. Which dye is known as Braziline dye?
   a. Brown dye b. Light brown dye
   c. Red dye d. Black dye

154. The dye obtained from *Ceasalpinia sappan* is known as?
   a. Santaline dye b. Braziline dye
   c. a is correct and b is wrong d. b is correct and a is wrong

155. Black dye from the bark is obtained from which species?

a. *Acacia concinna* b. *A. farnesiana*

c. *A. leucocephloea* d. All of them

156. Kamela dye is obtained from?

a. *Mallotus philippensis* b. *Mahuca longifolia*

c. *Acacia leucocephloea* d. a and b both

157. Kamela dye is obtained from which part of plant?

a. Seed dye b. Fruit dye

c. Flower dye d. Bark dye

158. Annatto dye of commerce is obtained from which plant?

a. *Bixa orellana* b. *Acacia mollissima*

c. *Acacia catchu* d. All of them

159. Bixin is obtained from which part of plant?

a. Seed b. Leaves

c. Fruit d. Flower

160. Dhak dye is the product of which plant?

a. *Bixa orellana* b. *Acacia mollissima*

c. *Butea monosperma* d. *Butea parviflora*

161. Dhak dye is popularly known as?

a. Seed dye b. Bark dye

c. Fruit dye d. Flower dye

162. The principle colouring matter of bixin is the product of which plant?

a. *Bixa orellana* b. *Butea monosperma*

c. *Butea parviflora* d. None of them

163. A valuable red dye (Marjit) is the product of which plant?

a. *Rubia cordifolia* b. *Toona ciliate*

c. *Shorea robusta* d. All of them

164. Marjit dye product is extracted from which part of plant?

a. Flower & Fruit b. Seed & Bark

c. Root & Stem d. Heartwood & sapwood

165. Which among the following is a root dye yielding plant?

a. *Berberis aristata* b. *Punica granatum*

c. *Morinda coreia* d. All of them

166. The dye produced from leaves of *Lawsonia inermis* is known as
a. Santaline dye
b. Kemela dye
c. Marjit dye
d. Henna dye

167. The Indian gum Arabica is the product of which plant?
a. *Acacia nilotica*
b. *A. catechu*
c. *A. auriculiformis*
d. All of them

168. *Acacia senegal* is the sources of which gum?
a. Indian gum Arabica
b. True gum Arabica
c. Gum kino
d. a and b both

169. *Pterocarpus massupium* is the sources of which gum?
a. Indian gum Arabica
b. True gum Arabica
c. Gum kino
d. Only Gum

170. *Pterocarpus massupium* gum contains _____ per cent of tannic acid?
a. 75
b. 55
c. 65
d. 45

171. Bengal kino is the product of
a. *Butea mononsperma*
b. *Butea parviflora*
c. a and b both
d. none of them

172. Jhingan gum is obtained from which plant?
a. *Lannea coromendelica*
b. *Butea parviflora*
c. *Artocarpos hetrophullus*
d. a and c both

173. Moringa gum is obtained from which plant?
a. *Morenga olifera*
b. *Butea parviflora*
c. *Artocarpos hetrophullus*
d. *Moring pterygosperma*

174. Salai gum is the product of
a. *Boswellia serrata*
b. *Madhuca indica*
c. *Artocarpos hetrophullus*
d. All of them

175. Resin yielding species of pine is
a. *Pinus roxburghii*
b. *P. wallichiana*
c. *P. Gerardiana*
d. All of them

176. Trade name of gum & resin exude from cracks/cut and solidify upon exposure to air is

a. Dammar b. Gammar

c. Damar d. a and b both

177. Tree dammar is obtained from which plant?

a. *Agathis loranthifolius* b. *Madhuca longifolia*

c. *Madhuca indica* d. a and b both

178. Black dammr is the product of which plant?

a. *Agathis loranthifolius* b. *Madhuca longifolia*

c. *Madhuca indica* d. *Canarium strictum*

179. *Hopea odorata* yields a resin known as?

a. White dammar b. Rock dammar

c. Hard dammar d. a and c both

180. Resin from *Vaterria indica* is popularly known as

a. White dammar b. Rock dammar

c. Hard dammar d. Red dammar

181. Gum extracted from *Boswellia serrata* is popularly known as

a. Salai gum b. Kino gum

c. Guggal gum d. a and c both

182. Source of gum resin gambage is

a. *Garcinia Morella* b. *Garcinia indica*

c. b is correct & a is wrong d. a is correct & b is wrong

183. Wild bees *Apis dorsata* and *A. indica* are source of ____ products?

a. Honey b. Wax

c. Food d. a and b both

184. Accumulated excrement of Bats guana found the in caves of forest area is a rich source of

a. Natural manures b. Artificial manures

c. Natural food d. a and b

185. Leaves of *Diospyrous melanoxylon* is mainly used for which purpose?

a. Manures b. Bidi

c. Fodder d. a and b

186. The nut of which species is used for soap purpose?
   a. *Sapindus mukorosii* b. *S. trifoliates*
   c. *Acacia concinna* d. All of them

187. Liquorice of commerce is the product of *Clycyrhiza globra*?
   a. Root b. Seed
   c. Flower d. Bark

188. Drug quinine is obtained from?
   a. *Cinchona ledgeriana* b. *C. hybrid*
   c. Both of them d. only a

189. Drug quinine is obtained from________ part of the plant?
   a. Bark b. Root
   c. Shoot d. Wood

190. Castor oil is yield by the seeds of _______plant?
   a. *Ricinus Communis* b. *Jatropha carcus*
   c. *Pongamia pinaata* d. All of them

191. Bark of *Albizia procera*, *Berberis aristata* and *Myrica esculenta* are used for
   a. Fish poison b. Fish food
   c. Fish medicine d. All of them

192. Rotenone a well known insecticide is the product of?
   a. *Pongamia pinaata* b. *Cinchona ledgeriana*
   c. *Milletia pachycarpa* d. b and c both

193. The process in which the impurities that impart a poor colour pulp are either removed or decolorized is
   a. Pulp bleaching b. Pulp cleaning
   c. Pulp beating d. a and b both

194. Mostly used chemical in single stage pulp bleaching is
   a. Calcium hypochlorite b. Calcium chloride
   c. a and b both d. Only a

195. In single stage pulp bleaching mostly used chemical is
   a. Chlorine gas b. Hypochlorite
   c. Chlorine dioxide d. All of them

196. Which among the following is used to size the paper?
   a. Rosin b. Aluminium sulphate
   c. Wax emulsion d. All of them

197. The process by which paper is made more or less impervious to the treatment of inks is known as
   a. Sizing b. Cleaning
   c. Beating d. Bleaching

198. Addition of non fibrous mineral matter to stock prior to sheet formation is known as
   a. Loading b. Mixing
   c. Beating d. Bleaching

198. Material used for loading in paper making are called as
   a. Shining agent b. Filler
   c. Supplement d. All of them

199. Which one is used as filler in paper industry?
   a. China clay b. Talc powder
   c. Titanium dioxide d. All of them

200. When heartwood of Acacia catechu is boiled in water, it gives?
   a. Cutch b. Katha
   c. None of them d. a and b both

201. The chief constituent of the catechin (katha) and catechu tannic acid (cutch) is obtained from?
   a. Sapwood b. Heartwood
   c. Heardwood d. Softwood

202. A third article of commerce obtained from a catechu tree in the shape of white powder is known as
   a. Khearsal b. Katha
   c. Insecticide d. a and b both

203. Laccifera lacca secreted a valuable resin known as
   a. Lac b. Honey
   c. Shellac d. a and c both

204. Which among the following is a lac host plants?
   a. *Butea monosperma* b. *Zizyphus mauritiana*
   c. *Schleichera oleasa* d. All of them

205. The two distinct strains of lac insect in India are

a. Kusmi  b. Rangeeni

c. Phaguni  d. a and b both

206. The species regularly tapped for resin in India is

a. *Garcinia Morella*  b. *Pinus roxburghii*

c. *Garcinia indica*  d. a and b both

207. Light continuous tapping method of resin is followed in trees having girth ............

a. >0.9 mm  b. <0.9 mm

c. 1.9 mm  d. a and b both

208. Heavy tapping of resin extraction is also known as

a. Tapping to death  b. Continuous tapping

c. Tapping of power  d. All of them

209. Saw dust of which species is having irritating nature.

a. *Albizia lebbck*  b. *Termenalia alata*

c. *Albizia procera*  d. *Acacia nilotica*

210. Which type of wood burns for longer duration?

a. Dense wood  b. Light wood

c. Porous wood  d. a and c both

211. Which constitute is responsible for more heat in wood?

a. Resin  b. Oil

c. Gum  d. All of them

212. Alignment of the fibre refers to

a. Grain  b. Longitudinal grain

c. Cross grain  d. All of them

213. Stain and decay type of defects in wood is due to

a. Insect attack  b. Fungal attack

c. Nematode attack  d. All of them

214. Wood is discoloured due to

a. Stain  b. Decay

c. Moisture  d. All of them

215. Fungi feeding on sapwood causes?
   a. Stain
   b. Decay
   c. a and b both
   d. All of them

216. Which species among the following is used for aircraft purpose?
   a. Sitka spruce
   b. Spruce
   c. Chir pine
   d. Champa

217. Which constitute is not good for battery separators?
   a. *Volatile acid*
   b. *Tannins*
   c. *Resin*
   d. All of them

218. Wood of which species among the following is good for motor bearings?
   a. Guaiacum officinale
   b. *G. Sanctum*
   c. *G. Indica*
   d. a and b both

219. Wood bearing is used in a machine having?
   a. High speed
   b. Slow speed
   c. Low pressure
   d. a and c both

220. Which wood is most suitable for ship building purpose?
   a. Teak
   b. Sal
   c. Sissoo
   d. Kadam

221. Match industry started in India in year?
   a. 1920
   b. 1921
   c. 1922
   d. 1923

222. The occurrence of fibre at an angle to the longitudinal surface of a timber is
   a. Spiral grain
   b. Diagonal grain
   c. Cross grain
   d. All of them

223. Wood having uniform annual rings is suitable for?
   a. Agricultural implements
   b. Bearing
   c. Musical Instruments
   d. All of them

224. Removal of moisture from wood is known as
   a. Drying
   b. Seasoning
   c. Heating
   d. a and b both

225. On the dry weight basis % of moisture under fibre saturation point is
a. 20-30 b. 10-20
c. 30-40 d. 15-25

226. How much % of moisture is left in air dried wood?
a. 0-5 b. 8-17
c. 10-18 d. 9-16

227. Shrinkage of wood is more in?
a. Dry weather b. Dry warm weather
c. Dry and cloudy weather d. a and b both

228. Warping in wood is due to
a. Only shrinkage b. Hanging drying
c. a and b both d. Unequal shrinkage

229. The best way to keep logs of wood in good condition is?
a. Storage in dry room b. Storage in teen shade
c. Storage in water d. and b both

230. Curvature of the plain of the face such that it becomes concave or convex across the grain is
a. Warping b. Bowing
c. Twist d. Cupping

231. Which wood is less durable?
a. Sapwood b. Hard wood
c. Heartwood d. a and c both

232. Impregnating wood with chemical preservative increases its
a. Strength b. Durability
c. Storage life d. Utilization capacity

233. Cedar oil used as wood preservative is effective against
a. Insect b. Nematode
c. Fungi d. Worms

234. The preservative from garlic boiled with vinegar is used against
a. Insect b. Nematode
c. Fungi d. Worms

235. Modern science of wood preservation was developed in which continent?
a. Asia
b. Europe
c. Africa
d. b and c both

236. In which year Kyan wood preservation method was developed?
a. 1822
b. 1852
c. 1842
d. 1842

237. The chemical used by Kyan as wood preservative was?
a. Mercuric chloride
b. Coal tar
c. Zinc
d. All of them

238. Person first used zinc chloride as wood preservative is?
a. Kyan
b. Bethel
c. a and b both
d. Sir William Burnett

239. Name of the scientist who developed novel method for wood preservation?
a. Dr. Boucherie
b. Bethel
c. Kyan
d. Sir William Burnett

240. Dr. Boucherie used.............water soluble inorganic salts as wood preservative
a. Copper sulphate
b. Zinc chloride
c. Only zinc
d. a and b both

241. Which latest development increased the value of treated wood?
a. Ship
b. Steam engine
c. Motor car
d. All of them

242. Which wood preservation method can increase the life of wood 5-10 times?
a. Chemical
b. Semi chemical
c. Indigenous
d. Mechanical (high vacuum & very high pressure.

243. Rattan is the commercial name of
a. Bamboo
b. Canes
c. Bamboo stick
d. a and b both

244. The resistance of wood to penetration by any other body is
a. Strength
b. Flexibility
c. Hardness
d. a and c both

245. Gum product obtained from *Bauhinia retusa* is known as

a. Gum Arabica b. Semla gum
c. Bengal Gum d. True gum

246. Chemical used in Bethel process under pressure for wood preservation is?

a. Zinc chloride b. Coal tar
c. Zinc d. Creosote

247. Which among the following is not a Lac host plant?

a. Terminalia b. *Butea*
c. *Zizphus* d. All of them

248. Name the tree which is used for making hockey sticks

a. Willow b. Shisham
c. Teak d. Mulberry

## Filling the blanks

1. *Picrorhiza kurroea* has active principle glucoside.........................
2. Poison abrin for poisoning cattle and other live stock and for homicidal purpose is ....................
3. Two principle alkaline process used for pulping are ..............................
4. Mechanical treatment viz bruising or cutting to fibres for sheet formation is .........................
5. Katha is an important ingredient for the preparation of chewing...............
6. A liquid constituent of crude pine resin is oil of.................
7. Solid constituent of crude pine resin is..............
8. Charcoal is carbonized ................
9. Valerian oil is used for ..............................
10. Which part of *Sapium sebiferum* yields wax ..................
11. The most important bark used in North India is that of ....................
12. Wattle box is obtained from ......................
13. Tan fruit of local value is ..........................., ...................... and ....................
14. Artocarpus is a ..............
15. The leaves of several species of indigifera contain a soluble glucoside known as ......................
16. Widely used creosote is ......................
17. Hardiproof and cupronol are two proprietar preservativs of.................type

18. Central Ply in Plywood is called ...............
19. The simplest structure of plywood is of ..................
20. The common thickness of rotator cut veneers are ..........; .............. and ..........
21. Glued laminated wood resulting for glued lamination is called ...............
22. Which part of saw is most important ............
23. Which saw is used for pruning purpose ...........
24. October to March is good timing for felling in which part of country ........
25. Floating depends upon ..............
26. Discoloration of Sapwood by fungi is known as...........
27. Outer protected zone of tree is known as ...........
28. Slow growth with thick wall is known as ..................
29. Spring wood is also known as ..................
30. Summer wood is also known as ................
31. Annual ring of broad leaved species is generally due to.............
32. Pores is also known as ..............
33. Fibre looks like tracheids of ..........
34. Which structure is responsible to performe conduction and mechanical functions ..............
35. Structure of tracheids looks like ..................
36. Tracheids are compressed in which type of wood ...............
37. Which type of wood vessels are large in size ....................
38. Thick type of vessels is present in which type of wood ................
39. Duct is little in size and scanty in which type of wood.................
40. Gummy deposits are help ful in ................
41. Function of parenchyma in softwood is ...........................
42. Function of wood ray or medullary ray are ........................
43. Which structure and system are responsible for radical conduction and storage of food in tree .....................
44. Where wood rays appear and in which shape ........................
45. Lusture is also known as ....................
46. Lusture or sheer depend on the ability of .....................
47. Drawback of lusture is ........................
48. Why climbers are more flexible ........................

49. Why elasticity is essential ...........................

50. Presence of ........................ substance keep away fungal and insect attack

### Answer Fill in the blanks

1. Picrorhiza
2. *Abrus precatorius*
3. Soda and sulphate
4. Beating and refining
5. Pans
6. Turpentine
7. Rosin
8. Wood
9. Flavouring and blending
10. Seed
11. *Acacia nilotica*
12. *Acacia mollissima*
13. *Acaia nilotica, Ceasalpinia coriaria* and *Zizyphus xylopyrus*
14. Wood dye
15. Indican
16. Coaltar creosote
17. Organic solvent type.
18. Core.
19. Plies
20. 1.25mm, 1.5mm, 2.5mm
21. Glulam
22. Tooth Shape
23. Pruning Saw
24. Plain
25. Specific gravity
26. Sap-stain
27. Bark
28. Late or Summer wood
29. Softwood
30. Hardwood
31. Pores
32. Vessels
33. Softwood
34. Tracheids
35. Spake of honey comb
36. Autumn Wood
37. Spring (Early wood)
38. Late Wood
39. Diffuse Porous Wood
40. Identification
41. Storage and Conduction of Food materials
42. Rising Sap and Transportation of food
43. Wood rays
44. Radical line and Horizontal ribbons
45. Sheer
46. Cell wall to reflect light
47. Do not take polish easily
48. Due to long straight loose fibers
49. Regain the original shape
50. Toxic

## Answer Key

| | | | | | | | | | |
|---|---|---|---|---|---|---|---|---|---|
| 1. | B | 2. | D | 3. | C | 4. | B | 5. | B |
| 6. | D | 7. | B | 8. | D | 9. | A | 10. | B |
| 11. | B | 12. | A | 13. | C | 14. | B | 15. | D |
| 16. | C | 17. | D | 18. | A | 19. | C | 20. | C |
| 21. | B | 22. | A | 23. | B | 24. | C | 25. | A |
| 26. | B | 27. | D | 28. | C | 29. | B | 30. | B |
| 31. | A | 32. | D | 33. | A | 34. | B | 35. | D |
| 36. | D | 37. | D | 38. | A | 39. | B | 40. | A |
| 41. | C | 42. | A | 43. | A | 44. | B | 45. | D |
| 46. | A | 47. | A | 48. | B | 49. | A | 50. | B |
| 51. | C | 52. | A | 53. | B | 54. | C | 55. | D |
| 56. | A | 57. | D | 58. | D | 59. | B | 60. | A |
| 61. | D | 62. | B | 63. | D | 64. | A | 65. | B |
| 66. | A | 67. | B | 68. | D | 69. | C | 70. | A |
| 71. | B | 72. | D | 73. | A | 74. | C | 75. | B |
| 76. | A | 77. | B | 78. | B | 79. | D | 80. | B |
| 81. | D | 82. | C | 83. | D | 84. | A | 85. | A |
| 86. | D | 87. | C | 88. | B | 89. | C | 90. | A |
| 91. | A | 92. | A | 93. | C | 94. | D | 95. | B |
| 96. | A | 97. | D | 98. | C | 99. | B | 100. | C |
| 101. | B | 102. | C | 103. | B | 104. | D | 105. | A |
| 106. | D | 107. | B | 108. | D | 109. | C | 110. | D |
| 111. | C | 112. | A | 113. | B | 114. | C | 115. | A |
| 116. | B | 117. | B | 118. | D | 119. | A | 120. | C |
| 121. | D | 122. | B | 123. | C | 124. | C | 125. | A |
| 126. | D | 127. | D | 128. | B | 129. | A | 130. | B |
| 131. | B | 132. | A | 133. | B | 134. | C | 135. | A |
| 136. | B | 137. | A | 138. | A | 139. | B | 140. | D |
| 141. | C | 142. | D | 143. | C | 144. | A | 145. | A |
| 146. | A | 147. | C | 148. | D | 149. | D | 150. | B |
| 151. | C | 152. | D | 153. | C | 154. | C | 155. | D |
| 156. | A | 157. | B | 158. | A | 159. | A | 160. | C |
| 161. | D | 162. | A | 163. | A | 164. | C | 165. | D |
| 166. | D | 167 | A | 168 | B | 169 | C | 170 | A |
| 171 | A | 172 | A | 173 | D | 174 | A | 175 | D |
| 176 | A | 177 | A | 178 | D | 179 | B | 180 | A |
| 181 | D | 182 | D | 183 | D | 184 | B | 185 | B |
| 186 | D | 187 | A | 188 | C | 189 | A | 190 | A |
| 191 | A | 192 | C | 193 | A | 194 | D | 195 | D |
| 196 | D | 197 | A | 198 | A | 199 | D | 200 | D |
| 201 | B | 202 | A | 203 | A | 204 | D | 205 | A |

| | | | | | | | | | |
|---|---|---|---|---|---|---|---|---|---|
| 206 | B | 207 | A | 208 | A | 209 | A | 210 | A |
| 211 | D | 212 | C | 213 | B | 214 | D | 215 | C |
| 216 | A | 217 | D | 218 | D | 219 | D | 220 | A |
| 221 | C | 222 | B | 223 | C | 224 | B | 225 | A |
| 226 | D | 227 | B | 228 | D | 229 | C | 230 | D |
| 231 | A | 232 | B | 233 | C | 234 | D | 235 | B |
| 236 | D | 237 | A | 238 | D | 239 | A | 240 | D |
| 241 | B | 242 | D | 243 | B | 244 | C | 245 | B |
| 246 | D | 247 | A | 248 | D | | | | |

# 5

# Forest Mensuration and Management

1. In most of the Common Wealth countries diameter is measured at a height of
   a. 1.35 m  b. 1.37m
   c. 1.6 m  d. 4 feet 4 inches
2. Spiegel relascope is provided with how much number of scales/bands to measure height of a tree?
   a. One  b. Two
   c. Three  d. Four
3. Smythies's hypsometer is based on the principle of
   a. Similar triangles  b.Trigonomery
   c. Probability proportional to size  d. Visual observation
4. Length of Christen's hypsometer is
   a. 33 mm  b. 33 cm
   c. 35 cm  d. 35 mm
5. While measuring height of a tree using Haga altimeter, if one reading is on right side of zero mark and other on left side, to get the total height of tree both the readings will be
   a. Subtracted  b. Added
   c. Added and divided by two  d. Subtracted and divided by two
6. Ravi multimeter differs from ravi altimeter in the way that it has
   a. Mirror and leveller  b. Aperture and turning knob
   c. None of them  d. Both (a) & (b) above
7. Which among the following is calculated in uneven aged forests?
   a. Crop height  b. Top height
   c. Mean height  d. Total height
8. Vertical point sampling for measuring crop height was developed by which scientist?
   a. Hirata  b. Brandis
   c. Shivnarayan  d. Odum

9. When basal area is measured at any convenient height and length of tree is taken above that point to calculate the form of the tree, the form factor so obtained is

a. Artificial form factor    b. Absolute form factor

c. True form factor    d. None of these

10. Point sampling is also called as

a. Bitterlich method    b. Pointless cruising

c. None of them    d. Both of these

11. Wedge prism is used to measure

a. Diameter    b. Basal area

c. Volume    d. Number of trees per unit area

12. Quarter girth formula for estimating volume of tree is also known as

a. Hoppus rule    b. Newton's formula

c. Hubers formula    d. None of these

13. Volume of the standing trees of forest is measured by

a. Hossfeld's and Urich's method    b. Hartig's and Draudt's method

c. Both of (a) & (b) is true    d. None of (a) & (b) true

14. Taking 1.41 m as crown spread which tree will be regarded as co-spaced tree among the following

a. Tree having 1 m crown spread    b. Tree having 0.5 m crown spread

c. Tree having 1.8 m crown spread    d. Tree having 0.6 m crown spread.

15. Floating periodic block was first introduced in

a. Germany    b. France

c. United Kingdom    d. India

16. The material that a forest can yield annually in perpetuity is known as

a. Progressive yield    b. Periodic yield

c. Sustained yield    d. Both (b) & (c)

17. Rotation under which a species yields the maximum material of a specified size for economic conversion is

a. Rotation of maximum volume production    b. Silvicultural rotation

c. Rotation of highest income    d. Technical rotation

18. Table showing the distribution of stems by diameter classes for each of a series of crop diameter is known as
    a. Yield table b. Volume table
    c. Stand table d. Money yield table
19. For a forest to provide sustained yield in perpetuity, it should have
    a. Normal increment b. Normal growing stock
    c. Normal series of age-gradation d. All of them
20. Rotation of maximum volume production is when
    a. MAI < CAI b. MAI > CAI
    c. MAI = CAI d. CAI negative
21. Floating Periodic Blocks are marked with which colour on map
    a. Green b. Black
    c. Blue d. Red
22. Langsaeter curves describes which of the following relation
    a. Effect of fertilizer on growth of tree b. Density on volume growth
    c. Density on soil properties d. Density on natural regeneration
23. Krajicek *et al.*, 1961 had developed which of the following stand density measures
    a. Relative density b. Quadratic mean stand diameter
    c. Crown Competition factor d. Relative stand density
24. Ratio of discounted value of all cash inflows to the discount value during the life of plantation is
    a. Net Present worth b. Benefit cost ratio
    c. Internal rate of return d. Net return
25. Forest mensuration is that branch of forestry which deals with the determination of ...................... of single tree, stand or whole or whole woods either standing or after felling
    a. Dimension b. Form
    c. Age & Increment d. All of the above
26. Foot, Pounds and Second system is also known as
    a. French system b. Metric system
    c. British system d. None of them

27. If greater accuracy is required, the unit of measurement should be........... rather than.........

a. cm & m
b. Foot & cm
c. gm & Decagram
d. Inch & mm

28. In universally adopted standard height for measuring girth, diameters and basal are of standing tree is

a. 4ft 3in
b. 4ft 5in
c. 4ft 6in
d. 4ft 4in

29. If the tree is leaning, dbh is measured ...............

a. Along the tree stem
b. Not vertically
c. Only a
d. a and b both

30. When the tree is forked above the breast height it is counted as

a. Two trees
b. One tree
c. a is wrong & b is correct
d. b is wrong & a is correct

31. Girth over bark can be converted into Girth under bark by using the formula

a. $g = g' - 2\pi t$
b. $g' = g - 2\pi t$
c. $t = g' - 2\pi t$
d. None of the above

32. The height of bole that is usually fit for utilization as timber is known as

a. Bole height
b. Height of standard timber bole
c. Commercial bole height
d. All of them

33. The height of the bole from the ground level upto the point where average diameter over bark is 20 cm

a. Bole height
b. Height of standard timber bole
c. Commercial bole height
d. None of them

34. If the vertical measurement of the crown of a tree from the tip to the point half way between the lowest green branches forming green crown all round and the lowest green branch on the bole

a. Crown height
b. Bole height
c. Crown length
d. All of them

35. If the height of the crown as measured vertically from the ground level to the point half way between the lowest green branch and the green branches forming green crown all round

a. Crown height
b. Bole height
c. Crown length
d. Total height

36. The formula used for determining form factor is

a. F=V/Sh  b. V=F/Sh

c. F=S/Vh  d. h=V/SF

37. Artificial form factor

a. True form factor  b. Breast height form factor

c. Normal form factor  d. a & c both

38. In normal form factor basal area is measured at .......... of the total height of tree

a. Constant proportion  b. Breast height form factor

c. Any convenient height  d. None of the above

39. In which type of form factor basal area is measured at any convenient height and the volume refers only to that part of the tree above the point of measurement.

a. True form factor  b. Breast height form factor

c. Normal form factor  d. Absolute form factor

40. An Australian forester A. Schiffel postulated that taper depends on what he called as

a. Form quotient  b. Form factor

c. Girth of tree  d. Basal area

41. In India, ...............meter height classes are generally used for classification of trees on the basis of height of trees

a. 4,5 or 6  b. 1,2 or 3

c. 2,4 or 6  d. 1,3 or 5

42. Generally height classes for species whose trees attain a height of more than 25 m at maturity

a. 2m  b. 5m

c. 4m  d. 1m

43. Generally height classes for species whose trees attain a height of between 15m and 25 m at maturity

a. 1m  b. 4m

c. 3m  d. None of the above

44. Generally height classes for species whose trees attain a height a less than 15 m at maturity

a. 5m  b. 3m

c. 2m  d. 1m

45. Ratio between the volume of the tree above the point of diameter or basal area measurement with the cylinder which has the same basal area and whose height is equal to the height of the tree above that point

a. Absolute form factor  b. Normal form factor
c. Artificial form factor  d. None of the above

46. In ..................... form factor basal area is measured at a constant proportion of the total height of the tree, e.g. $1/10^{th}$, $1/20^{th}$, etc. of the total height and the volume refers to the whole tree above ground level.

a. True form factor  b. Breast height form factor
c. Absolute form factor  d. None of the above

47. The basal area is measure at breast height and the volume refers to whole tree both above and below the point of measurement

a. Normal form factor  b. Artificial form factor
b. Absolute form factor  c. None of the above

48. The ratio between the volume of a tree to the product of basal area and height is known as

a. Form quotient  b. Form factor
c. Tree form factor  d. Stem timber form factor

49. In Britain quarter girth formula is also known as

a. Hoppus's rule  b. Smalians rule
c. Newtons formula  d. None of the above

50. Boring of a tree stem to determine increment of trees with annual rings is

a. Increment  b. Increment boring
c. Volume increment  d. None of the above

51. Which volume table is having all three variables?

a. Local volume table  b. Regional volume table
c. Form class volume table  d. Standard volume table

52. Which volume table is constructed based on the average volume of trees growing over a large geographical area

a. Standard volume table  b. General volume table
c. Regional volume table  d. Local volume table

53. Which volume table is applicable to a wide range of species?

a. Standard volume table  b. General volume table
c. Regional volume table  d. Local volume table

54. Which volume table show volume of trees by diameter classes and in each diameter class by height classes.
   a. Regional volume table b. Local volume table
   c. General volume table d. Standard volume table

55. Which volume table is used for deriving local volume tables
   a. General volume table b. Regional volume table
   c. Standard volume table d. Commercial volume table

56. In which volume tables the contents of round timber are given as volume measured down to a thin end diameter in which conversion is done, the stump volume being omitted
   a. Regional volume table b. Commercial volume table
   c. Standard volume table d. General volume table

57. The portion of the tree stem or log which is unmerchentable is known as
   a. Snag b. Cull
   b. Non-commercial log d. All of them

58. Instrument used for determine the age of tree is
   a. Pressler's increment borer b. Spigeal relescope
   c. Haga altimeter d. None of the above

59. The total increment up to a given age divided by that age is termed as
   a. PAI b. CAI
   c. MAI d. Total increment

60. The enumeration of the desired species above the specified diameter limit is carried out over the entire area of the forest unit is known as
   a. Complete enumeration b. Sample enumeration
   c. Partial enumeration d. None of the above

61. When the canopy density is 1.0 that means forest is
   a. Dense b. Thin
   c. Open d. Closed

62. When the canopy density is under 0.5 that means forest comes under which category?
   a. Open b. Dense
   c. Thin d. Closed

63. When the canopy density is between 0.75 and 1.0 than the forest comes under which class?
    - a. Closed
    - b. Thin
    - c. Dense
    - d. Open

64. When the canopy density is between 0.5 and 0.75 that means forest is
    - a. Dense
    - b. Thin
    - c. Open
    - d. Closed

65. Which table shows the distribution of stems by diameter classes for each series of crop diameter?
    - a. Stand table
    - b. Volume table
    - c. Yield table
    - d. None of the above

66. Type of enumeration practiced only in very valuable forest of limited extent?
    - a. Total enumeration
    - b. Partial enumeration
    - c. Sample enumeration
    - d. None of the above

67. The period between seedling felling and final felling on a particular area is?
    - a. Rotation interval
    - b. Regeneration interval
    - c. Regeneration period
    - d. b & c both

68. The percent ratio of normal yield to the NGS is?
    - a. Utilization period
    - b. Utilization value
    - c. Utilization percent
    - d. All of them

69. All material from thinning preceding the main felling in a regular forest is?
    - a. Yield
    - b. Total yield
    - c. Intermediate yield
    - d. All of them

70. In which year progressive yield was adopted?
    - a. 1948
    - b. 1958
    - c. 1940
    - d. 1950

71. Which scientist calculated increment from the volume of growing stock?
    - a. Pressler's
    - b. Schnider's
    - c. a and b both
    - d. none of them

72. Which scientist calculated increment from the diameter and annual ring?
    - a. Pressler's
    - b. Schnider's
    - c. Biolley's
    - d. a and b both

73. Which type of increment is independent of any increase in the price of forest produce?
    a. Increment  b. Total increment
    c. Quality increment  d. Value increment

74. Who calculated MAI based on the yield table attribute?
    a. Biolley's  b. Pressler's
    c. Schnider's  d. None of them

75. How many variables are used for construction of local volume table?
    a. 2  b. 1
    c. 4  d. 3

76. Analysis of a complete stem by measuring annual rings in order to determine past rate of growth
    a. Stump analysis  b. Stem analysis
    c. Branch analysis  d. Log analysis

77. The area obtained for reducing factor is
    a. Percent area  b. Reducing area
    c. Total area  d. All of them

78. The unit of yield regulation of both regular and irregular forest is a
    a. Felling  b. Felling cycle
    c. Felling series  d. All of them

79. The growing stock in a forest is termed as
    a. Value of forest  b. Forest capital
    c. Forest Items  d. a & b both

80. The sum of all the trees growing in the forest, or in a specified part is
    a. Biomass  b. Volume
    c. Growing stock  d. Timber

81. The increase in growth that takes place in a particular year is called
    a. MAI  b. CAI
    c. CAI & MAI  d. Only MAI

82. The MAI at rotation age is known as
    a. MAI  b. CAI
    c. Final MAI  d. Final CAI

83. How many times CAI and MAI coincide in the life of a crop
    a. 2 times  b. 3 times
    c. 1 times  d. All of them

84. CAI and MAI of a crop coincide once at the end of
    a. Second yr  b. Third yr
    c. Fourth yr  d. First yr

85. Criteria of fast growing species is
    a. $5m^3$/ha/annum  b. $15m^3$/ha/annum
    c. $20m^3$/ha/annum  d. $10m^3$/ha/annum

86. Which rotation is suitable for controlling the services?
    a. Physical  b. Silvicultural
    c. Technical  d. a and b both

87. The main objective of Physical and Silvicultural rotation is to control the
    a. Form  b. Service
    c. Height  d. Diameter

88. The main objective of technical rotation and rotation of maximum value of production rotation is to control on
    a. Output  b. Service
    c. Height  d. Diameter

89. Which one is considered as ideal state of forest condition?
    a. Abnormal forest  b. Normal forest
    c. Plantation forest  d. All of them

90. Normal series of age gradation, normal growing stock, and normal increment is termed as
    a. Perfect condition of forest  b. Managed forest
    c. Trinity of norms  d. a and b both

91. Analysis of a stump cross section by measuring annual rings to estimate age, past rate of diameter and basal area growth?
    a. Stem analysis  b. Log analysis
    c. Stump analysis  d. a and c both

92. CAI is decreases at?
    a. At maturity  b. At middle age
    c. With increasing age  d. a and c both

93. CAI and MAI also meet at the end of the?
    a. Maturity    b. Growing period
    c. Rotation Age    d. none of the above

94. In which type of forest age gradation is not present?
    a. Regular    b. Plantation
    c. Secondary    d. Irregular

95. If forests have Normal series of Age gradation and normal increment that means it has
    a. Normal growing stock    b. Normal forest
    c. Abnormal growing stock    d. Abnormal forest

96. Rotation which yield the highest net return on the invested capital is
    a. Maximum rotation    b. Financial rotation
    c. Technical rotation    d. Physical rotation

97. Rotation of forest rental is also known as
    a. Rotation of maximum production    b. Rotation of highest returns
    c. Rotation of maximum value    d. Rotation of highest income

98. Rotation of finance is also known as
    a. Rotation of economic rotation    b. Rotation of highest returns
    c. Rotation of maximum value    d. Rotation of highest income

99. Table in which yields are expressed in term of money instead of volume
    a. Money table    b. Yield table
    c. Volume table    d. Money yield table

100. The age at which CAI crosses MAI is the age of
    a. Maximum production    b. Total production
    c. Minimum production    d. Average production

101. A table showing the distribution of stem by diameter classes for each series of crop diameter, often auxiliary to a yield table
    a. Volume table    b. Stand table
    c. Growing stock table    d. a & b both

102. The rotation suitable for controlling the output of material from forest products in from or quantity is?
    a. Technical rotation    b. Maximum volume rotation
    c. Only b    d. a & b both

103. Rotation through which a species retain satisfactory vigour of growth and reproduction on a given site?

a. Technical rotation b. Maximum volume rotation
c. Silviculture rotation d. Physical rotation

104a. Rotation useful in forest management primarily for aesthetic and recreation al purpose?

a. Technical rotation b. Maximum volume rotation
c. Silviculture rotation d. Physical rotation

104. Rotation under which a species yields the maximum material of a specified size or suitability for economic conversion or for special use

a. Technical rotation b. Silviculture rotation
c. Financial rotation d. Physical rotation

105. Rotation which yield highest average annual gross or net revenue irrespective of the capital values of the forest

a. Rotation of forest rental b. Silviculture rotation
c. Financial rotation d. Technical rotation

106. Which rotations is important from overall national point of view?

a. Forest rental b. Rotation for highest income
c. Financial rotation d. All of them

107. Classification of forest as reserved, protected, village and unclassed is based on?

a. Classification based on protection b. Legal classification
c. Technical classification d. b & c both

108. Territorial classification of forests is

a. Block b. Compartment
c. Sub-compartment d. All of them

109. The Head quarter of inspector general of forest is located at

a. Chennai b. Kolkata
c. Dehra Dun d. Delhi

110. Written scheme of forest management is known as

a. Plan b. Plan of work
c. Working plan d. b & c both

111. A felling area usually one of an annual series unless otherwise stated as
a. Block
b. Stand
c. Beat
d. Coupe

112. A sub division of a felling series formed with the object of regulating cutting in some special manner is
a. Cutting cycle
b. Harvesting cycle
c. Cutting section
d. Cutting block

113. The period required to regenerate the whole of a periodic block is known as
a. Regeneration time
b. Regeneration period
c. Establishment period
d. a & b both

114. The part of a forest set aside to be regenerate or otherwise treated, during a specified period is
a. Block
b. Beat
c. Periodic block
d. a & c both

115. Which type of periodic blocks retain their territorial identity at any working plan revision is
a. Fixed periodic block
b. Permanent periodic block
c. Temporary periodic block
d. a & b both

116. Unit of working plan in India
a. District
b. Division
c. State
d. a and b both

117. Which principle is the backbone of forest management?
a. Yield regulation
b. Growing stock improvement
c. Sustained yield
d. All of them

118. The material that a forest can yield annually (or periodically) in perpetuity
a. Thinning material
b. Intermediate yield
c. Sustained yield
d. b & c both

119. The material or cash returns obtained from time to time from a forest not organized for continuous production
a. Thinning material
b. Forest product
c. Sustained yield
d. Intermittent yield

120. The concept of progressive yield was originally advocated by
a. Harting
b. Capt. Watson
c. Brandis
d. None of them

121. The mean volume of a tree or crop at the desired age is
a. Annual increment
b. Mean annual increment
c. Current increment
d. a & c both

122. The parameter of tree that can be estimated from the age beyond which quality of timber starts falling off
a. Ripeness
b. Maturity
c. a & b both
d. None of them

123. Timber, small wood and firewood fall under the category of
a. Minor forest product
b. Major forest product
c. a & b both
d. None of them

124. Category of forests on which villagers have no right?
a. Protected forest
b. Reserve forest
c. Private forest
d. All of them

125. National forest policy of 1952 suggested which classification of Indian forest?
a. Legal classification
b. Functional classification
c. Ownership classification
d. Classification based on age

126. All the material that counts against the prescribed yield derived from the main felling in a regular forest
a. Final product
b. Functional yield
c. Final yield
d. a & c both

127. Quantity of material per annum of a given species, that an area is capable of producing under normal condition, so long as the factors of locality remain unchanged
a. Production capacity
b. Harvesting capacity
c. Yield capacity
d. None of them

128. The term generally applied for determination of yield and the prescribed means of realizing it is
a. Yield calculation
b. Yield valuation
c. Yield regulation
d. a & c both

129. A document having systematic, obligatory and mandatory regulations for continuous management of a given forest property
a. Working cycle
b. Plan of management
c. Plan of work
d. Working plan

## Fill in the blanks

1. As per national forest policy 1952, how much forest area of forest is essential in hilly region..............................
2. In which year forest and wildlife are brought under concurrent list of constitution..................
3. Forest and wildlife are under the concurrent list of which schedule................
4. The interval between the formation and harvesting of forest crops is...........
5. Protection, national, village forest and tree lands are under the functional classification of Indian forest suggested in forest policy............
6. Reduced factor is also called....................
7. The factor by which each class must be multiplied to reduce it to the standard quality and / or density ....................
8. A written scheme of management aiming at continuity of policy and action and controlling the treatment of a forest ......................
9. Total enumeration is known as ..............................
10. Partial enumeration is known as ..............................
11. Flury's constant is denoted by..........
12. Schinedr's formula for increment % ...........
13. The total increment up to a given age divided by that age ...........
14. Average annual increment for any short period is .............
15. The CAI attains the maximum limit before the .............
16. Forest have normal series of age gradation, normal growing stock and normal increment is known as ........................
17. Which increment never reaches zero ..................
18. Normal series of Age gradation is not present in ............................
19. Virgin forest never comes under ............ ...... condition
20. Rotation suitable for controlling the financial rotation...................................
21. A change from one silviculture system or one (set of) species to another is.................
22. The period during which a change from one silviculture system to another ................
23. Rotation adopted particularly by industrial firms for the purpose of supplying raw materials ....................................
24. Rotation that yield maximum annual quantity of material ..........................
25. Rotation for highest value production is usually longer for ...........................

26. Rotation which yield highest average annual gross or net revenue irrespective of the capital value of the forest ..................................
27. Rotation which yield highest average annual gross or net revenue irrespective of the capital value of the forest ......................................
28. Main territorial division of the forest is ......................
29. Subordinate unit of each division is ......................
30. Forest guard is also known by the name of......................
31. Conservator of forest is the officer in-charge of ............................
32. DFO is the officer in-charge of .............................
33. The time which elapses between successive main felling on the same area .................
34. An age class with one year as the interval ...........................
35. Rotation which coincide with the natural lease of a life of a species on a given site ....................
36. Which rotation is applicable only in case of protection and amenity forest, park lands ....................
37. Practical application of the scientific, technical and economic principle of forest is known as ..............................
38. A person engaged in the profession of forestry .....................

## True and False

1. Income or annual increment of the forest is not distinct from the capital or the growing stock.
2. The national commission on agriculture NCA) was constituted in 1976
3. NCA suggested the need for a revised forest policy in their report in 1976
4. Forestry is a long term investment.
5. The NCA suggested 60% in the hills and 20% forest in the plains in revised forest policy.
6. The NCA suggested a revised forest policy should have 33% of the land under forest cover.
7. Increase in value per unit volume of the tree is quality increment
8. The increment can also be estimated from the CAI figures in the yield table by area method and per cent per tree method
9. In normal forest the no. of stem from one diameter class to next is described in De liocourt's law
10. Trees of all ages from one year old to rotation age are present in the forest in appropriate quantity is normal series of age gradation

11. Rotation is reduced in overstocked forest
12. Rotation is increased in under stocked forest

### Answer-Fill in the blanks

1. 60%
2. 1976
3. 7th
4. Rotation
5. 952
6. Modified factor
7. Reducing factor
8. Working plan
9. Complete enumeration
10. Sample enumeration
11. C
12. 400/nD
13. MAI
14. PAI
15. MAI
16. Normal forest
17. MAI
18. Irregular forest
19. Normal forest
20. Rotation of maximum gross and the financial rotation
21. Conversion
22. Conversion period
23. Technical rotation
24. Rotation of maximum volume production
25. Highest volume production
26. Rotation of highest income
27. Rotation of revenue
28. Block
29. Range
30. Beat officer
31. Circle
32. Forest division
33. Felling cycle
34. Age gradation
35. Physical rotation
36. Physical rotation
37. Forest management
38. Forester

## Answer Key

| | | | | | | | | | |
|---|---|---|---|---|---|---|---|---|---|
| 1. | B | 2. | C | 3. | A | 4. | B | 5. | B |
| 6. | D | 7. | C | 8. | A | 9. | B | 10. | D |
| 11. | B | 12. | A | 13. | C | 14. | A | 15. | B |
| 16. | C | 17. | D | 18. | C | 19. | C | 20. | C |
| 21. | C | 22. | C | 23. | D | 24. | D | 25. | D |
| 26. | C | 27. | A | 28. | C | 29. | D | 30. | B |
| 31. | A | 32. | C | 33. | B | 34. | C | 35. | A |
| 36. | A | 37. | B | 38. | A | 39. | D | 40. | A |
| 41. | D | 42. | B | 43. | C | 44. | D | 45. | A |
| 46. | A | 47. | B | 48. | B | 49. | A | 50. | B |
| 51. | C | 52. | B | 53. | B | 54. | C | 55. | A |
| 56. | B | 57. | B | 58. | A | 59. | C | 60. | A |
| 61. | D | 62. | A | 63. | C | 64. | B | 65. | A |
| 66. | A | 67. | B | 68. | C | 69. | C | 70. | A |
| 71. | A | 72. | B | 73. | C | 74. | C | 75. | B |
| 76. | B | 77. | B | 78. | C | 79. | B | 80. | C |
| 81. | B | 82. | C | 83. | A | 84. | D | 85. | D |
| 86. | D | 87. | B | 88. | A | 89. | B | 90. | C |
| 91. | C | 92. | C | 93. | C | 94. | D | 95. | A |
| 96. | B | 97. | D | 98. | A | 99. | D | 100. | A |
| 101. | B | 102. | D | 103. | C | 104. | C | 105. | A |
| 106. | A | 107. | B | 108. | D | 109. | D | 110. | C |
| 111. | D | 112. | C | 113. | B | 114. | C | 115. | D |
| 116. | D | 117. | C | 118. | C | 119. | D | 120. | A |
| 121. | B | 122. | A | 123. | B | 124. | B | 125. | B |
| 126. | C | 127. | C | 128. | C | 129. | D | 130. | A |

# 6

# Environment and Biodiversity

1. Global warming will lead to
   a. Shift of species to higher latitude
   b. Shift of species toward higher altitude
   c. a is true but b is false
   d. both a and b is true

2. United Nations Conference on Environment and Development held in June, 1992 is also known as
   a. Global summit
   b. De Janerio summit
   c. Janerio summit
   d. Earth summit

3. IPCC in 2001 had predicted that the global warming by the year 2100 will be in a range of
   a. 0.5 – 2.5°C
   b. 1.4 – 5.8°C
   c. 0.6 ± 0.2°C
   d. 1- 20

4. Variety and variability is known as
   a. Biodiversity
   b. Genetic resources
   c. Plant genetic resources
   d. None of the above

5. The world environment day is celebrated on
   a. 5th July
   b. 5th June
   c. 5th August
   d. 5th May

6. Relationship between environment and organisms is known as
   a. Ecosystem
   b. Environment
   c. Ecology
   d. Anthropology

7. Who coined the term ecology?
   a. Ernst Haeckel
   b. Darwin
   c. Thomas Edison
   d. a and b both

8. Fourteenth edition of ISFR was released in year
   a. 2009
   b. 2013
   c. 2011
   d. 2015

9. The average weather of an area over a decade is known as
   a. Temperature b. Environment
   c. Climate d. None of the above

10. The components of environment are
   a. Abiotic b. Biotic
   c. Only b d. a & b both

11. Which among the following is a Green house gas
   a. Carbon dioxide b. Oxygen
   c. Nitrogen d. Sulphur dioxide

12. Source of acid rain is
   a. Sulphuric acid b. Nitric acid
   c. Hydrochloric acid d. a & b both

13. Substances responsible for ozone depletion is
   a. Chlorofluoro carbons b. Lead
   c. a & b both d. None of the above

14. Gases responsible for increasing air temperature are called
   a. Green house gases b. Inert gases
   c. Both d. None of the above

15. The major gas in the earth's atmosphere is
   a. Oxygen b. Carbon dioxide
   c. Nitrogen d. a & c both

16. Chipko Movement was started by?
   a. Sunderlal Bahugun b. Rajendra Singh
   c. Anna Hazare d. Amrita Devi

17. Chipko movement took place in which region
   a. Tehri Garhwal b. Nainital
   c. Pauri Garhwal d. Almora

18. Chipko movement was started in which year
   a.1973 b. 1972
   c. 1962 d. 1982

19. Tehri Garhwal is situated in which state of India
   a. Uttar Pradesh b. Himachal Pradesh
   c. Uttrakhand d. Jammu & Kashmir

20. Van Mahotsava is related to
    a. Protecting tree
    b. Establishing garden
    c. Tree Plantation
    d. a & c both

21. Term Ecosystem was coined by
    a. Odum
    b. Arthur Tansley
    c. Mark Arthur
    d. a & b both

22. An Ecosystem consists of
    a. Only biotic component
    b. Only abiotic component
    c. Biotic and abiotic components
    d. None of the above

23. Biotic component of Ecosystem are
    a. Plants, Animals
    b. Producer
    c. Consumer
    d. None of the above

24. Percentage of world food produced from plants is about?
    a. 85
    b. 95
    c. 90
    d. 80

25. Major source of energy in the Ecosystem is
    a. Sun
    b. Moon
    c. Thermal
    d. None of the above

26. Transfer of energy from one trophic level to the next level is called
    a. Food web
    b. Energy transfer
    c. Food chain
    d. a & b both

27. Generally number of trophic levels in the food chain of an ecosystem is?
    a. 1-2
    b. 3-5
    c. 2-4
    d. 4-6

28. Network of food chain in an ecosystem is known as
    a. World of food
    b. Food system
    c. Food line
    d. Food web

29. Variety and variability among living organisms in a region is known as
    a. Species diversity
    b. Species richness
    c. Genetic diversity
    d. Biodiversity

30. Genetic variation within a species is called
    a. Species diversity
    b. Genetic diversity
    c. Ecosystem diversity
    d. Biodiversity

31. Availability of species in a region is known as
    a. Biodiversity b. Genetic diversity
    c. Ecosystem diversity d. Species diversity

32. Availability of habitat type and ecosystem in a region is known as
    a. Ecosystem diversity b. Genetic diversity
    c. Biodiversity d. Species diversity

33. Alpha diversity is also known as
    a. Point diversity b. Ecosystem diversity
    c. Biodiversity d. a & b both

34. The elimination of species is known as
    a. Extinction b. Expansion
    c. Extension d. a & b both

35. Species composition change along environmental gradient is known as
    a. Community diversity b. Genetic diversity
    c. Alfa diversity d. Beta diversity

36. Diversity of the habit type over the area is known as
    a. Alfa diversity b. Beta diversity
    c. Gama Diversity d. All of the above

37. Species available to a specific area is known as
    a. Endangered species b. Endemic species
    c. a & b both d. Extinct species

38. The organisation publishing Red Data Book is
    a. IUCN b. WWF
    c. A Tree d. a & b both

39. Number of hot spots in India are
    a. 1 b. 2
    c. 3 d. 4

40. Main criteria for gaining status of hot spots is
    a. Endemism of species b. Most species under endangered category
    c. a & b both d. None of the above

41. Major threat for biodiversity is
    a. Introduction of exotic
    b. Deforestation
    c. Industrialization
    d. All of the above

42. Introduction of species out of its natural range is known as
    a. Exotic species
    b. Endemic species
    c. Endangered species
    d. Extinct species

43. Most destructive exotic plants species in the country
    a. *Acacia auriculiformis*
    b. *Lantana camara*
    c. *Agave* Sp.
    d. a & b both

44. Full form of IUCN is
    a International union for conservation of nature
    b. International union for conservation of nature and natural resources
    c. a & b both
    d. None of the above

45. Full form of WWF is
    a. World water forum
    b. World wildlife fund
    c. Wildlife warning forum
    d. None of the above

46. Cryopreservation is a technique used for conservation of living tissue under which solution
    a. Nitrogen
    b. Hydrogen
    c. Oxygen
    d. All of the above

47. At which temperature living tissue is stored under liquid nitrogen?
    a. 196 °C
    b. 186 °C
    c. 176 °C
    d. 196 °C

48. Carnivores are -
    a. Usually primary consumers
    b. Usually secondary consumers
    c. Usually secondary or tertiary consumers
    d. Usually decomposers rather consumers

49. The word ecosystem was coined by
    a. Weaver and Clements
    b. A.G. Tansley
    c. R. Mishra
    d. E.P. Odum

50. Musk deers are residents of
    a. Dry deciduous forests of Odisha
    b. Tropical rain forests of Kerala
    c. High altitude Himalayan forests
    d. Thorny scrubs of Rajasthan

51. The importance of ecosystem lies in
    a. Cycling of materials
    b. Flow of energy
    c. Both the above
    d. None of the above

52. ISFR is released by
    a. FRI
    b. FSI
    c. MoEF
    d. ICFRE

53. As per 14th edition (2015) of ISFR % of forest cover of the country is
    a. 21.34 %
    b. 21.44 %
    c. 20.34 %
    d. 20.44 %

54. Ecosystems creates
    a. Food Chain
    b. Food web
    c. Any of the two
    d. None of the above

55. Pyramid of number in a grassland or a crop ecosystem is
    a. Upright
    b. Inverted
    c. a and b both
    d. None of the two

56. In tree ecosystem, pyramid of numbers is
    a. Upright
    b. Inverted
    c. Any of the two
    d. None of the two

57. In grassland and tree ecosystem pyramid of biomass is
    a. Always inverted
    b. Always Upright
    c. Sometimes inverted and sometimes upright
    d. Anything is possible

58. In pond ecosystem, pyramid of biomass is -
    a. Upright
    b. Inverted
    c. Anything is possible
    d. None is correct

59. Pyramid of energy in grassland or pond ecosystem is always
    a. Inverted
    b. First Inverted then upright
    c. Upright only
    d. Any of the above

60. An ecosystem consisting of hawks, mice, grasses and snakes is at dynamic equilibrium; which organism would be found at the bottom of an energy pyramid
    a. Hawks
    b. Mice
    c. Grasses
    d. Snakes

61. What is the best arrangement of an energy system consisting of hawks, mice, grasses and snakes
    a. Grasses, hawks, mice snakes
    b. Grasses, mice snakes, hawks
    c. Mice, snakes, grasses, hawks
    d. Snakes, grasses, mice, hawks

62. In most food webs, green plants are of prime importance because
    a. Most animals eat plants
    b. They contain chlorophyll
    c. They provide protection for animals
    d. They can convert light energy to chemical energy

63. Competition for food, light and space is probably most severe between
    a. Closely related species occupying the same niche
    b. Closely related species occupying different niche
    c. Unrelated species occupying the same niche
    d. Unrelated species occupying the different niche

64. In an ecosystem, the population of
    a. Primary producers is more than that of primary consumers
    b. Secondary consumers is the largest
    c. Primary consumers, outnumber the primary producers
    d. Primary consumers are least dependent upon primary producers

65. The food chain, in which micro organisms break down the energy rich compounds synthesized by producers is
    a. Predator food chain
    b. Parasitic food chain
    c. Detritus food chain
    d. Ecosystem

66. The numbers of primary producers within a specified area would be maximum in
    a. Pond ecosystem
    b. Grassland
    c. Desert
    d. Forest ecosystem

67. The cycling of elements in an ecosystem is called
    a. Biogeochemical cycle
    b. Geochemical cycle
    c. Chemical cycle
    d. Geological cycle

68. The source of energy in an ecosystem by bacteria is
   a. Decomposition of plants and animals by bacteria
   b. Photosynthesis by plants
   c. Fermentation of sugars
   d. Sunlight

69. The first link in any food chain is always, green plants, because
   a. They are widely distributed
   b. Only animals
   c. They alone can fix atmospheric $CO_2$ in the presence of sunlight
   d. There are more herbivorous animals than carnivores

70. Trophic levels are formed by
   a. Only plants
   b. Only animals
   c. Only carnivores
   d. Organisms linked in food chain

71. Biological equilibrium occurs among the
   a. Producers and consumers
   b. Producers, consumers and decomposers
   c. None of the above
   d. Producers and decomposers

72. A free floating exotic water weed in Indian rivers and lakes is
   a. Nile perch
   b. Dragonfly
   c. Water hyacinth
   d. None of the above

73. Which is most harmful for life on the globe
   a. Nuclear fallout
   b. Deforestation
   c. Increasing desert
   d. None of the above

74. The direct entry of gaseous pollutant may take place by?
   a. Stomata
   b. Root hair
   c. Stem
   d. Flowers

75. Which part of living cell is affected by sulphur oxide
   a. Nucleus
   b. Cell membrane
   c. Cell wall
   d. Plasmodesmata

76. Which among the following does not cause pollution
   a. Thermal power plant
   b. Automobiles
   c. Nuclear power plant
   d. Tree plantation

77. What is DDT

a. An antibiotic
b. A biodegradable pollutant
c. A nonbiodegradable pollutant
d. None of the above

78. Pollutant is a substance or factor which disturbs

a. Our balanced environment
b. Geochemical cycles
c. Flora of any region
d. Fauna of any region

79. Which statement is not correct

a. Carbon monoxide is main pollutant
b. All pollutants are not wastes
c. Water is polluted by nitrogen and magnesium
d. Lichens are indicators of pollution

80. Which is main source of water pollution

a. Smoke
b. Industrial effluents
c. Detergents
d. Ammonia

81. Which among the following is main air pollutant

a. Hydrogen
b. $SO_2$
c. $CO_2$
d. CO

82. Chilka lake is located in

a. West Bengal
b. Andhra Pradesh
c. Jhrakhand
d. Odisha

83. Which does not cause air pollution

a. Hydrogen
b. $SO_2$
c. $CO_2$
d. CO

84. Which of the following is an invaluable source of energy but is not air pollutant

a. Nuclear energy
b. Sun
c. Coal
d. Fuel wood

85. Which air pollutant is not released by motor vehicles

a. $SO_2$
b. Fly ash
c. Hydrocarbons
d. Lead

86. Which is most polluted country of Asia

a. China
b. Nepal
c. India
d. Bhutan

87. Which of the following is produced by a reaction of ultraviolet light

a. CO
b. $SO_2$
c. Ozone
d. Fluorides

88. Biomagnification is the phenomenon of

a. Culturing fungi in waste material for gain in protein rich biomass-
b. Culturing of fast growing trees to increase wood production
c. Increased nitrogen fixation by a combined growth of blue green algae and nitrogen fixing Bacteria.
d. Increase in the concentration of nonbiodegradable substances with passage through food chain within the body of organisms.

89. Which is an indicator of air quality

a. Lichens
b. Moss
c. Rhizopus
d. Virus

90. What do you understand by greenhouse effect?

a. Increase in temperature due to increase in $O_2$ concentration in the atmosphere.
b. Decrease in temperature due to decrease in $O_2$ concentration in the atmosphere.
c. Increase in temperature due to increase in $CO_2$ concentration in the atmosphere.
d. Decrease in temperature due to decrease in $CO_2$ concentration in the atmosphere.

91. Biosphere is composed of

a. Living organisms
b. Living organisms+ Lithosphere
c. Living organisms+ Lithosphere+ Atmosphere
d. Living organisms+ Lithosphere+ Atmosphere + Hydrosphere

92. The study of Environmental Science comprises of

a. Land
b. Atmosphere
c. Ocean
d. All of these

93. The highest layer of atmospheres is

a. Thermosphere
b. Mesosphere
c. Exosphere
d. Stratosphere

94. Which gas among the following constitutes minimum amount in air ?

a. Oxygen
b. Nitrogen
c. Argon
d. Carbon dioxide

95. The percentage of Oxygen in the atmosphere is

a. 50.947%
b. 30.947%
c. 20.947%
d. None the these

96. Lithosphere is composed of

a. Core and outer crust
b. Core and mantle
c. Core, mantle and outer crust
d. None of these

97. Worldwide, the source of maximum consumption of fuel is

a. Coal
b. Oil
c. Gas
d. Biomass

98. Soil is a complex mixture of

a. Sand and clay
b. Silt and Clay
c. Sand, clay and silt
d. Sand and silt

99. Kyoto Protocol was adopted in

a. 1977
b. 1977
c. 2002
d. 2007

100. Which layer of atmosphere maintains an almost uniform horizontal temperature?

a. Stratosphere
b. Troposphere
c. Thermosphere
d. Mesosphere

101. Coal burning power plants and factories are responsible for about 86 % of

a. CO in atmosphere
b. $SO_2$ in atmosphere
c. CI in atmosphere
d. $NO_2$ in atmosphere

102. Fall in temperature with increasing elevation is known as

a. Thermal anomaly
b. Thermal reduction
c. Temperature fall
d. Lapse rate

103. A powerful eye irritant present in smog is

a. Ozone
b. Nitric oxide
c. Proxy Acetyl Nitrate
d. Sulphur Dioxide

104. The official estimate of wasteland in India is nearly about
a. 15 million hectare
b. 45 million hectare
c. 55 million hectare
d. 63 million hectare

105. Biological oxygen demand measures
a. Industrial pollution
b. Dissolved oxygen needed by microbes
c. Polluting capacity of effluence
d. Air pollution

106. Prominent species which are endemic to Western Ghats
a. Crustancean
b. Protozoa
c. Amphibians
d. Algae

107. Pollution is not caused due to use of
a. Wood
b. $SO_2$
c. Solar energy
d. Unsaturated carbon

108. Ultraviolet radiations produce the photo-oxidant is
a. CO
c. $SO_2$
c. Ozone
d. Fluoride

109. Biological treatment of water pollution is done with the help of
a. Lichens
b. Fungi
c. Phytoplankton
d. All of these

110. Sulphur dioxide pollution is indicated by :
a. Ferns
b. Green algae
c. Lichens
d. Neem tree

111. First National air quality index was released in which state/UT
a. Delhi
b. Pudicherry
c. Chandigarh
d. Andaman

112. Acid rain is caused by high concentration of
a. Ozone and dust
b.CO and $CO_2$
c. $NH_2$ and $SO_2$
d. $NO_2$ and $SO_2$

113. Gas liberated in Bhopal gas tragedy was
a. Methyl isocynate
b. Phenyl isocynate
c. Ethylene
d. Acetylene

114. Ozonosphere is mainly depleted by
    a. Excess $CO_2$
    b. Excess CO
    c. Chloro-fluoro carbons
    d. Ozone

115. The critically endangered animal species in India
    a. Red Panda
    b. Asiatic Lion
    c. Pigmy Hog
    d. Bengal Tiger

116. Now-a-days DDT is not effective for killing mosquitoes because
    a. Mosquito population has become strong
    b. DDT is adulterated
    c. DDT has selection pressure on the genetic variability
    d. Mosquitoes have developed adaptive resistance to pesticides

117. The population of hawks and eagles is declining because
    a. of food scarcity
    b. of game lovers
    c. of excessive use of poisoned pesticides
    d. Very few dead animals are found in the fields

118. First National air quality index was released in year
    a. 2015
    b. 2014
    c. 2016
    d. None of the above

119. Ozone layer is chiefly disturbed by
    a. Large number of automobiles
    b. Large number of factories
    c. Supersonic jets
    d. Chimney exhausts

120. If BOD of a river is very low, this means water
    a. is clean
    b. is polluted
    c. Contains algae
    d. Contains other dissolved minerals

121. Nuclear power generates
    a. Photochemical pollution
    b. SO2 pollution
    c. Air pollution
    d. Thermal pollution

122. First National air quality index was released in new Delhi by
    a. President of India
    b. Prime Minister of India
    c. Vice-President of India
    d. All of them

123. When pollution load is more in the lakes they cannot take place self purification because

a. There is no $O_2$ to sustain microbial activity
b. No sunlight is present
c. Microbes die
d. Pollutants settle down automatically

124. Better method of pest control is

a. The use of chemical pesticide
b. The use of radioactive substance
c. By using pesticide taking into account number and composition of pest population
d. Use of steam

125. The pollution emitted by jet aeroplanes in outer atmosphere as fluorocarbons are known as

a. Photochemical oxidants
b. Aerosols
c. Ozone
d. Smog

126. Nuclear explosion causes mainly

a. Noise pollution
b. Soil pollution
c. Water pollution
d. Air pollution

127. MoEF has been renamed as

a. Ministry of Environment, Forest and Climate Change
b. Ministry of Environment and Climate Change
c. Ministry of Environment
d. Ministry of Forest and Climate Change

128. Which of the following is the main factor of water pollution?

a. Smoke
b. Industrial waste
c. Ammonia
d. Detergents

129. Ozone layer in upper atmosphere is destroyed by

a. HCI
b. Photochemical smog
c. $SO_2$
d. Chlorofluorocarbons

130. Natural pollution is caused by

a. UV rays
b. Erosion
c. Volcanoes
d. All of them

131. Expand NWDB
  a. National water and development board
  b. National Botanical development board
  c. National Wasteland development board
  d. None of them

132. Decomposition of domestic wastes under natural processes is known as
  a. Industrial pollution
  b. Termal pollution
  c. Biodegradable process
  d. Non-biodegradable process

133. Which of the following is secondary pollutant?
  a. $CCl_2F_2$
  b.DDT
  c. $C_2 H_2.4$ Pb
  d. PAN

134. Biochemical oxygen demand means
  a. Amount of oxygen taken up by the microorganisms present in the water
  b. Amount of oxygen released by the microorganisms present in the water
  c. Amount of nutrients taken up by the microorganisms present in the water
  d. None of these

135. The gas produced during paddy cultivation and cause global warming is
  a. $CH_4$
  b. Cl
  c. $CO_2$
  d. $H_2S$

136. Important initiatives regarding the management of nature is
  a. Earth summit
  b. Kyoto protocol
  c. Montreal protocol
  d. All of them

137. Photochemical smog is related to the pollution of
  a. Soil
  b. Water
  c. Noise
  d. Air

138. The classical literature which gives the message that resources should not be wasted out but should be conserved
  a. Isho Upanishad
  b. Atharva veda
  c. Artha Shastra
  d. All of them

139. Most important causative pollution of soil may be
  a. Plastics
  b. Iron junks
  c. Detergents
  d. Glass junks

140. The biological diversity act 2002 came in to force in

a. 2003 b. 2013

c. 2004 d. 2002

141. Green house effect is enhanced in the environment by the gas

a. $CO_2$ b. CO

c. CFC d. $SO_2$

142. Which is the main cause for desertification?

a. Developmental activities b. Tourism

c. Overgrazing d. Irrigated agriculture

143. Taj Mahal is threatened due to the effect of

a. Chlorine b. Sulphur dioxide

c. Oxygen d. Hydrogen

144. When huge amount of sewage is dumped into a river, the BOD will

a. Increase b. Remain unchanged

c. Slightly decrease d. Decrease

145. World day to combat desertification is celebrated every year on

a. $17^{th}$ June b. $17^{th}$ July

c. $17^{th}$ August d. $16^{th}$ June

146. Intensity of sound in normal conversation?

a. 10-20 decibel b. 30-60 decibel

c. 70-90 decibel d. 120-150 decibel

147. At present the most significant cause of dwindling biodiversity is

a. Biological magnification of DDT b. Global warming

c. Deterioration of ozone layer d. Destruction of habitat

148. The thickness of ozone layer is measured in

a. Dobson Units b. cm/sec.

c. mm/sec d. Pascal

149. Greenhouse effect with respect to global climate refers to

a. Cooling of earth b. Warming of earth

c. Increased rainfall and greenery d. Desertification

150. In which year, the Bhopal gas tragedy was caused

a. 1984 b. 1974

c. 1994 d. 1985

151. If there was no $CO_2$ in the earth's atmosphere, the temperature of earth's surface would be

a. Dependent on amount of $O_2$ in the atmosphere
b. Higher than the present
c. Less than the present
d. The same

152. The effect of global warming on crop production will be

a. Explosive weed growth
b. Increased incidence of insect & pest
c. Higher respiration rate
d. All of them

153. Formation of ozone hole is maximum over

a. Antarctica
b. Africa
c. Europe
d. India

154. Which one of the following organisms is used as indicator of water quality?

a. Biggiatoa
b. Chlorella
c. Azospirillum
d. Eschrichia

155. In the coming time, skin-related disorders might be more common due to

a. Use of detergents
b. Water pollution
c. Depletion of ozone layer
d. Air pollution

156. The major contribution of green house gases to the atmosphere is

a. Russia
b. Germany
c. Brazil
d. USA

157. Sewage drained into water bodies kills fishes because

a. It gives off a bad smell
b. It removes food eaten by fish
c. It increase competition for dissolved oxygen
d. Excess $CO_2$ is added in water

158. Narmada Sagar project is in

a. West Bengal
b. Uttar Pradesh
c. Rajasthan
d. Madhya Pradesh

159. In which of the following will you look for Escherichia coli ?

a. Milk
b. Water
c. Human intestine
d. Soil

160. The concentration of $O_3$ is highest during

a. August-September
b. November-December
c. February-April
d. March-April

161. Type of benefit provided by river valley project is
  a. Irrigation  b. Water supply
  c. Electric generation  d. All of above

162. Ozone umbrella is affected by
  a. CFC  b. $CO_2$
  c. Methane  d. PHN

163. The major aim of National Wasteland Development Board is
  a. Management of waste land  b. Check land degradation
  c. Increase biomass availability  d. All of them

164. Ozone hole refers to
  a. Reduction in thickness of ozone layer in troposphere
  b. Reduction of thickness of ozone layer in stratosphere
  c. Hole in ozone layers in stratosphere
  d. Increased concentration of ozone

165. Which one is not dangerous for life?
  a. Bio-pollutants
  b. Ionosphere
  c. Nuclear blast
  d. Deforestation

166. Major pollutant in the jet plane emission is
  a. Carbon tetrachloride  b. $SO_2$
  c. CO  d. Fluorocarbons

167. Sewage water is purified for recycling by the action of
  a. Light  b. Micro-organisms
  c. Aquatic plants  d. Fishes

168. One of the important effect of $SO_2$ and transformation products on plants is
  a. Plasmolysis  b. Destruction of chlorophyll
  c. Destruction of Golgi bodies  d. Destruction of cell wall

169. NGT stands for
  a. National Green tribunal  b. National Green Technology
  c. New Green Technology  d. None of the above

170. Leaf curling is caused by
   a. $SO_2$ b. $O_3$
   c. $H_2S$ d. CO

171. Air pollution effects are usually found on
   a. Roots b. Stems
   c. Flowers d. Leaves

172. Water pollution cause
   a. Increases oxygenation b. Decreases turbidity
   c. Increases turbidity and deoxygenation d. Increases photosynthesis

173. Carbon monoxide is a major pollutant of:
   a. Water b. Air
   c. Noise d. Soil

174. Plants are known as purifiers of air due to process of
   a. Respiration b. Transpiration
   c. Photosynthesis d. Desiccation

175. Acid rain is due to
   a. Sulphur dioxide pollution b. Carbon monoxide pollution
   c. Pesticide pollution d. Dust particles

176. The major source of methane in India is
   a. Rice fields b. Wheat fields
   c. Sugarcane plantation d. Fruit orchard

177. Acid rain occurs in areas where
   a. Citrus plants are grown b. Large plantations of Eucalyptus
   c. Large plantations of pine plants d. There are big industries and atmosphere is polluted with $SO_2$

178. USEPA stands for
   a. United States Environment Protection Agency
   b. United States Ecosystem Protection Agency
   c. United States Environment and Ecosystem Protection Agency
   d. All of them

179. The discoveries related to ozone destruction were made by
   a. Paul crutezen b. Sherwood Rowland
   c. Mario Molino d. All of them

180. Anti tobacco day is celebrated on
   a. 20 May
   b. 31 May
   c. 25 May
   d. 30 May
181. Smog is a combination of:
   a. Fire and wate
   b. Smoke and fog
   c. Water and smoke
   d. Air and water
182. The term biomagnifications refers to
   a. Increase in concentration of non-degradable pollutant through a food chain
   b. Increase in population size
   c. Growth of organisms due to food consumption
   d. Blowing up of environment issue by man
183. Photochemical smog always contains
   a. PAN and $O_3$
   b. $CH_4$ and $O_3$
   c. CO and $O_3$
   d. PAN and $CH_4$
184. Addition of solid waste to soil is called as
   a. Third pollution
   b. First pollution
   c. Second pollution
   d. All of them
185. The effect of exotic species is maximum on
   a. Island
   b. Crop land
   c. Forest land
   d. Wetland
186. The most biodiversity rich zone are
   a. North-East region
   b. Western Ghats
   c. Eastern Himalayas
   d. a & b both
187. As compared to tap water, BOD of water polluted with sewage waste would be
   a. High
   b. Low
   c. Normal
   d. Nil
188. Air pollution in metropolitan cities is mainly due to
   a. Burning of fossil fuels
   b. Thermal power plants
   c. Sewage
   d. Suspended particles
189. The indiscriminate use of fertilizers can cause
   a. Air pollution
   b. Water pollution
   c. Soil pollution
   d. None of these

190. One of the following is not a pollutant

a. $SO_2$ b. $CO_2$

c. CO d. $NO_2$

191. The most harmful environmental pollutants are

a. Human organic wastes b. Wastes from fields

c. Non-biodegradable d. Natural nutrients in excess

192. Increase in fauna and decrease in flora would be harmful due to increase in

a. Disease b. Insect

c. Radio active pollution d. Carbon di-oxide

193. The UV rays in atmosphere are checked by

a. $O_3$ b. $O_2$

c. $H_2$ d. $CI_2$

194. National Green Tribunal has been established on

a. 18th Oct, 2010 b. 18th Oct, 2011

c. 18th Oct, 2012 d. 18th Oct, 2013

195. National Green Tribunal has been established under

a. NGT Act 2010 b. NGT Act 2011

c. a and b both d. None of these

196. The effect of $SO_2$ and its transformation products on plants is

a. Destruction of Golgi apparatus b. Disintegration of proteins

c. Chlorosis d. None of these

197. The Ozone Depleting Substances (Regulation and Control Amendment Rules, 2014) had been notified in the Gazette of India in March

a. 2015 b. 2014

c. 2016 d. a & b both

198. Sound becomes a hazardous noise pollution if its level is above

a. 30 dB b. 80 dB

c. 120 dB d. 150 dB

199. In a ecosystem dispersion of energy is followed by

a. Loss of heat b. Gain of heat

c. a and b both d. None of them

200. The pollution discharged by jet planes is

a. Smoke b. Fog

c. Smog d. Aerosols

201. National Action Plan on climate change released in year
a. 2007
b. 2009
c. 2010
d. 2008

202. The nutrient enrichment is known as
a. Eutrophication
b. Neutrification
c. Nitrification
d. Acidification

203. Silent valley National is in which state?
a. Karnataka
b. Kerala
c. Andhra Pradesh
d. Telangana

204. BOD of a pond is related to.............in per unit volume of water
a. All the plants
b. All the nektons
c. All the microbes
d. All the animals

205. Madhumalai wildlife Sanctuary is in
a. Western Ghats
b. Nilgiris
c. Kodai kanal
d. b & c both

206. Depletion of ozone hole is responsible for
a. Deforestation
b. GHGs
c. Acid rain
d. Increased UV radiation

207. Hyperkeratosis is due to excess of which element in body
a. Arsenic
b. Lead
c. Chromium
d. All of them

208. If the fertilizers are added to water
a. Plants will die
b. Eutrophication will occur
c. Fish population will decrease
d. Overall animal population will increase

209. The ultraviolet radiations in the atmosphere are absorbed by
a. Oxygen
b. Ozone
c. Sulphur dioxide
d. Argon

210. Which is not true for a forest ecosystem?
a. Biotic and abiotic component
b. Number of primary producer is constant
c. Flow of energy is unidirectional
d. a & b both

211.Which forest ecosystem shows minimum species diversity?
a. Tropical rain forest
b. Evergreen forest
c. Deciduous fores
d. Alpine forest

212. First National park in India was established in?
a. Uttar Pradesh
b. Arunachal Pradesh
c. Madhya Pradesh
d. West Bengal

213.The World Forestry Day is celebrated on
a. 21$^{st}$ June
b. 21$^{st}$ March
c. 5$^{th}$ March
d. 5$^{th}$ June

214. The evolution of new species is known as
a. Specialization
b. Smog
c. Speciation
d. none of the above

215. The species diversity of a region is measured based on
a. Species richness
b. Equitability
c. Evenness
d. all of the above

216. The species determining the ability of large number of other species to persist in the community
a. Milestone species
b. Keystone species
c. Redstone species
d. none of the above

217. Diversity increases when we move from
a. High to low altitude
b. From poles to equator
c. From equator to pole
d. both a and b

218. Taxol is obtained from
a. *Taxus baccata*
b. *Taxus brevifolia*
c. both a and b
d. none of the above

219. Total forest and tree cover of the country as per 14th edition of ISFR is
a. 24.16 %
b. 24.00 %
c. 23.16 %
d. 23.00 %

220. The hotspot concept was developed by
a. Norman Vincent Peale
b. Norman Myers
b. Norman scot
d. None of the above

221. Arboreta is a

a. House b. Ship

c. Botanical garden d. Environment

222. Most undisturbed forest without any human impact

a. Residual forest b. Pristine forest

c. Deciduous forest d. All of the above

223. Ex-situ conservation of biodiversity can be done by

a. Germ plasma bank b. DNA bank

c. Gene bank d. All of the above

224. The storage of materials at ultralow temperature by very rapid cooling is useful for

a. Vegetative propaguales b. Seed

c. Tissue culture d. All of the above

225. The biosphere reserve was formulated by

a. UNESCO b.UNICEF

c. I.L.O d. IMF

226. A representative example of natural biome is

a. Sanctuary b. Biosphere reserve

c. Beach d. Lake

227. The characteristics feature which make a species susceptible to extinction are

a. Large body size b. Small population size

c. Feeding at high trophic levels d. All of the above

228. Morphine is obtained from

a. *Taxus baccata* b. *Chincona ledgeriana*

c. *Papaverum somniferum* d. All of the above

229. Which is anticancer drug among the following?

a. Morphine b. Taxol

c. Cinchona d. Quinine

230. Khejri is known as

a. *Ficus religiosa* b. *Ocimum sanctum*

c. *Prosopis cineria* d. Both a and b

231. The following is the active centre of evolution and exhibits a rich diversity of flowering plants

a. Eastern Himalayas
b. Satpuras
c. Vindhyas
d. Andamans

232. The higher diversity at community level provides the following

a. Stability
b. Strength
c. Higher productivity
d. both a and c

233. ----------- region which has severe climate with short growing period for plants

a. Tropical
b. Temperate
c. Mediterranean
d. none of the above

234. Reduction in diversity takes place in the following conditions

a. Drop in temperature
b. Seasonal variability
c. Cold
d. both a and b

235. A species with low genetic diversity results into-

a. Separation
b. diversion
c. Uniformity
d. both a and b

236. The subtle form of habitat degradation is

a. Environmental pollution
b. Synthetic compound usage
c. Spillover of oil in sea
d. none of the above

237. A biological community is sustained due to-

a. Cycling of nutrient
b. Flow of energy
c. Wind
d. both a and b

238. An organism with other individual of same species is known as

a. Population
b. Extrapolation
c. Biome
d. Genome

239. The environment is mutually related with

a. The organisms
b. Nature
c. Human being
d. all of the above

240. Vegetation and soil type of a region are determined by

a. Temperature
b. Precipitation
c. Pressure
d. both a and b

241. Groups of species exploiting a common resources are called
   a. Builds b. Guilds
   c. Community d. Population

242. Biological species are
   a. Non renewable b. Renewable
   c. Cannot predict d. Useful

243. Decline in forest is due to
   a. Unplanned felling b. Lack of foresight
   c. Increase in population d. all of the above

244. Deforestation is more prominent in
   a. Tropical region b. Temperate region
   c. Arctic region d. Subtropical region

245. If deforestation increases, the soil fertility will
   a. Increases b. Decreases
   c. Increases and decrease d. Difficult to predict

246. Soil erosion can be prevented by
   a. Overgrazing b. Afforestation
   c. Removal of vegetation d. Deforestation

247. The first movement against indiscriminate felling of trees in India took place in the year
   a. 1731 b. 1732
   c. 1733 d. 1734

248. Appiko movement took place in
   a. Karnataka b. Andhra Pradesh
   c. Himachal Pradesh d. Madhya Pradesh

249. The technical name of Earth Summit 1992 is
   a. Convention on Biological Diversity b. Montreal Protocol
   c. Helsinki Protocol d. All of them

250. The project tiger was initiated as per the advice of the PM of India
   a. I K Gujral b. Lal Bahadur Shastri
   c. Indira Gandhi d. Rajeev Gandhi

251. The element contained in smoke emitted by coal combustion

a. Lead b. Selenium
c. Polonium d. Titanium

252. Which of the following conference declared 5 June 2005 as the World Environment Day

a. London Conference b. Stockholm conference
c. Kyoto conference d. All of them

253. In India, Silicosis disease was first reported in

a. Kolar Gold Mine b. Korba aluminium complex
c. a and b both d. Khetri Copper Complex

254. Temperature inversion is responsible for the occurrence of

a. Acid rain b. GHGs
c. Smog D. All of them

255. Which of the following greenhouse gases is emitted in natural wetland?

a. Methane b. Carbon dioxide
c. CFC d. All of them

**Answer Key:**

| | | | | | | | | | |
|---|---|---|---|---|---|---|---|---|---|
| 1. | D | 2. | D | 3. | C | 4. | A | 5. | B |
| 6. | C | 7. | A | 8. | D | 9. | C | 10. | D |
| 11. | A | 12. | D | 13. | C | 14. | A | 15. | D |
| 16. | A | 17. | A | 18. | A | 19. | C | 20. | D |
| 21. | B | 22. | C | 23. | A | 24. | A | 25. | A |
| 26. | A | 27. | B | 28. | D | 29. | D | 30. | B |
| 31. | D | 32. | A | 33. | A | 34. | A | 35. | D |
| 36. | C | 37. | B | 38. | A | 39. | B | 40. | C |
| 41. | D | 42. | A | 43. | B | 44. | B | 45. | B |
| 46. | A | 47. | A | 48. | C | 49. | B | 50. | C |
| 51. | C | 52. | C | 53. | A | 54. | C | 55. | A |
| 56. | B | 57. | A | 58. | D | 59. | C | 60. | C |
| 61. | B | 62. | C | 63. | A | 64. | A | 65. | C |
| 66. | A | 67. | B | 68. | A | 69. | C | 70. | D |
| 71. | B | 72. | C | 73. | A | 74. | A | 75. | D |
| 76. | D | 77. | C | 78. | A | 79. | B | 80. | B |
| 81. | D | 82. | b | 83. | A | 84. | B | 85. | B |

| | | | | | | | | | |
|---|---|---|---|---|---|---|---|---|---|
| 86. | A | 87. | C | 88. | D | 89. | A | 90. | C |
| 91. | D | 92. | D | 93. | A | 94. | D | 95. | C |
| 96. | B | 97. | B | 98. | C | 99. | A | 100. | A |
| 101 | B | 102. | D | 103. | C | 104. | D | 105. | B |
| 106. | C | 107. | C | 108. | C | 109. | C | 110. | C |
| 111. | A | 112. | D | 113. | A | 114. | C | 115. | C |
| 116. | D | 117. | C | 118. | B | 119. | C | 120. | B |
| 121. | D | 122. | B | 123. | A | 124. | C | 125. | B |
| 126. | D | 127. | A | 128. | B | 129. | D | 130. | D |
| 131. | C | 132. | C | 133. | D | 134. | A | 135. | A |
| 136. | D | 137. | A | 138. | D | 139. | A | 140. | B |
| 141. | B | 142. | A | 143. | B | 144. | A | 145. | A |
| 146. | A | 147. | D | 148. | D | 149. | B | 150. | A |
| 151. | C | 152. | D | 153. | A | 154. | A | 155. | C |
| 156. | D | 157. | B | 158. | D | 159. | B | 160. | C |
| 161. | D | 162. | A | 163. | D | 164. | C | 165. | A |
| 166. | B | 167 | B | 168 | D | 169 | A | 170 | B |
| 171 | D | 172 | B | 173 | B | 174 | C | 175 | A |
| 176 | A | 177 | D | 178 | A | 179 | D | 180 | A |
| 181 | B | 182 | A | 183 | A | 184 | A | 185 | A |
| 186 | d | 187 | B | 188 | D | 189 | B | 190 | D |
| 191 | C | 192 | D | 193 | A | 194 | A | 195 | A |
| 196 | C | 197 | B | 198 | B | 199 | B | 200 | D |
| 201 | D | 202 | A | 203 | B | 204 | C | 205 | B |
| 206 | D | 207 | A | 208 | B | 209 | B | 210 | B |
| 211 | D | 212 | A | 213 | B | 214 | C | 215 | A |
| 216 | B | 217 | D | 218 | C | 219 | A | 220 | B |
| 221 | C | 222 | B | 223 | D | 224 | B | 225 | A |
| 226 | B | 227 | D | 228 | C | 229 | B | 230 | C |
| 231 | A | 232 | B | 233 | B | 234 | D | 235 | C |
| 236 | A | 237 | D | 238 | B | 239 | B | 240 | D |
| 241 | B | 242 | A | 243 | D | 244 | A | 245 | B |
| 246 | B | 247 | A | 248 | A | 249 | A | 250 | C |
| 251 | B | 252 | B | 253 | A | 254 | C | 255 | A |

# 7

# Social Science and Others

1. Which of the following is not a type of frequency distribution?
   a. U shaped b. J shaped
   c. S shaped d. Multimodal
2. Which of the following is not a central tendency?
   a. Harmonic mean b. Geometric mean
   c. Median d. Standard deviation
3. Degree of departure from symmetry of the data is referred to as
   a. Kurtosis b. Mode
   c. Skewness d. Both a & c. are true
4. Which of the following is not a univariate theoretical distribution?
   a. Poisson b. Binomial
   c. Hypergeometric d. Correlation
5. Which of the following is not a type of correlation?
   a. Spearman's rank b. Kendall's rank
   c. Grade d. Dunken's rank
6. Simplest measure of dispersion is
   a. Mean b. Mode
   c. Range d. Median
7. The square of the standard deviation is known as
   a. Variance b. Variable
   c. a and b both d. Median
8. The process of selecting a sample is known as
   a. Sampling b. Selection
   c. Process d. All of them
9. Simplest probability distribution in measure of dispersion is
   a. Poisson b. Binomial
   c. a and b both d. None of them

10. Normal distribution is also known as
    a. Gaussian distribution
    b. Single distribution
    c. Sample distribution
    d. All of them

11. Which distribution occurs commonly?
    a. Normal distribution
    b. Single distribution
    c. Sample distribution
    d. Multiple distribution

12. The standard deviation of the sampling distribution of a statistics is called
    a. Error
    b. Standard error
    c. Sampling error
    d. All of them

13. *F*-distribution is also known as
    a. Fisher test
    b. Z-test
    c. T-test
    d. a & c both

14. Working hypothesis is known as
    a. True hypothesis
    b. Null hypothesis
    c. Alternative hypothesis
    d. All of them

15. Symbol of null hypothesis is
    a. $H_0$
    b. $H_1$
    c. H
    d. a and b both

16. Symbol of alternative hypothesis is
    a. $H_0$
    b. $H_1$
    c. H
    d. a and b both

17. If more than two variables are involved, the correlation is known as
    a. Simple correlation
    b. Multiple correlation
    c. Mixed correlation
    d. b and c both

18. When variables move in the same direction, the correlation is termed as
    a. Simple correlation
    b. Positive correlation
    c. Mixed correlation
    d. Negative correlation

19. Negative correlation is also known as
    a. Inverse correlation
    b. Positive correlation
    c. Mixed correlation
    d. All of them

20. The index of the degree of relationship between two continuous variables is known as

a. Correlation b. Coefficient of correlation
c. Correlation of coefficient d. None of them

21. The correlation coefficient is known as

a. Rank correlation b. Pearson's correlation coefficient
c. Spearman correlation of coefficient d. none of them

22. The range of correlation is

a. 0 to 1 b. 1 to 2
c. 1 to +1 d. None of them

23. The functional relationship between two variables is known as

a. Correlation b. Regression
c. a and b both d. None of them

24. When only two variable are involved then the functional relationship is known as

a. Simple regression b. Mixed regression
c. Multiple regression d. Single regression

25. When more than two variable are involved then the functional relationship is known as

a. Simple regression b. Mixed regression
c. Multiple regression d. Single regression

26. The basic principle of the experimental design is

a. Replication b. Randomization
c. Local control d. All of them

27. The most commonly used tests are

a. LSD b. DMRT
c. CD d. All of them

28. In which condition the null hypothesis is rejected?

a. Non significant of F b. Signification of F
c. a and b both d. None of them

29. In which condition CRD is applied

a. Field condition b. Lab condition
c. Artificial condition d. None of them

30. The term 'Extension' has originated from
    a. Latin c. Persian
    a. Greek d. Sankrit

31. The Latin roots for the word 'Extension' is
    a. Ex and tension c. ex and tension
    b. Ex and lucea d. ex and termo

32. The term 'University Extension' was first used in
    a. 1866 b. 1972
    c. 1901 d. 1921

33. The person considered as father of extension is
    a. James Stewatt b. Seaman A Knapp
    c. Edgar Dale d. Paul Leagans

34. The term 'Extension Education' was first coined in
    a. USA b. UK
    c. Netherland d. India

35. The first use of the word extension was done by
    a. Vorhees b. Seaman A Knapp
    c. Edgar Dale d. Paul Leagans

36. The person considered as father of extension in India
    a. Adivi Reddy b. K N Singh
    c. O P Dahama d. J B Chitambar

37. The father of demonstration in extension is
    a. Seaman A Knapp b. Robert Chambers
    c. Gabriale De Thorde d. James Stewatt

38. The use of computer in technology transfer is known as
    a. Eamncipatory extension b. Cyber extension
    c. Broad based extension d. Participatory extension

39. Extension can be considered as
    a. Teaching and Learning Process b. Applied behavioral science
    c. Decision oriented science d. All of the above

40. Naturally occurring inorganic substances having definite chemical formula and specific structure is known as

a. Mixture | b. Mineral
c. Manure | d. All of them

41. Disintegration and decomposition of rocks and minerals is called

a. Weathering | b. Decomposition
c. a is correct & b is wrong | d. B is correct & a is wrong

42. Disintegration and decomposition of rock fragments without changing its chemical composition is

a. Physical Weathering | b. Chemical weathering
c. Natural weathering | d. All of them

46. Configuration of land surface is known as

a. Topology | b. Geology
c. Topography | d. a and c both

47. Soil colour is determined by using?

a. Munsell colour chart | b. Colour char
c. Soil colour Chart | d. All of them

48. Dominant special colour in munsell colour chart is referred as

a. Blue | b. Hue
c. Grey | d. Red

49. Relative hotness and coolness of the soil is

a. Soil temperature | b. Soil colour
c. Soil texture | d. Soil structure

50. The water drained by gravity force when soil is fully saturated with water is known as

a. Gravitational water | b. Ground water
c. Surface water | d. Capillary water

51. Amount of exchangeable cations present in the unit weight of dry soil is CEC

a. CCE | b. CEC
c. ECC | d. All of them

52. Cohesion of organic nitrogen into inorganic nitrogen through decomposition by microbes is known as

a. Acidification | b. Ammonification
c. a and b both | d. None of them

53. The headquarter of ITTO situated at

a. Yokohama | b. Boger
c. Rome | d. Vienna

54. Tropical savannah is a part of

a. Desert | b. Woodland
c. Forest | d. Grassland

1. Match the following

| | |
|---|---|
| 1. Herbivores | a. Lion, Tiger |
| 2. Carnivores | b. Micro consumers |
| 3. Decomposers | c. Eat other animals |
| 4. Top Carnivores | d. Feed on plants |

2. Match the following

| | |
|---|---|
| 1. Forests | a. Food Chain |
| 2. Wildlife | b. Milk, Meat and Wool |
| 3. Grassland | c. Timber |

3. Match the following

| | |
|---|---|
| 1. Weather | a. Grinnel |
| 2. Climate | b. The Place |
| 3. Habitat | c. Temperature |
| 4. Niche | d. Arthur Tansely |

4. Match the following

| | |
|---|---|
| 1. Ecology | a. Khejri trees |
| 2. Bishnoi Women | b. Haekel |
| 3. Ecosystem | c. Charles Elton |
| 4. Ecological | d. Arthur Tansely |

5. Match the following

| | |
|---|---|
| 1. Pyramid of energy | a. Norman Myers |
| 2. Hot spots | b. Odum |
| 3. Minamata disease | c. Richter scale |
| 4. Earth quake intensity | d. Contaminated Fish with mercury |

6. Match the following

| | |
|---|---|
| 1. Incineration | a. Australia |
| 2. Willy Willy | b. Ponds |
| 3. Johada | c. Green house gas |
| 4. Methane | d. 85 D DC |

7. Match the following

| | |
|---|---|
| 1. Alpha diversity | a. Vulnerable but at risk |
| 2. Taxol | b. Within the community |
| 3. Rare | c. Anti Cancer drug |
| 4. Anthropogenic | d. Man made |

8. Match the following

| | |
|---|---|
| 1. Benzo pyrene | a. Gujarat |
| 2. Fluorosis | b. Tobacco |
| 3. Sardar Sarovar | c. Teeth deformity |
| 4. Chloroflurocarbons | d. Ozone depletion |

9. Match the following

| | |
|---|---|
| 1. Xerophytes | a. Syphilis |
| 2. STD | b. Himanchal Pradesh |
| 3. Shikari Devi Sanctuary | c. Plants in dry soil |
| 4. Floating Plants | d. Pistia |

10. Match the following

| | |
|---|---|
| 1. Macrophytes | a. Bharatpur |
| 2. Detritus | b. Routed plants found in shallow water |
| 3. Keoladeo Sanctuary | c. Irritation of eyes |
| 4. Peroxy Acetyl Nitrate | d. Dead plant parts and animals |

11. Match the following

| | |
|---|---|
| 1. Extinction | a. 40 db (night) |
| 2. Specification | b. Elimination |
| 3. Green house gas | c. Evolution of new species |
| 4. Silent Zone | d. Methane |

12. Match the following

| | |
|---|---|
| 1. Montreal protocol | a. 2000 |
| 2. National population policy | b. 66 |
| 3. Hot spots | c. 1987 |
| 4. Life expectancy | d. 25 |

13. Match the following

| | |
|---|---|
| 1. Itai Itai | a. Fluorine excess |
| 2. Blue baby syndrome | b. Black foot disease |
| 3. Arsenic | c. Cadmium |
| 4. Flurosis | d. Excess nitrate |

14. Match the following

| | |
|---|---|
| 1. Decomposers | a. Organic substances |
| 2. Abiotic Component | b. Diversity of habitat over total land scape |
| 3. Gamma diversity | c. Hot spots |
| 4. Eastern Himalayas | d. Actinomycetes |

15. Match the following

| | |
|---|---|
| 1. Indian Bustard | a. Earth worm farming |
| 2. Vermiculture | b. $CO_2$ |
| 3. Most abundant greenhouse gases | c. Reproducing capacity |
| 4. Fertility | d.Endangered species |

16. Match the following

| | |
|---|---|
| 1. Morphine | a. *Ocimum sanctum* |
| 2. Quinine | b. *Taxus baccata* |
| 3. Taxol | c. *Papaverum somniferum* |
| 4. Tulsi | d.*Cinchona ledgeriana* |

17. Match the following

| | |
|---|---|
| 1. Sultanpur lake bird Sanctuary | a. Assam |
| 2. Kaziranga national park | b. 150gm/litre |
| 3. BOD | c. Weed |
| 4. Water hyacinth | d. Gurgaon |

18. Match the following

| | |
|---|---|
| 1. Endangered | a. Conservational method |
| 2. Transitional zone | b. Red Panda |
| 3. Germ bank | c. 75dB |
| 4. Industrial zone | d. Outer part of biosphere reserve |

19. Match the following

| | |
|---|---|
| 1. Western ghats | a. Alexander Graham |
| 2. Global warming | b. Air |
| 3. Samira | c. Ozone layer depletion |
| 4. Decibel | d. Hot spots |

20. Match the following

| | |
|---|---|
| 1. Kyoto protocol | a. Ozone layer destruction |
| 2. Sherwood Rawland | b. Living matter at different trophic levels |
| 3. Standing crop | c. Excessive plantation of trees |
| 4. Afforestation | d. Green house emission level |

21. Match the following

| | |
|---|---|
| 1. World environment day | a. $16^{th}$ September |
| 2. Earth day | b. $5^{th}$ June |
| 3. Anti tobacco day | c. $31^{st}$ May |
| 4. Ozone day | d. $22^{nd}$ April |

22. Match the following

| | |
|---|---|
| 1. Organism | a. Local population |
| 2. Biome | b. Distinct unit of life |
| 3. Climate | c. Regional unit-desert |
| 4. Ecotype | d. Seasons |

23. Match the following

| | |
|---|---|
| 1. Niche | a. Gause's Hypothesis |
| 2. Competitive Exclusion | b. Crowded ciries |
| 3. Urbanization | c. Crust of earth |
| 4. Lithosphere | d. Grinnel |

24. Match the following

| | |
|---|---|
| 1. Tropical rain forests | a. Pine and Deodar |
| 2. Desert | b. Diptcrocarpus |
| 3. Coniferous | c. Cacti |
| 4. Grassland | d. Cynadon |

25. Match the following

| | |
|---|---|
| 1. 13000 genes | a. Magnolia |
| 2. Anti cancer drug | b. Humans |
| 3. Exotic species | c. Yew free |
| 4. Primitive genes | d. *Lantana camara* |

26. Match the following

| | |
|---|---|
| 1. Kaziranga National Park | a. Tiger |
| 2. Corbett National Park | b. Lion |
| 3. Gir National Park | c. Rhinoceros |
| 4. Bandipur | d. Sambhar |

27. Match the following

| | |
|---|---|
| 1. Biosphere | a. Grass, Sea weed |
| 2. Endemic | b. Threatened species |
| 3. Red Book | c. Confined to a place |
| 4. Producers | d. Ecosphere |

28. Match the following

| | |
|---|---|
| 1. Fusion material | a. Uranium- 235 |
| 2. Fission material | b. Lithium |
| 3. Earth quake | c. Madhya Pradesh |
| 4. Bodghat Project | d. Seismology |

29. Match the following

| | |
|---|---|
| 1. Royal Park | a. Elton |
| 2. Key industry animals | b. Consumers |
| 3. Standing Stage | c. Abiotic material |
| 4. Phargotrophs | d. Australia |

30. Match the following

| | |
|---|---|
| 1. Producers | a. Malaria |
| 2. Quinine | b. Transducers |
| 3. Penicillin | c. Ficus religiosa |
| 4. Pipal | d. Antibiotic |

31. Match the following

| | |
|---|---|
| 1. Solar energy | a. Methane and $CO_2$ |
| 2. Minerals | b. Agroforestry |
| 3. Taungya system | c. Mining |
| 4. Derelict land | d. Inexhaustible |
| 5. Biogas | e. Exhaustible |

32. Match the following

| | |
|---|---|
| 1. Ecology | a. Bacteria and Fungi |
| 2. Niche | b. Earth crust |
| 3. Edaphic | c. Soil |
| 4. Lithosphere | d. Haeckel |
| 5. Decomposers | e. Grinnel |

33. Match the following

| | |
|---|---|
| 1. Earth summit | a. Malaria |
| 2. Kyoto protocol | b. Transducers |
| 3. Antarctica | c. Ficus religiosa |
| 4. Kautilya | d. Antibiotic |
| 5. National forest policy | e. World's first forest conservation programme |

34. Match the following

| | |
|---|---|
| 1. Planktons | a. Dicanthium |
| 2. Floating | b. Cephalanthus |
| 3. Woodland | c. Lemma |
| 4. Sedge or marsh | d. Cyanobacteria |

35. Match the following

| | |
|---|---|
| 1. Birmotibagh wildlife Sanctuary | a. Assam |
| 2. Dachigam Sanctuary | b. West Bengal |
| 3. Jaldapara Sanctuary | c. Patiala |
| 4. Manas wild life Sanctuary | d. Srinagar |

36. Match the following

| | |
|---|---|
| 1. Rice | a. *Prosopis cineraria* |
| 2. Khejri | b. *Oryza sativa* |
| 3. Pipal | c. *Ficus sanctum* |
| 4. Tulsi | d. *Ficus religiosa* |

37. Match the following

| | |
|---|---|
| 1. Exotic species | a. Flying bird |
| 2. Draught | b. Cadmium |
| 3. Inorganic pollutant | c. Alien species |
| 4. California condor | d. Dryness |

37. Match the following

| | |
|---|---|
| 1. Organic farming | a. Cover with crop residue and litter |
| 2. Crop rotation | b. Increased organic input to soil |
| 3. Contour ploughing | c. Growing different crops |
| 4. Mulching | d. Alternate furrows and ridges |

## Fill the blanks

1. Rocks formed from the solidification of molten magma are..........................
2. The direction towards which slope faces is known as.....................
3. Relative purity of strength of the spectral colour in munsell colour chart is referred as ...........................
4. Relative proportion of different soil components such as sand, silt and clay in a soil is...................
5. Arrangement of soil particles into groups or aggregates is known as.....................
6. Arrangement of soil aggregates in thin horizontal plane is.......................
7. Unit weight of soil which include pore spaces is .......................
8. Unit weight of solids in a soil which does not include pore space is.....................
9. Water retained in the capillary pores by the force of cohesion and adhesion is .........
10. The conversion of ammonia into nitrates is .........................................
11. Reduction of nitrites into nitrogen gas is known as...................................
12. Potential ability of the rainfall to cause erosion is...............................
13. Vulnerability or susceptibity of the soil to get eroded is known as.....................
14. Separation of individual soil particles from the soil system by the erosive agents is called.....................
15. Formula of universal soil loss equation is ............................
16. A natural geohydrological unit where by all streams are draining into a

common point is known as...........................

17. The national watershed atlas is published by ..................................
18. Place where sensors are mounted is known as ...............................
19. NDVI stands for ......................................................
20. Satellite based navigation system that provide continuous real time, 3 dimensional positioning, navigation and timing worldwide ............................
21. Any act which affects or have an adverse effect on forest or that interfere with forest control is ..............................
22. Act of possession of forest land illegally is termed as .......................
23. Maximum number of animals that can graze on a specific area and a given period of time without causing any adverse effect ..............................
24. The term 'Ecology' was coined by______________
25. The study of reciprocal relationship between organisms and their environment is called _____________
26. ____________ can be visualized as a thin life supporting belt on and around earth
27. The microscopic, photosynthetic organisms that float on water surface are called______________
28. The ecological factors related to soil and substratum is called_____________ factors.
29. The solid or dry crust of the earth that forms the contents and other land masses is called___________
30. The water mantle of the earth is known as______________
31. The ability of some animals to blend with the surrounding is known as ____________
32. The study of soil and its related aspects is known as ______________
33. _____________are group of species exploiting a common resource in a similar fashion
34. ______________showed that closely related birds could occues together due to difference in their nesting and feeding habits
35. Bisons of Asia, Kangaroos of Australia and Zebra of Africa are_______
36. Physical space occupied by and organisms is_____________
37. The physical space occupied by and organism, population, community is called_______________
38. The term 'Niche' was first introduced by in the year_____________&_____
39. The first atomic bomb explosion was done in ______and second in_______

40. Prolonged exposure to noise of ___________ or more may lead to impairing hearing
41. Degradation of organic waste by microorganisms in presence of oxygen is known as_______________
42. The process of controlled burning of the waste at high temperature of $850^0$C in known as____________
43. The magnitude or intensity of energy released by an earthquake is measured by_____________________
44. Tropical cyclones in Caribbean sea is called as_____________
45. Property of certain elements to emit protons or electrons is known as____________
46. Ozone is formed in the atmosphere by_______
47. Tobacco smokes contains a hydrocarbon called_____________
48. Petroleum used in automobiles contains_______________ as a antiknock agent
49. _______________ is the most abundant hydrocarbons in the atmosphere.
50. Increase in concentration of soluble salts in soil is called_____________
51. Minamata disease is caused due to biomagnifications of ______________
52. The total land mass of India is ____________ million hectares.
53. Deposition of acids (Sulphuric acid/ nitric acid. on the earth from atmosphere is known as____________
54. The unit of measurement of sound is____________
55. Excess of nitrates in drinking water causes _____________ in humans
56. The radioactive gases are also called___________
57. The thinning of stratospheric layer during spring time is called ___________
58. The management of rainfall with resultant runoff is called________________
59. The type of vegetation found in temperature forests is______
60. Deep channel worn by water are called_____________
61. Soil on river bank is poor in nutrients because of _______________
62. A land for grazing is known as____________
63. The three component of environment are________________________
64. The difference between number of birth and that of death is known as_____________
65. The replacement level is developed and deloping countries

are_____________

66. The total fertility rates in developed countries is close to _____________
67. Replacement level in developing countries is always higher than 2.0 because_____________
68. The number of children a couple must produce to replace themselves is called _____________
69. The movement of individuals into a place or country is known as___________
70. The time required for a population to double itself is known as____________
71. The number of babies produce per thousand individuals is known as____________________
72. Biochemical oxygen demand measures_______
73. __________ can serve as indicators to detect pollution of air by SO
74. Sound becomes hazardous noise pollution at decibels___________
75. Taj Mahal at Agra is damaged by___________
76. Preservation of living tissues/parts of plants in liquid nitrogen at temperature of -196$^0$C is known as_______
77. An exotic plant species which has posed threat to the native species is_____
78. The total number of National Parks in India are___________
79. Derivative chemicals synthesized from plant products are called__________
80. The diversity of communities along the environment gradient is _________
81. Oak species are predominantly found in____________ forests
82. The pioneer plant of xerarch is___________
83. The primary source for all living organisms is___________
84. The ecological pyramids were devised by_____________
85. The plant species that invade the bare habitat initially are known as ________
86. Graphic representation of ecological parameters at each trophic level in an ecosystem is_____________
87. Interconnected matrix of food chain in an ecosystem is known as_____________
88. A protected area where multiple use of the land is permitted by dividing it into certain zone is known as___________
89. The richest and most threatened reservoirs of plant and animal life on earth is known as______________

90. Excess fluoride in drinking water causes______________
91. The ability of the reproductively active individuals to produce babies is known as__________
92. If the individuals of a species remain alive only in captivity or other human controlled conditions, the species is said to be___________
93. The increased concentration of green house gases in the atmosphere leads to____________
94. A glass house used for raising delicate plant is called___________
95. _____________is a product of incomplete decomposition caused by a group of bacteria called ethanogens.

## Answer key

| | | | | | | | | | |
|---|---|---|---|---|---|---|---|---|---|
| 1 | D | 2 | D | 3 | C | 4 | D | 5 | C |
| 6 | C | 7 | A | 8 | A | 9 | B | 10 | A |
| 11 | A | 12 | B | 13 | A | 14 | B | 15 | A |
| 16 | B | 17 | B | 18 | B | 19 | A | 20 | C |
| 21 | B | 22 | C | 23 | B | 24 | A | 25 | C |
| 26 | D | 27 | D | 28 | B | 29 | B | 30 | A |
| 31 | A | 32 | A | 33 | A | 34 | B | 35 | A |
| 36 | B | 37 | A | 38 | B | 39 | D | 40 | B |
| 41 | C | 42 | A | 43 | C | 44 | A | 45 | B |
| 46 | A | 47 | A | 48 | B | 49 | B | 50 | A |
| 51 | B | 52 | B | 53 | A | 54 | B | | |

## Answers key-Match

1. 1 (d., 2 (c., 3 (b., 4 (a.
2. 1 (c., 2 (a., 3 (b.
3. 1 (c., 2 (d., 3 (b., 4 (a.
4. 1 (b., 2 (a., 3 (d., 4 (c.
5. 1 (b., 2 (a., 3 (d., 4 (c.
6. 1 (d., 2 (a., 3 (b., 4 (c.
7. 1 (b., 2 (c., 3 (a., 4 (d.
8. 1 (b., 2 (c., 3 (a., 4 (d.
9. 1 (c., 2 (a., 3 (b., 4 (d.
10. 1 (b., 2 (d., 3 (a., 4 (c.
11. 1 (b., 2 (c., 3 (d., 4 (a.
12. 1 (c., 2 (a., 3 (d., 4 (b.
13. 1 (c., 2 (d., 3 (b., 4 (a.
14. 1 (d., 2 (a., 3 (b., 4 (c.
15. 1 (d., 2 (a., 3 (b., 4 (c.
16. 1 (c., 2 (d., 3 (b., 4 (a.
17. 1 (d., 2 (a., 3 (b., 4 (c.
18. 1 (b., 2 (d., 3 (a., 4 (c.
19. 1 (d., 2 (c., 3 (b., 4 (a.
20. 1 (d., 2 (a., 3 (b., 4 (c.
21. 1 (b., 2 (d., 3 (c., 4 (a.
22. 1 (b., 2 (c., 3 (d., 4 (a.
23. 1 (d., 2 (a., 3(b., 4 (c.
24. 1 (b., 2 (c., 3 (a., 4 (d.
25. 1 (b., 2 (c., 3(d., 4 (a.
26. 1 (c., 2 (a., 3 (b., 4 (d.
27. 1 (d., 2 (c., 3 (b., 4 (a.
28. 1 (b., 2 (a., 3 (d., 4 (c.

29. 1 (d., 2 (a., 3 (c., 4 (b.
30. 1 (b., 2 (a., 3 (d., 4 (c.
31. 1 (d., 2 (e., 3 (b., 4 (c., 5 (a.
32. 1 (d., 2 (e., 3 (c., 4 (b., 5 (a.
33. 1 (c., 2 (d., 3 (a., 4 (e.,5(b.
34. 1 (d., 2 (c., 3 (a., 4 (b.
35. 1 (c., 2 (d., 3 (b., 4 (a.
36. 1 (b., 2 (a., 3 (d., 4 (c.
37. 1 (c., 2 (d., 3 (b., 4 (a.
38. 1 (b., 2 (c., 3 (d., 4 (a.

**Answer**

1. Igneous
2. Aspect
3. Chroma
4. Texture
5. Structure
6. Platy structure
7. Bulk density
8. Particle density
9. Capillary water
10. Nitrification
11. Denitrification
12. Erosivity
13. Erodibility
14. Detachability
15. A=R×K×LS×C×P
16. Watershed
17. All India soil and land use
18. Platform
19. Normalized differential vegetation indices
20. Global positioning system
21. Forest offences
22. Encroachment
23. Carrying capacity
24. Ernst Haeckel
25. Ecology
26. Biosphere
27. Phytoplanktons
28. Edaphic
29. Lithosphere
30. Hydrosphere
31. Camouflage
32. Pedalogy
33. Guilds
34. Lack
35. Ecologically equivalent
36. Spatial
37. Habitat
38. Grinnel, 1917
39. Nagasaki, Hirooshima\
40. 80 dB
41. Composting
42. Incineration
43. Richter scale
44. Hurricanes
45. Radioactivity
46. Photochemical reaction
47. Benzo pyrene
48. Tetra ethyl lead
49. Methane
50. Salination
51. Mercury
52. 305
53. Acid rain
54. Decibel

55. Mathamoglobinema- Blue baby syndrome
56. Green house gases
57. Ozone hole
58. Watershed management
59. Conifers mixed with broad leaved trees
60. Gullies
61. Leaching
62. Pasture
63. Productive system, protective system and waste assimilative system
64. Rate of natural increase
65. 2.1 and 2.7
66. Replacement level
67. Some children die before recing reproductive stage
68. Replacement level
69. Immigration
70. Double time
71. Natality by microbes to decompose
72. Dissolved oxygen needed organic waste
73. Lichens
74. Above 80
75. Sulphur dioxide
76. Cryopreservation
77. Lantana camara
78. 89
79. Botano chemicals
80. Beta diversity
81. Temperate broad leaf
82. Lichens
83. Sun
84. Charles Elton
85. Pioneer species
86. Ecological Pyramids
87. Food web
88. Biosphere reserve
89. Hotspot
90. Fluorosis
91. Fertility
92. Extinct in the wild
93. Global warming
94. Green house gases
95. Methane

# 8

# Exercise Paper –I

1. The response of plants to elevate concentration of $CO_2$ is known as ________

2. Collecting and storage of rain water for future use is known as ________

3. Spot the wrong one

   a. Chlorofluorocarbons b. $CO_2$

   c. Methane d. Oxygen

4. Identify the odd one out

   a. Nandadevi b. Nilgiris

   b. Periyar d. Pachmarhi

5. Identify the odd one out

   a. Keoladeo b. Mudumalai

   b. Chilka d. Simplipal

6. Identify the odd one out

   a. *Susalvinius* b. *Aliurns fulgens*

   c. *Barberis nilghiriensis* d. *Antilope cervicapra*

7. Identify the odd one out

   a. Stronitum b. Cesium

   c. Arsenic d. Iodium

8. Identify the odd one out

   a. X- rays b. Cosmic Rays

   c. Atomic Rays d. Infra Red rays

9. Identify the odd one out

   a. Kautilya b. Earth Summit

   c. Kyoto Protocol d. Montreal treaty

10. Identify the odd one out

    a. Producers b. Consumers

    c. Decomposers d. Abiotic components

11. Identify the odd one out
    a. Lichen stage
    b. Moss stage
    c. Herb stage
    d. Parent stage
12. Identify the odd one out
    a. Reaction
    b. Co-action
    b. Stabilisation
    d. Drama
13. Identify the odd one out
    a. Phytoplankton
    b. Zooplankton
    c. Grasslands
    d. Fish
14. Identify the odd one out
    a. Photochemical smog
    b. Brown air
    c. White air
    d. Grey air
15. Identify the odd one out
    a. Coal
    b. $SO_2$
    c. Petroleum
    d. Gas
16. Identify the odd one out
    a. Sundarlal Bahuguna
    b. Amrita Devi
    c. Salim Ali
    d. Indira Gandhi
17. Most Biotic resources are_________
18. The practice of felling and burning of forests followed by cultivation of crop for few years is called_______________
19. The first movement against tree felling was fought by a Bishnoi women of Keharili Village named_______________
20. In Karnatka, Chipko movement is known as_____________
21. Our big dams were called " The temple of modern India" by our late Prime Minister__________
22. Chipko movement in Tehri Garhwal region was initiated by ____________
23. The practice of farming with increased organic input to the soil is known as_______________
24. The land that has been destroyed due to mining is known as_____________
25. Conversion of grass lands/forests into deserts is known as____________
26. The practice of growing agriculture crops between rows of planted tree is known as __________

27. Identify the odd one out
    a. Coal
    b. Forests
    c. Water
    d. Wildlife

28. Identify the odd one out
    a. Over grazing
    b. Removal of vegetation
    c. Afforestation
    d. Deforestation

29. Raising of plant species having high calorific value and growth rate is known as ______________

30. The book lost containing a record of threatened species is ________________

31. The most rich biodiversity zones of India are________________

32. Match the following

| | |
|---|---|
| 1. Red data book | a. 19% |
| 2. Land under forest | b. data of threatened species |
| 3. Fluorosis | c. 15-44 years |
| 4. Reproductive age | d. 1.5 parts per million |

33. The population growth when birth and death rates are equal is known as .........

34. The life expectancy of people on Zambia is_______________

35. UNESCO stands for______________

36. World Wildlife week is celebrated during_____________

37. The two very much complex interdependent mutually reactive entities are ____

38. The various principles, that govern the relationships between the organisms and environment is called________________

39. The term 'Ecology' was first time introduced by________________

40. Lithosphere, Hydrosphere and the atmosphere will constitute the ____________

41. The basic unit of ecological hierarchy is known as______________

42. Competition, mutualism and predation are the interaction occurring between ____________

43. The assemblage of population of plants, animals, bacteria and fungi that live in and is known as ______________

44. The unit of land with a natural boundary having a mosoic of patches is known as_________

45. A large regional unit characterized by a major vegetation type and associated fauna found in a specific climate zone is known as________________

46. ________ extends to about 22.5 km in thickness from ocean to mountain tops.

47. The solid earth crust is known as__________

48. The surroundings in which the organisms live is known as____________

49. Short term properties of atmosphere is known as______________

50. The climate is largely determined by the __________and of an area

51. Because of their small size, decomposers are known as_____________

52. The minerals and atmospheric gases enter into biotic system and after the death and decay of organisms return to the soil and atmosphere. This is known as________________

53. The rate of increases in the biomass of consumers per unit and time is called_________

54. The largest carnivores prey upon the primary carnivores are called_________

55. All types of ecosystems possess two types of food chain, they are__________

56. Ecological pyramids were first devised by a British ecologist_____________

57. A semi-closed coastal body of water that has a free connection with sea is known as______________

58. The sequence of succession stage on a bare rock are called as________________

59. The last and stable community in the area is called as____________

60. The first arrivals in a bare area are called ________________

61. The sequence of successional stages on sand are known as__________

62. The sequence of successional stages of secondary succession is called ________

63. A byproduct of paper industry resembling raw dust is known as__________

64. The acidic water received through rain, for and snow is known as_________

65. Plants which are non-green, grow on other plants and obtain food from the host are known as ______________

66. An area which is strictly reserved for the welfare of wild life and activities like forestry, grazing and cultivation are not allowed is known as_________________

67. The first national park established in India was___________

68. The species is considered _____ when no member of the species remains alive.

69. The most undisturbed forests without any human impact are known as________

70. The major drawback of incineration is________

71. The major disappearance of species from the face of earth due to human activities is known as ___________

72. ___________ is the most comprehensive inventory of the global conservation status of plant and animal species

73. Growing ornamental and fruit trees in urban area alongside roads is known as______________

74. Using the same land for farming and forestry is known as________

75. About ¾ of the earth's surface is occupied by___________

76. On an average, the residence time of water in the air is only about_____________

77. Kaveri rivers sharing water dispute is between______________

78. The dam across the river Nile in Egypt is ____________

79. The biomass can be used to obtain fuels like_____

80. Biogas is a mixture of two gases namely_____________

81. The study that deals with the origin, formation and geographic distribiution of the soil is known as________________

82. ________________ converts direct solar energy into electricity.

83. All material originating from photosynthesis are known as_______________

84. The energy produced from kinetic energy of water falling from a height is known as___________

85. Breaking down of rock into small particles is known as_

86. Maturation of soil through development of humus is known as_____________

87. The removal of top soil from its place by various physical agencies is called___________

88. Men folk opposing the large scale felling of forests trees, the movement was known as______________

89. Chipko movement was started in ____________

90. The main objectives of Appiko movement were______________

91. A special programme of tree plantation is held every year in the country is

known as______________

92. The measures and practices taken to protect the soil against loss is known as___________

93. Water logging and application of non – degradable chemicals leads to loss of ____________________

94. Planting of crops in rows or strips to check flow of water is called______

95. The best soil for healthy growth of most plants is _____________

96. Both power and manure are provided by_____

97. The successful establishment of a species after reaching to new area, as a result of adjustment with the condition prevailing there is known as_______________

98. Successive replacement of communities in an area over a period of time is known as___________

99. Autotrophic plankton are called________

100. A primary succession on bare rock starts with________

101. Tropical forests occur in India in __________

102. The rate of biomass or organic matter production by the organisms is known as __________

103. The food chain in which microorganisms breakdown dead producers is called _________

104. Anthropogenic or man made ecosystem basically agriculture fields is knows as ______________

105. The pyramid of __________ is always right

106. New approaches of conservation of environment is the establishment of _____

107. The area reserved for welfare of wildlife is called_____________

108. The totality of genes, species and the ecosystem of a region are known as ________

109. The whole sequences of communities that replace one another in the given area is called ____________

110. Formation of different layers or strata of different species in a community is known as _____________

111. A population as able to adapt to its environment and respond to natural selection due to its___________

112. The evenness in the no of individuals of a species is known as_________

113. Nile perch is an exotic predatory_____

114. Water hyacinth is a free floating exotic_____

115. The extinction of species in the geological past is called____________

116. Chilka lake bird sanctuary is in__________

117. The two main centers of biological diversity in Western Ghats are________

118. Animals having high protection prospects are______________

119. The main natural sources of air pollution are______________

120. Burning of plastic producers___________

121. The widely used aerosol propellant and refrigerant is ____________

122. ______ dissolves silver and lead paints.

## Answers

1. Carbon dioxide fertilization effect
2. Rain water harvesting
3. d) oxygen
4. c) Periyar
5. d) Simplipal
6. c) Barberis nilghiriensis
7. c) Arsenic
8. d) Infra Red rays
9. a) Kautilya
10. d) Abiotic component
11. d) Parent stage
12. d) Drama
13. c) Grasslands
14. c) White air
15. b) Sulphur dioxide
16. d) Indira Gandhi
17. Renewable
18. Jhum (Shifting cultivation)
19. Amrita Devi
20. Appiko movement

21. Pandit Jawaharla Nehru
22. Sunderlal Bahuguna
23. Organic farming
24. Mine spoil
25. Desertification
26. Taungya cultivation
27. a) Coal
28. c) Afforestation
29. Energy plantation
30. Red data book
31. Western Ghats and North East
32. 1(b), 2(a), 3(d), 4(c)
33. Zero population growth
34. 37 years
35. United Nations Education Scientific and Cultural Organication
36. 1st – 7th October
37. Organisms and Environment
38. Ecology
39. Ernst Haeckel
40. Physical Environment
41. Organisms
42. Different population in an area
43. Biological Community
44. Landscape
45. Biome
46. Biosphere
47. Lithosphere
48. Environment
49. Weather
50. Temperature and Rainfall
51. Micro Consumers
52. Biogeochemical cycle
53. Seconadary Productivity
54. Third order consumers or secobdary carnivores

55. Grazing food chain and detrirus food chain
56. Charles Elton
57. Estuary
58. Lithosphere
59. Climax community
60. Pioneers or pioneer colonizers
61. Psammosere
62. Subsere
63. Bregoli
64. Wet deposition
65. Parasites
66. National Park
67. Jim Corbett national park, Nainital
68. Extinct
69. Pristine forests
70. That it release a number of toxic chemicals in the atmosphere
71. Antropogenic extinction
72. 2000 IUCN Red list
73. Urbal forestry
74. Agroforestry
75. Ocean
76. 10 days
77. Karnatka and Tamil Nadu
78. Aswan Dam
79. Methanol and Ethanol
80. Methane and Carbon dioxide
81. Pedology
82. Photovoltaic cell
83. Biomass
84. Hydropower
85. Weathering
86. Pedogenesis
87. Soil erosion
88. Chipko movement

89. Tehri garhwal region of Uttarakhand
90. Ulisu, Belesu and Balasu
91. Van mahotsava
92. Soil conservation
93. Soil fertility
94. Strip cropping
95. Loamy soil
96. Biogas plants
97. Ecesis
98. Succession
99. Phytoplankton
100. Lichens
101. Kerala and Assam
102. Productivity
103. Detritus food chain
104. Agroecosystem
105. Energy
106. Biosphere reserves
107. National park
108. Biodiversity
109. Sere
110. Stratification
111. Genetic diversiry
112. Equitability
113. Fish
114. Water weed
115. Background extinction
116. Balagaon (orissa)
117. Agastryamalai hills, Silent valley and the new Ammambalam reserve
118. Himalayan bear and musk deer
119. Volcanic eruptions and solar flames
120. Polychlorinated biphenyls
121. Chlorofluoro methane
122. Hydrogen sulphide

# 9

# Model Paper –I

1. The tree species suitable for Agroforestry in hot and arid climate is
   a. *Prosopis cineraria* b. *Albizia lebbeck*
   c. *Salix alba* d. *Eucalyptus globulus*

2. *Acacia Senegal* is suitable for Agroforestry in
   a. Hill soils b. Alluvial soils
   c. Laterite soils d. Desert soils

3. Find the odd man out with reference to suitability of the species to a particular site factor?
   a. *Prosopis chilensis* b. *Acacia tortilis*
   c. *Acacia nilotica* d. *Juglans regia*

4. The following species like Eucalyptus hybrid, *Prosopis chilensis*, *Gliricidia maculata* and *Cassia siamea* are suitable for Agroforestry system because of
   a. The species are generally not grazed b. Deciduous in nature
   c. Nitrogen fixing d. All of these

5. *Casuarina equisetifolia* is preferred for Agroforestry because it is
   a. Atmospheric nitrogen fixer in the soil b. The bole is upright and straight
   c. None of these d. Both of these

6. Agrisilvicultural system classification of Agroforestry is based on
   a. Nature of components b. Arrangement of components
   c. Functional basis d. Ecological basis

7. Taungya system is a
   a. Agrisilvicultural system b. Silvipastoral system
   c. Agrosilvopastoral system d. All of these

8. The Agroforestry system that is based mainly on temporal arrangement of components is
   a. Home gardens b. Shifting cultivation
   c. Tea gardens d. None of these

9. Local name for Sweden Agriculture in India

   a. Milpa  b. Lading

   c. Jhum  d. Chena

10. ICRAF came into existence in which year

   a. 1975  b. 1985

   c. 1977  d. 1980

11. Ratio of height and width in shelter belts should be roughly

   a. 1:15  b. 1:10

   c. 1:20  d. 1:5

12. Minimum length of a shelter belt should be about how many times its height?

   a. 20  b. 15

   c. 25  d. 30

13. A wind break of 20 m height will give protection from

   a. 100-500 m  b. 200- 800 m

   c. up to 1 km  d. up to 2 km

14. Most dominating agroforestry system in Humid tropics is

   a. Silvipasture  b. Silvihorticulture

   c. Homegardens  d. Hortipasture

15. To allow more light inside the agroforestry system the rows of trees should be planted in which direction

   a. East- West  b. North-south

   c. South-west  d. North-west

16. Headquarter of ICRAF located at which country

   a. Australia  b. Kenya

   c. New Zealand  d. India

17. Suitable tree species for Agroforestry

   a. NFT  b. MPTS

   c. a and b  d. None of the above

18. Major cause of soil erosion

   a. Deforestation  b. Mining

   c. a and b  d. None of the above

19. Major cause of deforestation

   a. Human habitation  b. Agriculture

   c. Dam  d. None of the above

20. Oldest agroforestry system of the world
    a. Block plantation
    b. Taungya system
    c. Shifting cultivation
    d. a and c both

21. Taungya system was started at
    a. Burma
    b. South Africa
    c. India
    d. None of the above

22. Who introduced Taungya system in India?
    a. Brandis
    b. Swaminathan
    c. Tipu Sultan
    d. Maclland

23. In which state Taungya system was first introduced in India
    a. West Bengal
    b. Sikkim
    c. Uttar Pradesh
    d. Kerala

24. Shifting cultivation mostly practiced in which region
    a. North-East Region
    b. Eastern Region
    c. Western Region
    d. Southern Region

25. Agroforestry work was started during which five year plan
    a. First five year
    b. Third five year
    c. Six five year
    d. Seventh five year

26. Land without crops in called
    a. Taungya
    b. Fallow land
    c. a and b
    d. None of the above

27. Objective of improved fallow species in shifting cultivation is
    a. Sustain the crop yield
    b. Recover depleted soil nutrients
    c. Increase forest cover
    d. None of the above

28. Institute responsible for agroforestry research in India
    a. ICFRE & FRI
    b. ICAR & NRCAF
    c. a and b
    d. None of the above

29. How many broad agroecological regions in India?
    a. 10
    b. 8
    c. 5
    d. 9

30. How many agroclimatic regions in India?
    a. 15
    b. 11
    c. 12
    d. 13

31. Which agroforestry system practiced without capital input?
    a. Taungya
    b. Shifting cultivation
    c. Silvipastoral system
    d. Aquaforestry

32. Present day fallow period is shorter due to
    a. Adequate rainfall
    b. Accurate land shortage
    c. a and b
    d. None of the above

33. Alley cropping is also known as
    a. Intercropping
    b. Hedgerow intercropping
    c. Mixed cropping
    d. None of the above

34. Main aim of alley cropping system is
    a. Sustain crop yield
    b. Improvement of soil & microclimate
    c. Reducing soil erosion
    d. a and b

35. Hedgerow should be planted in which direction
    a. North-South
    b. South-West
    c. East-West
    d. North-East

36. Several row of trees established at right angles to prevailing wind is known as
    a. Wind break
    b. Alley cropping
    c. Shelter belt
    d. a and c

37. Main aim of shelter belt is
    a. Protect crop from insect & Pest
    b. Reduce rainfall
    c. Reduce wind velocity
    d. None of the above

38. Ideal shape for shelter belt is
    a. Rectangular
    b. Triangular
    c. Both a and b
    d. None of the above

39. Ideal width of shelter belt in India is
    a. 15 m
    b. 20 m
    c. 50 m
    d. 40 m

40. Wind breaks reduce the open wind speed
    a. 25 times of tree height
    b. 35 times of tree height
    c. 45 times of tree height
    d. 15 times of tree height

41. Wind breaks should be planted in which direction
    a. East-West
    b. North-South
    c. North-East
    d. Perpendicular to wind direction

42. When woody plant is combined with pasture the system is called
    a. Silvopastoral
    b. Silvo-Agro-Pastoral
    c. Agropastrol
    d. Both a and b

43. Silvopastoral system mostly practiced in which area
    a. Cold
    b. Dry
    c. Rainy
    d. None of the above

44. Living fence of fodder trees & hedge is under which agroforestry system
    a. Alley cropping
    b. Silvopastoral
    c. Hortipastrol
    d. Block plantation

45. Spatial arrangement is the main feature of which agroforestry system
    a. Improved fellow
    b. Shifting cultivation
    c. Taungya
    d. Home garden

46. Which agroforestry system supports higher diversity?
    a. Home garden
    b. Taungya
    c. Shifting cultivation
    d. None of the above

47. Which state has highest area under arid condition?
    a. Rajasthan
    b. Haryana
    c. Punjab
    d. Gujarat

48. Which type of characteristic is required for arid agroforestry species?
    a. Deep root system & Wax coating on leaf
    b. Only deep root system
    c. Covered stomata on leaves
    d. Both a and c

49. Best time for tree planting for agroforestry in arid zone is
    a. Beginning of rain
    b. Beginning of winter
    c. After rain
    d. None of the above

50. Major problem in arid zone agroforestry is
    a. Availability of moisture
    b. Soil fertility
    c. Both a and b
    d. None of the above

51. First university to stared PG programme in Agroforestry is
    a. YSPHF, Solan
    b. Gujarat Agricultural University
    c. GB Pant Agricultural University
    d. CCS Agricultural University

52. The standard length of last section of a log is not more than
    a. 6 m
    b. 4.5 m
    c. 5 m
    d. 3.5 m

53. Which tree species is suitable for shifting sand-dunes in arid area?
    a. Eucalyptus
    b. Prosopis
    c. Mango
    d. Neem

54. Which is suitable agriculture crop for arid area?
    a. Pearl-millet
    b. Maize
    c. Both a and b
    d. None of the above

55. Which is suitable horticultural plant for arid area?
    a. *Zizyphus mauritiana*
    b. Mango
    c. Papaya
    d. None of the above

56. Preferred agroforestry system for wetland is
    a. Aquaforestry
    b. Hortipastrol
    c. Both a and b
    d. Silvopastoral

57. Which types of measures should be taken to improve the condition of wetland?
    a. Ditching
    b. Terracing
    c. Contour
    d. both a and b

58. Block planting of tree is known as
    a. Forest
    b. Agroforestry
    c. Wind breaks
    d. Woodlot

59. Which land use system sequester highest carbon
    a. Agriculture
    b. Agroforestry
    c. Wind breaks
    d. Forest

60. Farm forestry should be practiced in which type of land
    a. Farmers land
    b. Community land
    c. Government land
    d. None of the above

61. Which type of species selected for farm forestry
    a. Short rotation
    b. Medium rotation
    c. Both a and b
    d. None of the above

62. Community forestry should be practiced in which type of land
    a. Waste land
    b. Community/Public land
    c. Both a and b
    d. Road side land

63. Main aims of community forestry is
    a. Production of Fuel wood
    b. Production of fodder
    c. Both a and b
    d. Production of timber

64. United Nations Conference on Environment and Development held in June, 1992 is popularly known as
    a. Global summit
    b. De Janerio summit
    c. Janerio summit
    d. Earth summit

65. When efforts are directed towards development of pest-resistant strains of tree, the activity will be categorized under which term
    a. Forest tree breeding
    b. Forest genetics
    c. Tree improvement
    d. All of them

66. Groups of populations that generally interbreed with one another and that intergrade more of less continuously is referred to as
    a. Population
    b. Family
    c. Race
    d. Seed orchard

67. Which among the following has a role in reducing variability in natural stands?
    a. Migration
    b. Gene flow
    c. Natural selection
    d. Both a and b are true

68. Average performance of the progeny of an individual when it is mated to a number of other individuals in the population is known as
    a. Specific combining ability
    b. Heritability
    c. General combining ability
    d. Additive genetic value

69. Average phenotypic value of the selected individuals, expressed as a deviation from the population mean is known as
    a. Genetic gain
    b. Broad sense heritability
    c. Narrow sense heritability
    d. Selection differential

70. Which of the following is not a multitrait selection procedure
    a. Independent culling
    b. Selection index
    c. Tandem selection
    d. Both b. & c

71. A tree which had been proven to be genetically superior by means of progeny testing is known as

a. Plus tree b. Check tree
c. Elite tree d. Superior tree

72. Broader genetic base will be in which types of seed orchards

a. Seedling orchards b. Vegetative orchards
c. Both of a& b. d. None of a.& b..

73. Which of the following is not a complete pedigree mating design for tree improvement?

a. Nested design b. Factorial design
c. Single pair mating d. None of these

74. When each parent is crossed with other in all possible combinations except reciprocal crosses such system of mating is

a. Systematic diallels b. Half diallels
c. Full diallels d. Progressive diallel

75. Limited spread of genetic material from one species into another species as a result of hybridization followed by backcrossing of the hybrid and its progeny is known as

a. Hybrid swarms b. Hybridization
c. Introgression d. Hybrid vigour

76. Which of the following is not a type of frequency distribution?

a. U shaped b. J shaped
c. S shaped d. Multimodal

77. Which of the following is not a central tendency?

a. Harmonic mean b. Geometric mean
c. Median d. Standard deviation

78. Degree of departure from symmetry of the data is referred to as

a. Kurtosis b. mode
c. Skewness d. Both a and c are true

79. Which of the following is not a univariate theoretical distribution?

a. Poisson b. Binomial
c. Hypergeometric d. Correlation

80. Which of the following is not a type of correlation?
    a. Spearman's rank
    b. Kendall's rank
    c. Grade
    d. Dunken's rank

81. In most of the Common Wealth countries diameter is measured at a height of
    a. 1.27 m
    b. 1.37 m
    c. 1.57 m
    d. 1.47 m

82. Spiegel relascope is provided with how much number of scales/bands to measure height of a tree?
    a. One
    b. Two
    c. Three
    d. Four

83. Smythies's hypsometer is based on the principle of
    a. Similar triangles
    b. Trigonometry
    c. Probability proportional to size
    d. Visual observation

84. According to Girder theory the growth materials of the tree are deposited at
    a. Base
    b. Middle
    c. Top
    d. Root

85. While measuring height of a tree using Haga altimeter, if one reading is on right side of zero mark and other on left side, to get the total height of tree both the readings will be
    a. Subtracted
    b. Added
    c. Added and divided by two
    d. Subtracted and divided by two

86. Ravi multimeter differs from Ravi altimeter in the way that it has
    a. Mirror and leveller
    b. Aperture and turning knob
    c. Only one among a & b above
    d. Both a & b. above

87. Which among the following is calculated in uneven aged forests?
    a. Crop height
    b. Top height
    c. Mean height
    d. Total height

88. Vertical point sampling for measuring crop height was developed by which scientist?
    a. Hirata
    b. Brandis
    c. Shivnarayan
    d. Odum

89. When basal area is measured at any convenient height and length of tree is taken above that point to calculate the form of the tree, the form factor so obtained is
    a. Artificial form factor b. Absolute form factor
    c. True form factor d. None of these

90. Point sampling is also called as
    a. Bitterlich method b. Pointless cruising
    c. None of these d. Both of these

91. Wedge prism is used to measure
    a. Diameter b. Basal area
    c. Volume d. Number of trees per unit area

92. Quarter girth formula for estimating volume of tree is also known as
    a. Hoppus rule b. Newton's formula
    c. Huber's formula d. None of these

93. Volume of the standing trees of forest is measured by
    a. Hossfeld's and Urich's method b. Hartig's and Draudt's method
    c. Both a and b are true d. None of them

94. Taking 1.41 m as crown spread which tree will be regarded as co-spaced tree among the following
    a. Tree having 1 m crown spread b. Tree having 0.5 m crown spread
    c. Tree having 1.8 m crown spread d. Tree having 0.6 m crown spread.

95. A non-leguminous nitrogen fixing tree species is
    a. *Leucaena leucocephala* b. *Casuarina equisetifolia*
    c. *Albizia lebbeck* d. *Acacia nilotic*

96. Clear felling system of forest management is
    a. Diffused regeneration system b. Accessory system
    c. Concentrated regeneration d. Both b and c are true

97. Clear felling system was for the first time introduced in 19th century on commercial scale. The system was introduced by
    a. Heinrich Von Cotta b. Henry Von Cotta
    c. Troup d. D. Brandis

98. In Shelter wood system, during seeding felling in deodar (Cedrus deodara) the number of seed bearer to be kept per hectare is

    a. 12- 18 b. 45 – 50

    c. 25 – 30 d. 35 – 45

99. Floating periodic block was first introduced in

    a. Germany b. France

    c. United Kingdom d. India

100. In India minimum number of trees used for general volume table preparation is

    a. 100 b. 1000

    c. 10000 d. 500

## Answer Key

| 1 | a | 2 | d | 3 | d | 4 | a | 5 | d | 6 | a |
|---|---|---|---|---|---|---|---|---|---|---|---|
| 7 | a | 8 | b | 9 | c | 10 | a | 11 | c | 12 | c |
| 13 | a | 14 | c | 15 | a | 16 | b | 17 | c | 18 | c |
| 19 | b | 20 | c | 21 | a | 22 | a | 23 | a | 24 | a |
| 25 | d | 26 | b | 27 | b | 28 | c | 29 | b | 30 | a |
| 31 | b | 32 | b | 33 | b | 34 | b | 35 | c | 36 | c |
| 37 | c | 38 | b | 39 | c | 40 | a | 41 | d | 42 | a |
| 43 | b | 44 | b | 45 | d | 46 | a | 47 | a | 48 | D |
| 49 | a | 50 | a | 51 | a | 52 | b | 53 | b | 54 | A |
| 55 | a | 56 | a | 57 | d | 58 | d | 59 | d | 60 | A |
| 61 | a | 62 | c | 63 | c | 64 | d | 65 | c | 66 | D |
| 67 | c | 68 | c | 69 | c | 70 | c | 71 | c | 72 | A |
| 73 | a | 74 | b | 75 | c | 76 | d | 77 | d | 78 | D |
| 79 | d | 80 | c | 81 | b | 82 | c | 83 | a | 84 | A |
| 85 | b | 86 | b | 87 | a | 88 | a | 89 | a | 90 | A |
| 91 | b | 92 | c | 93 | a | 94 | a | 95 | b | 96 | A |
| 97 | a | 98 | b | 99 | c | 100 | b | | | | |

# 10

# Model Paper –II

1. Dauerwald system of managing forest was first used by which of the following
   a. Alfred Moller in year 1920
   b. Alfred Moller in year 1900
   c. Harting in year 1920
   d. Harting in year 1900.

2. Light intensity at which amount of $CO_2$ taken up in photosynthesis exactly equals the amount concurrently given off in respiration is known as
   a. $CO_2$ compensation point
   b. $CO_2$ saturation point
   c. Light compensation point
   d. light saturation point

3. Turgor-pressure gradient theory for movement of sugars in plant system was proposed by
   a. Shiroya
   b. Canny
   c. Roberts
   d. Munch

4. In genus Juniperus the shoot growth is
   a. Indeterminate
   b. Determinate
   c. Both fixed and free growth
   d. None of these

5. When crop density is 1.5 then it is known as
   a. Closed
   b. Dense
   c. Fully stocked
   d. Over stocked

6. Intensity of light in southern aspect is ______ time's higher than northern aspect.
   a. 0.5 – 0.9
   b. 2.4 – 3.0
   c. 1.6 – 2.3
   d. 2.8  3.2

7. The term 'forest succession' was first used by
   a. Clements
   b. Richard peters
   c. Dawson
   d. Thoreau

8. In hills secondary succession starts with which species?
   a. *Woodfordia fruticosa*
   b. *Cedrus deodara*
   c. *Macaranga*
   d. *Acrocarpus fraxinifolius*

9. Which of the species is climatic climax in North Indian Tropical Moist Deciduous Forests?
   a. Teak b. Terminalia
   c. Sal d. Hardwickia

10. Which of the following species is a edaphic climax in Himalayan moist temperate forest (Type 12/E1) due to presence of limestone
   a. *Cedrus deodara* b. *Cupressus*
   c. *Alnus* d. *Pinus roxburghii*

11. Which of the following species is a biotic climax?
   a. *Cedrus deodara* b. *Pinus roxburghii*
   c. *Toona ciliata* d. *Picea smithiana*

12. When forest are classified into forest types on the basis of growth form and seasonal changes in vegetation such basis is called as
   a. Structure b. Function
   c. Floristic d. Physiognomy

13. Northern tropical wet evergreen forest is found in which of the following state?
   a. West Bengal b. Himachal Pradesh
   c. Uttrakhand d. Uttar Pradesh

14. Forest growing at or near the sea shore is known as
   a. Swamp forest b. Littoral forest
   c. Riparian forest d. Fringing forest

15. Scientific name of 'Kharsu oak' is
   a. *Quercus incana* b. *Quercus leucotricophora*
   c. *Quercus dilatata* d. *Quercus semecarpifolia*

16. Dry Alpine scrub forest is found in which State?
   a. West Bengal b. Sikkim
   c. Arunachal Pradesh d. None of these

17. To maintain the genetic continuity between protected areas, linking the protected areas through corridors were suggested in which National Forest policy?
   a. 1894 b. 1952
   c. 1966 d. 1988

18. Forest conservation act came into being in the year
   a. 1988 b. 1980
   c. 1998 d. 1981

19. Global warming will lead to
    a. Shift of species to higher latitude
    b. Shift of species toward higher altitude
    c. a. is true but b. is false
    d. both a. and b. is true

20. IPCC in 2001 had predicted that the global warming by the year 2100 will be in a range of
    a. 0.5 – 2.5°C
    b. 1.4 – 5.8°C
    c. 0.6±0.2°C
    d. 1- 2°C

21. Peculiar feature of forestry enterprise is
    a. Income and capital are separate
    b. Income and capital is not distinct
    c. Both a and b are true
    d. both a and b are false

22. National Commission on Agriculture was constituted in the year
    a. 1970
    b. 1976
    c. 1973
    d. 1972

23. Timber calculators generally give an idea about
    a. Volume of trees
    b. Basal area of trees
    c. Volume of logs
    d. Basal area of logs

24. A forest area which is under one silvicultural system and one set of working plan prescription is known as
    a. Coupe
    b. Working circle
    c. Compartment
    d. Block

25. The material that a forest can yield annually in perpetuity is known as
    a. Progressive yield
    b. Periodic yield
    c. Sustained yield
    d. both b and c are true

26. Rotation under which a species yields the maximum material of a specified size for economic conversion or specific use is known as
    a. Rotation of maximum volume production
    b. Silvicultural rotation
    c. Rotation of highest income
    d. Technical rotation

27. Table showing the distribution of stems by diameter classes for each of a series of crop diameter is known as
    a. Yield table
    b. Volume table
    c. Stand table
    d. Money yield table

28. For a forest to provide sustained yield in perpetuity, it should have
    a. Normal increment
    b. Normal growing stock
    c. Normal series of age-gradation
    d. All of them

29. Rotation of maximum volume production is when
    a. MAI < CAI
    b. MAI > CAI
    c. MAI = CAI
    d. CAI negative

30. The variation in volume of aggregate check shouldn't exceed
    a. 2 %
    b. ≥ 1 %
    c. ≤ 1 %
    d. 1.5 %

31. Method of removing all the branches below a prescribed point on the stem is known as
    a. Selective pruning
    b. Variable-lift pruning
    c. Fixed-lift pruning
    d. None of these

32. Which among the following is a key feature of Diagnosis and Design?
    a. Flexibility
    b. Productivity
    c. Sustainability
    d. Adoptability

33. Which among the following is true while designing agroforestry system?
    a. Design and evaluation precedes diagnostic stage
    b. Planning stage precedes Design and evaluation stage
    c. Planning stage precedes prediagnostic stage
    d. Design and evaluation precedes planning stage

34. Criteria of good agroforestry design are
    a. Productivity and sustainability
    b. Sustainability and adoptability
    c. Productivity and adoptability
    d.Productivity, adoptability and sustainability

35. Which among the following is a systematic design for laying out agroforestry trials?
    a. 'Y' design
    b. Beehive design
    c. Fan design
    d. Nearest neighbor

36. Which among the following doesn't match with rest of the choices?
    a. Homegardens
    b. Agrisilvipasture
    c. Multitier agroforestry system
    d. Homestead gardens

37. A species which is of relatively little silvicultural importance in a forest is known as
    a. Auxiliary species  b. Accessory species
    c. Principal species  d. both a. & b. are true.

38. A forest area which had been provided limited degree of protection under chapter IV of Indian Forest Act, 1927 is called as
    a. Reserved forest  b. Protected forest
    c. National park  d. Social forest

39. National Commission on Agriculture proposed how many classes of forest?
    a. 4  b. 3
    c. 5  d. 6

40. In Maurya period head of the forest department was called as
    a. Vanapalas  b. Kupyadhyaksha
    c. Nawabs  d. Jagirdars

41. In British period the first ever forestry commission was established in the year
    a. 1800  b. 1887
    c. 1890  d. 1850

42. Central Board of Forestry was constituted in which year?
    a. 1950  b. 1975
    c. 1948  d. 1952

43. Which of the following is a shade bearer species?
    a. *Mesua ferrea*  b. *Xylia xylocarpa*
    c. *Rhododendron*  d. *Cedrus deodara*

44. Dominated tree are those trees which have a height of
    a. 5/8th of the tallest trees  b. ½ of the tallest trees
    c. 3/4th of the tallest trees  d. 5/6th of the tallest trees

45. A forest is called as dense when the canopy density is
    a. 0.5 – 0.75  b. 0.75 – 0.8
    c. 1.0  d. 0.75 – 1.0

46. The size of circular sample plots should be of
    a. 1-2 ha  b. 2-5 ha
    c. 0.5-1.0 ha  d. 0.05-0.1 ha

47. In Indo-gangetic plains of India with increase in one degree latitude the temperature variation will be
    a. Increase of 0.55°C
    b. Decrease of 0.55°C
    c. Increase of 1°C
    d. Decrease of 10°C.

48. Frost occurring in night when the sky is clear is known as
    a. Advective frost
    b. pool frost
    c. Radiation frost
    d. convection frost

49. Which of the following species is frost hardy?
    a. *Tectona grandis*
    b. *Boswellia serrata*
    c. *Garuga pinnata*
    d. *Hardwickia binnata*

50. Frost resistance of a plant is as a result of
    a. Large sized cell
    b. More osmotic concentration
    c. Less water binding colloids
    d. None of these

51. High nitrogen application will
    a. Reduce frost hardiness
    b. Increase frost hardiness
    c. No effect on frost hardiness
    d. Both can happen

52. Resistance of plants to heat will
    a. Decrease with low water content and high sugar
    b. Increase with low water content and high sugar
    c. Decrease with high water and high sugar
    d. Increase with low water and low sugar

53. A rainy day is a day when a minimum amount of rainfall is
    a. 2.0 mm
    b. 2.5 mm
    c. 3.0 mm
    d. 3.5 mm

54. A month is referred to as dry month when rainfall is
    a. >50 mm
    b. < 50 mm
    c. <100 mm
    d. >100 mm

55. Intensity of light on southern aspect is
    a. 2.0 – 2.5 times higher than northern aspect
    b. 1.6 – 2.3 times higher than northern aspect
    c. 2.0 – 2.5 times higher than western aspect
    d. 1.6 – 2.3 times higher than western aspect

56. Process of laterization will lead to which of the following processes
   a. Leaching of Iron b. Accumulation of Iron
   c. Leaching of aluminum d. Both a & b are true.

57. In Parbatti valley of Himachal Pradesh chir pine occurs at higher altitude then deodar due to
   a. Lime stone b. Climate
   c. Quartzite d. Laterites

58. Secondary immature soil which is derived from soil material of older origin is known as
   a. Aeolian soil b. Alluvial soil
   c. Sedentary soil d. Colluvial soil

59. Which of the following ratio (clay: silt: sand) will give rise to a course-textured soil?
   a. 2:3:3 b. 1:3:4
   c. 4:2:2 d. 4:3:1

60. Capillary water is amount of water which is retained around the soil particle and capillary pores in the soil at forces between
   a. pF 2.0 – 3.5 b. pF 3.5 – 5.5
   c. pF 2.7 – 4.5 d. pF 1 – 2.6

61. Increase in pH of soil will leads to decreased availability of
   a. Calcium b. Magnesium
   c. Molybdenum d. Iron

62. Availability of nitrogen to plants is correlated with C/N ratio. In which ratio nitrogen will become immobilized?
   a. 17:1 b. 33:15
   c. 33:1 d. None of these

63. *Hoplocerambyx spinicornis* is an insect of which species
   a. Teak b. Deodar
   c. Sal d. Toon

64. A fast growing species is one which gives a minimum yield of ____ per hectare per annum in a short rotation
   a. $15m^3$ b. $20\ m^3$
   c. $10\ m^3$ d. $5m^3$

65. Which of the following is not included in tending operations?
    a. Soil working b. Cleaning
    c. Weeding d. Pruning

66. Which of the following is Glover's formula for mechanical thinning; where D is spacing of trees in feet and d is diameter of trees in inches?
    a. D=1.5d b. D = 2d
    c. D = d d. D = 2.5 d

67. In which of the following species "German thinning" will be applied?
    a. Teak b. Deodar
    c. Sal d. None of these

68. Selection thinning will be applied to which of the following crops?
    a. Even aged crops b. Uneven-aged crop
    c. Even aged irregular crop d. Uneven-aged irregular crop

69. In which of the following species dormancy is due to immature embryo?
    a. *Swietenia mahagoni* b. *Zizyphus jujube*
    c. *Ginkgo biloba* d. *Plantanus* spp.

70. Which of the following can be tested for viability through cutting test?
    a. Eucalyptus b. Populus
    c. Fraxinus d. Toona

71. Which of the following species has orthodox seed?
    a. Acacia b. Pinus
    c. Cassia d. All of them

72. Rudimentary embryo dormancy occurs in which of the following species?
    a. *Gingko biloba* b. *Ilex opaca*
    c. *Fraxinus* spp. d. All of them

73. Which of the following species had double dormancy?
    a. *Dalbergia latifolia* b. *Fraxinus excelsior*
    c. *Trewia nudiflora* d. *Pinus silvestris*

74. Which of the following is a cut worm?
    a. Agrotis ipsilon b. Apogonia
    c. Melolontha d. Granida

75. Which of the following species causes damping-off diseases in nursery?
    a. *Rhizoctonia solani* b. *Botryodiplodia theobromae*
    c. *Uncinula* spp. d. all of these

76. In batten board the thickness of the strips of wood in the core should be
    a. 2.5 cm b. 7.5 cm
    c. 2.5 mm d. 7.5 mm

77. Stem analysis in trees is done to determine
    a. Age b. Volume
    c. Past rate of growth d. All of these

78. Which of the following is not a water soluble wood preservative?
    a. Zinc-chloride b. Mercuric chloride
    c. Cuprinol d. Zinc-meta-arsenite

79. Modern paper making started in India in which of the following year?
    a. 1850 b. 1830
    c. 1930 d. 1950

80. In which of the following process of pulping sodium sulphide is used?
    a. Soda process b. Sulphate process
    c. Sulphite process d. All of the them

81. Which among the following is not the principal effect of beating process in paper making?
    a. Decrease in fibre length b. Formation of fibrils
    c. Retardation of drainage d. Decrease in fibre flexibility.

82. Which of the following is an edible bamboo species?
    a. *Bambusa balcooa* b. *Dendrocalamus asper*
    c. *Dendrocalamus strictus* d. *Bambusa tulda*

83. Palmrosa oil is extracted from which species?
    a. *Aquilaria agallocha* b. *Vetivera zizanioides*
    c. *Eucalyptus globules* d. *Cymbopogon martini*

84. Which of the following species is a source of leaf tannin?
    a. *Carissa spinarum* b. *Gmelina arbore*
    c. *Bixa orellana* d. All of them

85. 'Gum Kino' is obtained from which species
  a. *Acacia modesta*  b. *Pterocarpus marsupium*
  c. *Butea monosperma*  d. *Moringa pterygosperma*

86. Which of the following species produces 'white dammar'?
  a. *Canarium strictum*  b. *Vateria indica*
  c. *Shorea robusta*  d. *Hopea odorata*

87. Langsaeter curves describe which of the following relation?
  a. Effect of fertilizer on growth of tree  b. Density on volume growth
  c. Density on soil properties  d. Density on natural regeneration

88. Krajicek et al., 1961 had developed which of the following stand density measures
  a. Relative density  b. Quadratic mean stand diameter
  c. Crown Competition factor  d. Relative stand density

89. Ratio of discounted value of all cash inflows to the discount value during the life of plantation is
  a. Net Present worth  b. Benefit cost ratio
  c. Internal rate of return  d. Net return

90. In which of the following situations double trench soil working techniques will be employed?
  a. Salt impregnated soil  b. Stony and sloppy soil
  c. Low and ill distributed rainfall zone  d. Clayey soil

91. Which of the following silvicultural system is also called as system of "successive regeneration felling"?
  a. Alternative strip system  b. clear strip system
  c. Shelter wood system  d. Dauerwald system

92. How many months does it take from first appearance to ripening of cones of Cedrus deodara?
  a. 12-13 months  b. 10 -11 months
  c. 14-15 months  d. 15-16 months

93. Which of the following has hypogenous germination?
  a. *Cedrus deodara*  b. *Pinus roxburghii*
  c. *Populus ciliata*  d. *Artocarpus hirsuta*

94. Which of the following species do not have parthenocarpic fruits?

a. *Acer*  b. *Ulnus*
c. *Betula*  d. *Populus*

95. As many as 500 different plant species can be found in one forest patch in

a. Eastern Ghats  b. Amazon
c. Chhattisgarh  d. North American plains

96. Industrialization resulted in loss of what % of forests?

a. 9.3 %  b. 3.9 %
c. 19.3 %  d. 13.9 %

97. Colonial state regarded forests as

a. No man's land  b. Unproductive and wilderness
c. Source of revenue  d. Sign of balanced eco-system

98. Why did colonists need durable timber?

a. To build ships for the Royal Navy  b. To construct bridges
c. For furniture  d. To build beautiful homes

99. Each mile of railway track requires

a. Between 1670-2200 sleepers  b. 3000-5000 sleepers
c. 1760-2000 sleepers  d. 35000 trees

100. Which of the following was the reason for forests disappearing near railway tracks?

a. Wood was used to make railway sleepers
b. 'Scorched earth' policy of Imperialist
c. Indiscriminate exploitation by tribal's
d. Indiscriminate cutting of trees by contractors

**Answer Key**

| | | | | | | | | | | | |
|---|---|---|---|---|---|---|---|---|---|---|---|
| 1 | c | 2 | D | 3 | d | 4 | a | 5 | d | 6 | c |
| 7 | a | 8 | A | 9 | c | 10 | b | 11 | b | 12 | d |
| 13 | b | 14 | B | 15 | b | 16 | b | 17 | d | 18 | b |
| 19 | d | 20 | A | 21 | b | 22 | b | 23 | c | 24 | a |
| 25 | c | 26 | D | 27 | c | 28 | d | 29 | c | 30 | c |
| 31 | c | 32 | A | 33 | b | 34 | d | 35 | c | 36 | b |
| 37 | b | 38 | D | 39 | a | 40 | a | 41 | b | 42 | a |
| 43 | a | 44 | D | 45 | d | 46 | d | 47 | a | 48 | c |
| 49 | d | 50 | B | 51 | a | 52 | b | 53 | b | 54 | b |
| 55 | b | 56 | B | 57 | c | 58 | d | 59 | b | 60 | d |
| 61 | c | 62 | A | 63 | a | 64 | c | 65 | a | 66 | c |
| 67 | b | 68 | D | 69 | c | 70 | c | 71 | d | 72 | a |
| 73 | b | 74 | A | 75 | a | 76 | c | 77 | c | 78 | b |
| 79 | b | 80 | A | 81 | a | 82 | b | 83 | d | 84 | a |
| 85 | a | 86 | D | 87 | b | 88 | c | 89 | c | 90 | a |
| 91 | a | 92 | D | 93 | d | 94 | a | 95 | b | 96 | a |
| 97 | b | 98 | A | 99 | a | 100 | d | | | | |

# 11

# Model Paper –III

1. Potential biofuel plants are
   a) Jatropha, Karanja  b) Jatropha, Neem
   c) Jatropha, Mahua  d) Karanja, Mahua, Neem
   e) Tribals were encouraged to settle in forest villages

2. Biodiversity Conservation Policy of India came into existence
   a) 2000  b) 2001
   c) 2002  d) 2003

3. The best forests are
   a) Protected forests  b) Village forests
   c) State forests  d) Reserved forests

4. The headquarters of ICFRE is at
   a) Dehra Dun  b) Mussoorie
   c) Bangalore  d) Shimla

5. Which of the following is not a feature of shifting cultivation?
   a) Parts of the forest are cut and burnt in rotation
   b) Seeds are sown in the ashes
   c) Plots cleared are cultivated for a few years and then left fallow
   d) Single crop is grown on these plots

6. Which of the following species of trees are suited for building ships and railways?
   a) Sal and Semul  b) Teak and Mahogany
   c) Rosewood and Sal  d) Teak and Sal

7. The Central minister for Ministry of Environment and Forest at present is
   a) Jayanti Natarajan  b) Jayaram Ramesh
   c) Anil Madhav Dave  d) Prakash Javdkar

8. Who among the following was leader of rebel foresters in Andhra Pradesh?
   a) Birsa Munda b) Siddhu Kanu
   c) Alluri Sita Ram Raju d) None of these

9. Bastar people believe each village was given land by
   a) The British b) The Gods
   c) The Earth d) The Chief

10. Birsa Munda belonged to
   a) Andhra Pradesh b) Maharashtra
   c) Konker d) Chhotanagpur

11. Detergents can affect surface tension of water to
   a) Decrease b) Increase
   c) either (a) or (b) d) No effect

12. Itai-itai disease is due to toxicity of
   a) Cadmium b) Nickel
   c) Arsenic d) Chromium

13. Example of a volatile herbicide is
   a) Trifluralin b) 2-4-D
   c) PCNB d) PNCB

14. Which of the following is a new development in forestry?
   a) Conservation of forests b) Collecting timber
   c) Scientific forestry d) Keeping communities away from forests

15. Which among the following is the main reason for survival of some dense forests in India?
   a) Conservationists b) Environmentalists
   c) Scientific forestry d) Protected them as sacred grooves

16. Sacred grooves are known as
   a) Sarnas, kan, rai, devarakudu b) Dhya, penda, bewar
   c) Nevad, jhum, podu d) Siadi, semur, Chena, tavi

17. Absorptivity of 2-4-D in soil is
   a) Very weak b) Very strong
   c) Strong d) Moderate

18. The tree species suitable for Agroforestry in hot and arid climate is
    a) *Prosopis cineraria*  b) *Albizia lebbeck*
    c) *Salix alba*  d) *Eucalyptus globulus*

19. *Acacia Senegal* is suitable for Agroforestry in
    a) Hill soils  b) Alluvial soils
    c) Laterite soils  d) Desert soils

20. Find the odd man out with reference to suitability of the species to a particular site factor?
    a) *Prosopis chilensis*  b) *Acacia tortilis*
    c) *Acacia nilotica*  d) *Juglans regia*

21. A non-leguminous nitrogen fixing tree species is
    a) *Leucaena leucocephala*  b) *Casuarina equisetifolia*
    c) *Albizia lebbeck*  d) *Acacia nilotica*

22. The species like *Eucalyptus hybrid, Prosopis chilensis, Gliricidia maculata* and *Cassia siamea* are suitable for Agroforestry system because of
    a) The species are generally not grazed  b) Deciduous in nature
    c) Nitrogen fixing  d) All of these

23. *Casuarina equisetifolia* is preferred for Agroforestry because it is
    a) Atmospheric nitrogen fixer in the soil
    b) The bole is upright and straight
    c) None of these
    d) Both of these

24. In some parts of India, *Eucalyptus Hybrid, Populus deltoids, Leucaena leucocephala* and *Casuarina equisetifolia* became popular because these species could be harvested within a period of eight years.
    a) The statement is correct
    b) The statement is partially correct as harvest period mentioned is higher than mentioned
    c) The statement is partially incorrect as all the species mentioned are not popular
    d) The statement is incorrect

25. Agrisilvicultural system classification of Agroforestry is based on
    a) Nature of components  b) Arrangement of components
    c) Functional basis  d) Ecological basis

26. Taungya system is a
    a) Agrisilvicultural system
    b) Silvipastoral system
    c) Agrosilvopastoral system
    d) All of these

27. The Agroforestry system that is based mainly on temporal arrangement of components is
    a) Home gardens
    b) Shifting cultivation
    c) Tea gardens
    d) None of these

28. Solar energy is
    a) Continuous resource
    b) Flow resource
    c) Stock resource
    d) Extrinsic resource

29. Fickle resources are
    a) Continuous and available
    b) Capable of natural regeneration
    c) Available in finite quantities
    d) Extrinsic resources

30. The stock of fresh water to the total water available on earth surface is
    a) 0.45 %
    b) 0.55 %
    c) 0.65 %
    d) 2.15 %

31. The per capita requirement of clean water in litres daily is
    a) 1.7
    b) 3.7
    c) 2.7
    d) None

32. The prime use of fresh water is in
    a) Domestic
    b) Industry
    c) Power generation
    d) Agricultural purposes

33. The major cause of destruction of forest resources is
    a) Hunting and trade
    b) Pollution
    c) Introduction of alien species
    d) None of these

34. The states/Union Territory whose forest cover is above 80 % is
    a) Arunachal Pradesh, Mizoram, Nagaland
    b) Andaman & Nicobar Islands Arunachal Pradesh, Manipur
    c) Andaman & Nicobar Islands Mizoram, Manipur
    d) Arunachal Pradesh, Mizoram, Assam

35. The globe's major share of energy is from
    a) Oil
    b) Coal
    c) Natural gas
    d) Lignite

36. Among the identified species, the organisms dominating the earth in terms of species richness is

a) Plants b) Vertebrates

c) Insects d) Micro organisms

37. Of the prescribed drugs, the majority has its origin from

a) Plant Sources b) Synthetic sources

c) Animal sources d) Micro organisms

38. The major cause of forest destruction in India is

a) River Valley projects b) Agriculture

c) Industries d) Roads and communications

39. The maximum loss of tropical forest is in

a) Brazil b) Malaysia

c) Indonesia d) Zaire

40. The maximum loss of vegetation occurred in

a) Rain forests b) Moist deciduous forests

c) Hill and mountain forests d) Dry deciduous forests

41. The species are decreasing and may be left with fewer individuals if unfavorable conditions continue is

a) Endangered b) Vulnerable

c) Rare d) Threatened

42. The amendment into the Indian Constitution which allowed the states to protect and improve the environment for safeguarding public health, forests and wildlife is

a) 41st b) 43rd

c) 44th d) None of these

43. The disease that is most prevalent and causes maximum death worldwide is

a) Diarrhoea b) Malaria

c) Parasitic worm infections d) Respiratory diseases.

44. Public agencies only consider risk greater than________ individual(s) in one million populations to be significant risks warranting action

a) 10 b) 1

c) 100 d) 1000

45. The EIA conducted comprehensively for a particular region to establish the baseline environmental status is

a) Comprehensive EIA
b) Sectoral EIA
c) Rapid EIA
d) None of these

46. The environment act enforced in the year 1991 to provide insurance for purpose of providing immediate relief to the persons by accident handling with any hazardous substances was

a) National Environmental Tribunal Act
b) National Environment Appellate Authority Act
c) Public Liability Insurance Act
d) Cess Act

47. The 1st International investigation taken up to advance the understanding of the protection of nature is

a) Earth watch Program
b) International Biological Program
c) Earth scan
d) Man and Biosphere Program

48. The World Ocean's Day falls on

a) June 8
b) June 5
c) May 22
d) March 22

49. Duties of the citizen to protect and preserve the environment and prevent environmental damage is drafted in part _____ of the Charter for Human Rights and Environment.

a) I
b) II
c) III
d) IV

50. The given names indicate- Amrapali, Lenghra, Himsagar and Fazli

a) Genetic diversity
b) Species diversity
c) Ecosystem diversity
d) None of these

51. Lesser known Indian Rhinoceros is

a) Extinct
b) endangered
c) Threatened
d) None of these

52. There are ____ megadiversity countries.

a) 9
b) 12
c) 15
d) 21

53. Which is not a Megadiversity country?
    a) India b) China
    c) Australia d) New Zealand

54. Which is not an endangered mammal?
    a) *Axis axis* b) *Presbytis geei*
    c) *Moschus moschiferus* d) *Macaca assamensis*

55. The national avian species is
    a) *Pavo cristatus* b) *Choriotis nigriceps*
    c) *Grus luecogeranus* d) *Buceros bicornis*

56. Which of the species is extinct?
    a) Manipur brown-antlered deer b) Indian Cheetah
    c) Nilgiri tahr d) Nilgiri langur

57. The extent of radiation is measured in units of
    a) Gray b) Bar
    c) Decibel d) None of them

58. The International Convention that deals with ozone hole is
    a) Montreal Protocol b) Kyoto Protocol
    c) Basel Convention d) Ramsar Convention.

59. The national animal of India is
    a) *Panthera tigris* b) *Panthera leo*
    c) *Panthera pardus* d) None.

60. In India, any new project or expansion or modernization of any existing industry or project should submit a __________ report along with application to the Secretary, ministry of Environment and Forests, New Delhi.
    a) Rapid Environmental Impact Assessment
    b) Comprehensive Environmental Impact Assessment
    c) Strategic Environmental Impact Assessment
    d) Sectoral Environmental Impact Assessment

61. Which one of these is not a mechanical method of birth control?
    a) Diaphragm b) IUD
    c) Condoms d) Spermicides

62. A food chain can have a maximum number of trophic levels as
    a) 4 b) 5
    c) 6 d) 3

63. This is a National Park in North Bengal
    a) Gorumara b) Buxa tiger Reserve
    c) Mahananda d) Chilapata.

64. At 1992 Earth Summit was held in
    a) Argentina b) USA
    c) Brazil d) United Kingdoms.

65. Bonn Convention was on
    a) Atmospheric ozone management b) Conserve migratory species
    c) Transboundary movements of hazardous wastes d) Conserve wetlands
    .

66. The headquarter of Food and Agricultural Organization is in
    a) New York b) Geneva
    c) Paris d) Rome

67. World Environment Day falls on
    a) May 5 b) June 6
    c) May 6 d) June 5

68. The first National park in India
    a) Ranthambor National Park b) Kanha National Park
    c) Jim Corbett National Park d) Kazhiranga National Park

69. Hotspots are designated on the basis of
    a) Area of primary forest b) Degree of endemism
    c) Numbers of endangered species d) All of these

70. In India the hotspots are
    a) Western and Eastern Ghats b) Western Ghats and North eastern states
    b) Eastern Ghats and North eastern states d) Conserve wetlands

71. Bishnois, a tribe in Rajasthan protect which animal placing religious values
    a) Nilghai b) Black Buck
    c) Cheetal/Spotted Deer d) Sambhar

72. Chipko movement was associated with protecting
    a) Trees b) Rivers
    c) Wildlife d) Mountains

73. Kaoledeo National Park in Rajasthan is famous for
    a) Siberian Crane b) Sarus Crane
    c) Migratory birds d) both (a) and (c)

74. The only abode of Asiatic Lion is
    a) Bir Buneherhari National Park b) Rajaji National Park
    c) Gir National Park d) Jim Corbett National Park

75. *Nephanthis khasiana* is endemic to
    a) Sikkim b) Western Ghats
    b) Meghalaya c) West Bengal

76. Recent Himalayan tsunami created disaster in which state
    a) Uttarakhand b) Sikkim & Darjeeling Himalayas
    c) Jammu and Kashmir d) All of these

77. As agronomy is to agriculture, _______________ is to forestry
    a) Dendrology b) Silviculture
    c) Agroforestry d) Wood technology

78. Taxol, a remedy for cancer is extracted from
    a) *Cedrus deodara* b) *Texas baccata*
    d) *Pinus khasiana* c) *Picea smithiana*

79. Triphala, a popular ayurvedic formulation contain fruits of
    a) *Terminalia chebula* b) *Terminalia bellirica*
    c) *Embellica officinalis* d) All of these

80. Bamboo is
    a) Grass b) Tree
    c) Shrub d) None of these

81. Lianas are
    a) Woody climbers b) Herbaceous climber
    c) Ground Creepers d) None of these

82. An endemic tree species to India

a) *Ficus religiosa* b) *Tectona grandis*

c) *Shorea robusta* d) None of these

83. Organism with highest life span

a) Tree b) Mammals

c) Amphibians d) Birds

84. Largest and biggest living creature in earth

a) Blue Whale b) African Elephant

c) Giant Redwood tree d) A fungus recorded from Amazon forest

85. Pedology is study of

a) Rocks and minerals b) Soil

c) Both of these d) None of these

86. Which is not your friend?

a) *Rhizobium* sp. b) *Saccharomyces cereviacea*

c) *Penicillium notatum* d. *Escherichia coli*

87. Not an essential element for plant

a) Ca b) S

c) Si d) Fe

88. An international organization responsible for updating the status and enlisting the wild animals and plants every year

a) IUCN b) FAO

c) WWF d) CITES

89. Tiger in India is

a) Endangered b) Vulnerable

c) Rare d) No problem

90. Biomagnification is

a) Increase in concentration of nonbiodegradable chemical in food chain

b) Increase of pollution load in biosphere

c) Accumulation of poisonous chemicals in plant system

d) Increase in soil toxicity

91. A summer deciduous tree

a) *Zizyphus mauritiana* b. *Populous deltoides*

b) *Tectona grandis* c. *Terminalia arjuna*

92. An international organization was awarded Nobel Prize for peace for creating awareness and fighting against climate change

a) Green Peace b) WWF

c) IPCC d) No such Nobel was awarded

93. Vanamahatsava week is celebrated from

a) July 1-7 b) Oct 1-7

b) June 1-7 c) Sept 1-7

94. The first actual confirmed death from AIDS was reported from

a) Africa b) Asia

c) Europe c) North America

95. Minamata disease occur due to toxicity of

a) Mercury b) Cadmium

c) Arsenic d) Iron

96. A mercury bearing fungicide is

a) Agalol b) Atrazine

c) Monouron d) Paraquat

97. Soil can act as a physical filter to resist the entry of pollutant by the process of

a) Buffering b) Sieving

c) Decomposition d) All of these

98. Organic substances in water

a) Deplete $O_2$ b) Increase $O_2$

c) No effect on $O_2$ d) Initially increases than decreases

99. Waste foods are

a) Garbage b) Rubbish

c) Both of these c) None of these

100. Soil adsorption of pesticides is higher at

a) Acidic pH b) Alkaline pH

c) Any pH d) Neutral to alkaline

## Answers

| | | | | | | | | | | | |
|---|---|---|---|---|---|---|---|---|---|---|---|
| | | | | 1 | d | 2 | c | 3 | a | 4 | a |
| 5 | d | 06 | d | 07 | a | 08 | c | 09 | b | 10 | d |
| 11 | a | 12 | a | 13 | a | 14 | a | 15 | d | 16 | a |
| 17 | d | 18 | a | 19 | d | 20 | d | 21 | b | 22 | a |
| 23 | d | 24 | a | 25 | a | 26 | a | 27 | b | 28 | a |
| 29 | d | 30 | c | 31 | c | 32 | d | 33 | d | 34 | a |
| 35 | a | 36 | c | 37 | a | 38 | b | 39 | a | 40 | c |
| 41 | b | 42 | d | 43 | a | 44 | a | 45 | d | 46 | c |
| 47 | d | 48 | d | 49 | d | 50 | a | 51 | a | 52 | b |
| 53 | d | 54 | d | 55 | a | 56 | b | 57 | b | 58 | a |
| 59 | a | 60 | a | 61 | d | 62 | b | 63 | a | 64 | c |
| 65 | c | 66 | d | 67 | d | 68 | c | 69 | d | 70 | b |
| 71 | b | 72 | a | 73 | a | 74 | c | 75 | b | 76 | a |
| 77 | b | 78 | b | 79 | d | 80 | a | 81 | a | 82 | a |
| 83 | a | 84 | d | 85 | a | 86 | d | 87 | c | 88 | a |
| 89 | a | 90 | a | 91 | a | 92 | c | 93 | a | 94 | a |
| 95 | a | 96 | a | 97 | b | 98 | a | 99 | a | 100 | a |

# Annexures

## Annexure 1

| | Important Event/Milestones | Year |
|---|---|---|
| 1. | 103 Number of National Parks | 2016 |
| 2. | 535 number of wildlife sanctuaries | 2016 |
| 3. | 730 number of protected areas | 2016 |
| 4. | Fourteenth assessment of ISFR | 2015 |
| 5. | Forest cover of the country is 701,673 sq. km which is 21.34 percent of the geographical area. | 2015 |
| 6. | The total forest and tree cover of the country is 794,245 sq. km which is 24.16 percent of the geographical area of the country. | 2015 |
| 7. | The total carbon stock in the country's forest is estimated to be 7,044 million tones, | 2015 |
| 8. | First National air quality index is released in New Delhi | 2014 |
| 9. | MoEF has been renamed as the Ministry of Environment, Forest and Climate Change. | 2014 |
| 10. | National Agroforestry Policy | 2014 |
| 11. | Panna Biospehere reserve | 2011 |
| 12. | Seshachalam biospehere reserve (4755.997) Seshachalam hill ranges in Eastern Ghats encompassing part of Chittoor and Kadapa districts in Andhra Pradesh. | 2010 |
| 13. | Establishment of the National Green Tribunal | 2010 |
| 14. | The total number of JFMCs in the country as on 2010 are 112, 896 and the forest area brought under it is 24.6 million ha, till March 2010 | 2010 |
| 15. | Cold Desert biosphere (7,770) Pin Valley National Park and surroundings; Chandratal & Sarchu; and Kibber Wildlife sanctuary in Himachal Pradesh. | 2009 |
| 16. | National Action Plan on climate change released | 2008 |
| 17. | The Panchayati Raj Act, PESA, and the FRA | 2006 |
| 18. | Tribal Forest rights Act | 2006 |
| 19. | Tribal Forest Protection Act | 2004 |

| | | |
|---|---|---|
| 20. | Biological Diversity Rules | 2004 |
| 21. | The Biological Diversity Act 2002 came into force in | 2003 |
| 22. | The Biological Diversity Act | 2002 |
| 23. | Guidelines for Strengthening JFM | 2000 & 2002 |
| 24. | Notification for JFM Network | 2000 |
| 25. | Biodiversity Bill, 2000 introduced in the Parliament. Forest Survey on India publishes the 7th state of Forest Report (1999) of India. Kanchanjanga (Sikkim) declared as the 12th Biosphere Reserve in the Country | 2000 |
| 26. | Ministry of Environment and Forests prepares a National Policy and Macro level Action Strategy on Biodiversity through a consultative process | 1999 |
| 27. | Terms of Reference Notification, Sharing of experiences of JFM implementation as each state has passed its own resolutio for Monitoring of JFM programmes | 1999- |
| 28. | JFM Cell Creation Notification, Standing Committee Notification | 1998 |
| 29. | Seeds Act passed | 1996 |
| 30. | Siberian Crane Project Started at Bharatpur (Rajasthan) | 1995 |
| 31. | Great Indian Bustard started | 1993 |
| 32. | Project Elephant started | 1992 |
| 33. | Public Liability Insurance Act | 1991 |
| 34. | Ibex and Musk deer Projects are started | 1991 |
| 35. | The Circular (first) Concerning JFM, | 1990 |
| 36. | Third National Forest Policy passed in the Parliament. New Seed Development Policy also passed | 1988 |
| 37. | The Montreal Protocol was agreed on 16 September 1987 | 1987 |
| 38. | Forest Survey of India publishes its First State of forest Report of India, Indian Council of Forest Research and Education established at Dehradun, Indira Gandhi National Forest Academy, Dehradun established | 1987 |
| 39. | Environment (Protection) Act passed, JFM is started in Gujarat, Indira Vrikshamitra Award is Instituted by the Ministry. | 1986 |
| 40. | B.Sc (Forestry) courses started in State Agriculture Universities, National Wasteland Development Board established, Department of Environment, Forest and Wildlife within the Ministry of Environment and Forest is created | 1985 |
| 41. | Ministry of Environment and Forest created | 1984 |

42. Indian Institute of Forest Management in Bhopal is established, Wildlife Institute of India established 1982

43. Forest (Conservation) Act passed. Department of Environment constituted on 1st November 1980 1980

44. Social Forestry Project started 1979

45. Central Crocodile Breeding Institute in Hyderabad is established. Joint Forest Management is started in West Bengal. Reptile skin and ivory export banned 1978

46. Temperate Forest Research Institute at Shimla is established 1977

47. Forest and Wildlife brought on Concurrent List in the Seventh Schedule by 42nd Amendment to Constitution. India becomes a member of CITES. National Commission on Agriculture Report Published 1976

48. CITES was Effective : 1975

49. The Crocodile Breeding and Management Project 1975

50. CITES signed on Signed: 3 March 1973 1973

51. Project Tiger started, Sundarlal Bahuguna start Chipko Movement, UNESCO starts Man & Biosphere Programme 1973

52. Gujarat – First state in India to start Social Forestry Programme outside the conventional forest and National Commission on Agriculture is setup. Project Hangul is started at J&K 1970

53. Champian and Seth classify the Forests of India into 16 Forest types. Westby coin the term "Social Forestry" in World Forestry Conferences held in India 1968

54. Pre-investment Survey of Forest Resources (PISFR) publish the Forest Type Map of India 1965

55. Forest Seed testing started at FRI, Dehradun. Large scale Industrial wood plantation also get started 1962

56. Logging branch established at FRI, Dehradun. Hailey National Park renamed as Corbett National Park 1957

57. Hill Area (Preservation) Act passed. Indian Forest College renamed as Northern Forest Range College and Madras Forest College 1955

58. Grassland survey in India conducted. Word "Minor Forest Products" coined in World Forest Conference 1954

59. Indian Forest Policy passed. 33% of total geographical area to be under forest is stressed. Indian Board for Wildlife is established. 1952

60. Vanmahotsav – The Tree planting festival is started by K.M.Munshi 1950

61. Forest Colleges handed over to The Government of India. Central Board of Forestry is setup. 1948

62. Research in Indian Forest soil is started 1939

| | | |
|---|---|---|
| 63. | United Provinces National Park Bill approved. First National Park of India named after Hailey and established in United Province | 1936 |
| 64. | Bamboo Paper Industry (Protection) Act Passed. Rangeland Classified. Teak stump planting started in Madras | 1932 |
| 65. | Ornithological Survey in India conducted | 1929 |
| 66. | Royal Commission on agriculture India is set up | 1928 |
| 67. | Indian Forest Act Passed | 1927 |
| 68. | Board of Forestry set up | 1914 |
| 69. | Wild birds and animal preservation act passed | 1912 |
| 70. | Madras college of forest is started at Coimbatore | 1912 |
| 71. | Ruther appointed as conservator of Forest | 1906 |
| 72. | Imperial forest school again renamed as Imperial College | 1906 |
| 73. | Gass forest Museum established in Madras | 1901 |
| 74. | Vedanthangal declared as a wildlife sanctuary | 1898 |
| 75. | Nilambur working plan is completed | 1895 |
| 76. | Indian forest policy is passed | 1894 |
| 77. | Dr Voelkar starts a study on Indian agricultural Problems | 1890 |
| 78.. | Eucalyptus grandis introduced in Kerala | 1884 |
| 79. | Forest School renamed as Imperial Forest School | 1884 |
| 80. | Schlich is the second Inspector General of Forest | 1883 |
| 81. | Bombay Natural History Society established | 1883 |
| 82. | Elephant Prevention Act | 1879 |
| 83. | Revised Indian Forest Act | 1878 |
| 84. | Forest School at Dehra Dun | 1878 |
| 85. | Gamble started research on NTFPs | 1878 |
| 86. | Working plant is stared and cattle trespass act is passed | 1871 |
| 87. | Indian forest service started | 1867 |
| 88. | Indian forest act passed | 1865 |
| 89. | Dietrich Brandis appoint first inspector general of Inida | 1864 |
| 90. | *Eucalyptus pinnata* introduced by Champell at Madras | 1843 |
| 91. | Conolly collector of Malabar along with Chathu menon establish nilambur teak plantation | 1842 |
| 92. | Captain Watson appointed as first conservator of forest by Madras Govt. | 1806 |
| 93. | Royalty on teak tree was started | 1805 |
| 94. | Commission on forestry appointed to check the availability of Teak in Malabar region. The commission also recommended felling of teak <21 inches is prohibited | 1800 |
| 95. | Eucalyptus introduced in Nandhi hills, Maysore by Tipu Sultan | 1790 |

| Sl. No. | First in Indian Forestry and Associates | | Year |
|---|---|---|---|
| 1. | First Silviculturist in India | Troup | 1909 |
| 2. | First Biosphere Reserve in India | Nilgiri | 1986 |
| 3. | First Chief Conservator of Forest | Ruther | 1906 |
| 4. | First Conservator of Forest to Become a MLA | A T Shuttle Worth | - |
| 5. | First Conservator of Forest | Police Office Watson | 1806 |
| 6. | First Director of the Forest School | F. Bailey | 1878 |
| 7. | First National Forest Act | Indian Forest Act | 1865 |
| 8. | First Forest Entomologist | Stebbing | 1901 |
| 9. | First Forest Movement | Chipko Movement (Sunder Lal Bahu-guna) | 1973 |
| 10. | First Forest Policy (Pre Independence) | Indian Forest Policy | 1894 |
| 11. | First Forest Policy (Post Independence) | Indian Forest Policy | 1952 |
| 12. | First Indian Inspector General of Forest | M. D. Chaturvedi | 1949 |
| 13. | First Inspector General of Forest | Dietrich Brandis | 1864 |
| 14. | First Issue of Indian Forester (Issued By) | Powel and Schlich | 1875 |
| 15. | First National Park | Hailey National Park | 1936 |
| | | (Now Corbett) UP | |
| 16. | First President of Forest Research Institute and College (Dehra Dun) | S Eardley Wilmot | 1906 |
| 17. | First Regular Conservator of Forest | Cleghom | 1856 |
| 18. | First Special Assistant Conservator of Forest | Ribben Trop and W. Schlich | 1867 |
| 19. | First Wildlife Sanctuary in India | Vedanthangal Wildlife Sanctuary, Madras, Presidency | 1898 |
| 20 | First Working Plan in India | Nilambur Forest Working Plan | 1895 |
| 21. | First Zoo in India | Calcutta Zoo, WB | 1854 |
| 22. | First Prime minister Released Air Pollution Tolerance Index of India | Narendra Modi | 2014 |

National and International Organization working in field of Forestry

| S. No. | Short Name | Institute Name | State/Country |
|---|---|---|---|
| | | **National** | |
| 1. | ACSFER | Advance centre of social forestry and eco-Rehabilitation | Allhabad UP |
| 2. | AFRI | Arid forest research institute | Jodhpur (Rajasthan) |
| 3. | | Biotechnological centre for tree improvement | Triupathy, Andhra Pradesh) |
| 4. | CAZRI | Central Arid Zone Research Institute | Jodhpur (Rajasthan) |
| 5. | CPCB | Central Pollution Control Board | New Delhi |
| 6. | CERT | Centre for Ecological Research and Training | Bangalore, Karnataka |
| 7. | CEE | Centre for Environmental Education | Ahmedabad, Gujarat |
| 8. | CEMDE | Centre for Environmental Management of Degraded Ecosystem | New Delhi |
| 9. | CME | Centre for Mining Environment | Dhanbad, Jharkhand |
| 10. | DFE | Directorate of Forest Education | Dehra Dun |
| 11. | FRI | Forest Research Institute | Dehra Dun |
| 12. | FSI | Forest Survey of India | Dehra Dun |
| 13. | GBPI-HED | G. B. Pant Institute of Himalayan Environment and Development | Almora, Uttrakhand |
| 14. | ICFRE | Indian Council of Forestry Research & Education | Dehra Dun |
| 15. | IIB | Indian Institute of Biodiversity | Itanagar, Arunachal Pradesh |
| 16. | IIFM | Indian Institute of Forest Management | Bhopal, MP |
| 17. | IPIRTI | Indian Plywood Industries Research and Training Institute | Bangalore, Karnataka |
| 18. | IGNFA | Indira Gandhi National Forest Academy | Dehra Dun |
| 19. | IFGTB | Institute of Forest Genetics and Tree Breeding | Coimbatore, Tamilnadu |
| 20. | IFP | Institute of Forest Productivity | Ranchi, Jharkhand |
| 21. | IRMDFR | Institute of Rain and Moist Deciduous Forest Research | Jorhat, Assam |
| 22. | IWSRDT | Institute of wood Science & Research, Development and Training | Bangalore, Karnataka |
| 23. | IWST | Institute of wood Science and Technology | Bangalore, Karnataka |
| 24. | NEERI | National Environmental Engineering Research Institute | Nagpur, Maharashtra |
| 25. | TFRI | Temperate Forest Research Institute | Shimla, Himachal Pradesh |
| 26. | TFRI | Tropical Forest Research Institute | Jabalpur, MP |

| | | | |
|---|---|---|---|
| 27. | NRCAF | National Research Centre for Agroforestry (NR-CAF) | Jhansi, UP |
| 28. | AWB | Animal welfare Board | Chennai, Tamil Nadu |
| 29. | BNHS | Bombay Natural History Society | Mumbai |
| 30. | CZA | Central Zoo Authority | Delhi |
| 31. | SACON | Salim Ali Centre for Ornithology and Natural History | Coimbatore, Tamil-nadu |
| 32. | WII | Wildlife Institute of India | Dehra Dun |
| 33. | WPS | Wildlife preservation Society of India | Dehra Dun |
| 34. | WPS | Wildlife protection Society | New Delhi |
| 35. | WWF | World wide fund for nature (India) (WWF) | New Delhi |
| | | **International** | |
| 1. | FAO | Food and Agriculture Organization | Rome |
| 2. | UNDP | United Nations Development Program | Nairobi, Kenya |
| 3. | ITTO | International Tropical Timber Organization | Yokohama |
| 4. | CIFOR | Central for International Forestry Research | Bogor, Indonesia |
| 5. | IUFRO | International Union of Forestry Research Organization | Vienna |
| 6. | WWF | World Wildlife fund | Switzerland |
| 7. | WB | World Bank | Washington |
| 8. | ADB | Asian Development Bank | Manila, Philippines |
| 9. | DID | Department of International Development | London |
| 10. | IUCN | International Union for Conservation of Nature and Natural Resources | Switzerland |
| 11. | IIED | International Institute for Environment and Development | Britain |
| 12. | IISD | International Institute for Sustainable Development | Canada |
| 13. | EC | Earth Council | Costa Rica |
| 14. | FORSPA | Forest Research Supporting Programme for Asia and Pacific | Indonesia |
| 15. | ICRAF | International Centre for Research in Agroforestry | Nairobi, Kenya |
| 16. | IRRI | International Rice Research Institute | Manila, Philippines |
| 17. | IFAD | International Fund for Agricultural Development | Rome, Italy |
| 18. | UNFCCC | United Nations Framework Convention on Climate Change | Bonn, Germany |
| 19. | UNESCO | United Nations Educational, Scientific and Cultural Organization | Paris, France |
| 20. | UNC-CDD | United Nations Framework Combat Desertification | Bonn, Germany |
| 21. | UNEP | United Nations Environment Programme | Nairobi, Kenya |
| 22. | WFP | World Food Programme | Rome, Italy |

Harmful insects in plantation and natural forests and their control measures

| | Insect Local Name | Scientific Name |
|---|---|---|
| **Borers** | | |
| 1. | Sal heart wood borer | *Haplocerambyx spinicornis* |
| 2. | Root borer (Sal) | *Lophosternus hugelii* |
| 3. | Bamboo borer | *Dinoderus brevis* |
| 4. | Teak borer | *Diphammus cervinus* |
| 5. | Shisham borer | *Dichomeris eridantis* |
| 6. | Babul borer | *Celosterna scrabator* |
| 7. | Toon borer | *Hypsipyla robusta* |
| 8. | Tendu stem borer | *Plocaederus ferrugineous* |
| 9. | Poplar stem borer | *Aprioma cinerea* |
| 10. | Bark eating caterpillar | *Indarbela quadrinotata* |
| 11. | Semul shoot borer | *Tonica niviferana* |
| **Defoliators** | | |
| 12. | Teak defoliator | *Hyblaea puera* |
| 13. | Sal defoliator | *Lymantria Mathura* |
| 14. | Tendu defoliator | *Hypocola rostrata* |
| 15. | Shisham defoliator | *Plecoptera dichormis* |
| 16. | Deodar defoliator | *Ectropis deodarae* |
| 17. | Gmelina defoliator | *Calopepla leayana* |
| 18. | Chir defoliator | *Lebeda nobilis* |
| 19. | Ailanthus defoliator | *Eligma narcissus* |
| 20. | Poplar defoliator | *Clostera cupreata* |
| 21. | Kadam defoliator | *Arthroschista hilaralis* |
| **Others** | | |
| 22. | Sal sem- looper | *Ahaea janata* |
| 23. | Gmelina tingids | *Tingis beesoni* |
| 24. | Teak skeletoniser | *Eutectona machaeralis* |
| 25. | Ailanthus web worm | *Atteva fabriciella* |
| 26. | Casuarina bag worm | *Clania crameri* |
| 27. | Tendu gall former | *Trioza obsolete* |
| 28. | Bark eating caterpillar | *Indarbela quadrinotata* |
| 29. | Phassus borer | *Phassus malabaricus* |
| 30. | Red borer | *Zeuzera coffeae* |

| | | |
|---|---|---|
| 31. | Chafer beetle | *Apogania coriaceae* |
| 32. | Canker grub | *Dihammus cervinus* |
| 33. | Mosquito bug | *Helopeltis antonii* |
| 34. | Gmelina miner | *Phyllocnistis amydropa* |

Important Diseases of tree and their causal organism

| | Diseases | Organism |
|---|---|---|
| 1. | Chestnut blight | *Endothia parasitica* |
| 2. | Dutch Elm disease | *Cerotocystis ulmi* |
| 3. | Stem blister rust (pines) | *Cronartium rubicola* |
| 4. | Dothiostroma blight | *Dothiostroma pini* |
| 5. | Swertia felt rust (pines) | *Cronartium himalayense* |
| 6. | Wilt disease | *Fusarium oxysporium* |
| 7. | Root rot | *Ganoderma spp* |
| 8. | Root | *Fomes annosus* |
| 9. | Butt rot | *Armillaria mellea* |
| 10. | Polyporus root rot | *Polyporus shoreae* |
| 11. | Armillaria root rot | *Armillaria mellea* |
| 12. | White root rot | *Fomes lignosus* |
| 13. | Red root rot | *Ganoderma pseudoferreum* |
| 14. | Stump rot | *Fomes lignosus* |
| 15. | Heart rot | *Hymenomychaetes* |
| 16. | Punk knots | *Fomes caryophylli* |
| 17. | Stem wilt (Casuarina) | *Trichosporium vesiculosum* |
| 18. | Bamboo blight | *Sacrocladium oryzae* |
| 19. | Damping off | *Rhizoctonia, Pythium, Fusarium* |

Some Important diseases and their effects on trees

| Name of the disease | Causal organisms | Affected tree spp | Effect on tree/ plant |
|---|---|---|---|
| Damping - off | *Rhizoctonia, Pythium, Fusarium* | Pinus, Deodar, Eucalyptus | Death of seedlings |
| Heart rot | *Hymenomychaetes, Fomes caryophylli, Fomes badius* | Sal, Khair, Teak and others | Loss in growth and damage to heartwood |
| Root and Butt rot | *Heterobasidion annosum* | Deodar | Death of trees |
| Stem blister rust | *Cronatrium ribicola* | Deodar | Death of trees |
| Wilt disease | *Fusarium spp* | Blue pine | Exudation of resin |
| Root rot | *Ganoderma spp* | Khair, Babul, Deodar, Siris, Chir | Loss of growth and death of plants |
| Pink disease | *Corticum salmonicolor* | Eucalyptus spp | Top drying and loss in growth |
| Spike disease | *Mycoplasma like organisms* | Sandal | Loss of growth and death of plants |
| Powdery mildew | *Uncinula tectonae* | Teak | Leaf shedding |
| Leaf spot | *Cercospora tectonae* | Teak | White spot on the leaves |

## List of some NTFPs

Wood oils:

| Products | Trees responsible | Plant Part use |
|---|---|---|
| | **Essential Oils** | |
| Agar oil | *Aquillaria agallocha* | Wood |
| Lonoloe oil | *Bursera penicillata* | |
| Sandal oil | *Santalum album* | |
| Deodar oil | *Cedrus deodara* | |
| Turpentine oil | *Pinus roxburghii* | |
| Camphor oils | *Cinnamomum camphora* | Leaf |
| Citriodara oil | *Eucalyptus citriodara* | |
| Patchouli oil | *Pogostemon cablin* | |
| Pine needle oil | *Pinus roxburghii* | |
| Cinnamomum oil | *Cizeylanicum* | |
| Eucalyptus oil | *Eucalyptus globules* | |
| Mint oil | *Mentha spp* | |
| Citronella oil | *Cymbopogon nardus* var. *winterianus* | Grass |
| Ginger oil | *C.martini* var. *sofia* | |
| Lemon grass oil | *C. flexuosus* | |
| Palmorosa oil | *C. martini* var. *motia* | |
| Vetiver oil | *Vetivera zizonoides* | |
| Costus oil | *Saussurea lappa* | Root |
| Indian Valarian oil | *Valarian jatamansi* | |
| Curcuma oil | *Curcuma aromatic* | |
| Rose oil | *Rosa dauriascena* | Flower |
| Jasmine oil | *Jasmine officinale* | |
| Keora oil | *Pandanus tectorius* | |
| Ylang-ylang oil | *Cananga odorata* | |
| Others | *Michelia champaca, Juniper macropoda, Mimusops elangu* | |

| | Family | Plant Name | Products |
|---|---|---|---|
| 1. | Stercuiaceae | *Sterculia urens* | Fibers |
| | | *S. villosa* | |
| | | *S. foetida* | |
| 2. | Asclepediaceae | *Calotropis gigantean* | |
| | | *C. procera* | |
| 3. | Tiliaceae | *Grewia teliafolia* | |
| | | *G. oppositifolia* | |
| 4. | Ulmaceae | *Trema orientalis* | |
| 5. | Moraceae | *Morus alba* | |
| | | *Ficus religiosa* | |
| | | *F. bengalensis* | |
| 6. | Leguminosae | *Bauhinia vahlii* | |
| | | *B. racemosa* | |
| | | *Hardwickia binnata* | Flosses |
| 7. | Bombacaceae | *Ceiba pentandra* | |
| | | *Bombax ceiba* | |
| | | *Cochlospermum religiosum* | |
| | | *Calotropis procera* | |
| | | *C.gigantea* | |

| | Species | Type of products | |
|---|---|---|---|
| 1. | *Acacia mearnsii* | | |
| 2. | *A.nilotica* | | |
| 3. | *Cassia fistula* | | |
| 4. | *C. aruiculiformis* | Bark tan | |
| 5. | *Rhizophora mucronoides* | | |
| 6. | *Ceriops roxburghiana* | | |
| 7. | *Terminalia arjuna* | | |
| 8. | *Terminalia chebula* | Fruit tan | |
| 9. | *T.bellerica* | | |
| 10. | *Acacia nilotica* | | |
| 11. | *Emblica officinalis* | | |
| 12. | *Zizyphus xylocorpus* | | |
| 13. | *Caesalpinea coriarea* | | |
| 14. | *Anogeissus latifolia* | Leaf tan | |
| 15. | *Emblica officinalis* | | |
| 16. | *Carissa spinatum* | | |
| 17. | *Tamarix spp* | Gall tan | |
| 18. | *Cassia sappan* | Wood dye | |
| 19. | *Acacia catechu* | | |
| 20. | *Pterocarpus santalinus* | | |
| 21. | *Artocarpus heterophyllus* | | |
| 22. | *Acacia leucophloea* | Bark dye | |
| 23. | *A. coincinna* | | |
| 24. | *A. farnesiana* | | |
| 25. | *Terminalia alata* | | |
| 26. | *Manilkara littoralis* | | |
| 26. | *Rubia cordifolia* | | |
| 27. | *Bixa orellena* | Flower and Frut dye | *Annota dye* |
| 28. | *Mallotus phillippensis* | | *Kamala dye* |
| 29. | *Toona ciliate* | | |
| 30. | *Butea monosperma* | | |
| 31. | *Wrightia tinctoria* | | |
| 32. | *Nyctanthus arbortristis* | | |
| 33. | *Rubia cordifolia* | Root dye | |
| 34. | *Punica granatum* | | |

| | | | |
|---|---|---|---|
| 35. | *Lawsonia inermis* | Leaf dye | |
| 36. | *Indigofera tinctoria* | | |
| 37. | *Butea monosperma* | Gum | Bengal gum |
| 38. | *Boswellia serrata* | | Salai gum |
| 39. | *Acacia Senegal* | | Gum Arabica |
| 40. | *Pterocarpus santalinus* | | Kino gum |
| 41. | *Sterculia urens* | | Gum traganth |
| 42. | *A. nilotica* | | Indian gum Arabic |
| 43. | *A. modesta* | | |
| 44. | *A. catechu* | | |
| 45. | *Sopia sebiferum* | Waxes | |
| 46. | *Rhus succedarea* | | |
| | | **Resins** | |
| 47. | *Canarium strictum* | | Black dammar |
| 48. | *Shorea tumbuggaia* | | Green dammar |
| 49. | *Hopea odorata* | | Rock dammar |
| 50. | *Vateria indica* | | White dammar |
| 51. | *Pinus succinifera* | True resins | Amber |
| 52. | *Rhus vernicifera* | | Lacquer |
| 53. | *Laccifera lacca* (insect) | | Shellack |
| 54. | *Pistacia leutiscus* | | Mastic |
| 55. | *Callitiris quadrivalvis* | | Sand arac |
| 56. | *Boswellia serrata* | Oleoresins | Salai gum |
| 57. | *Ferula assafoetida* | Gum resins | Asafoetida |
| 58. | *Garcenia spp* | | Gambage |
| 59. | *Ferula galbaniflua* | | Galbanum |
| 60. | *Commiphera spp* | | Myrrah |

1. **Oil seeds**

   *Melia azadirach, Azadirachta indica, Pongamia pinnata, Calophyllum innophyllum, Mesua ferrea, Shores robusta, Madhuca latifolia, Garcinia indica, Mallotus philippensis, Vateria indica* etc

2. **Beed seeds**

   *Adenanthra pavonia, Eleocarpus serratus*

3. **Soap nut**

   *Sapindus emarginatus, Semecarnus anacardium*

4. **Edible forest products**

   a) **Flower**

   *Madhuca indica. Musa spp, Bombax ceiba, Ficus glomerata, Alangium saxinifolium*

   b) **Leaves**

   Agave americana, Moringa oleifera, Antidegma diandrum

   c) **Fruits**

   *Ancardium occidentale, Psidium gujava, Syzygium cumini, Borassus flabellifer, Mangifera indica, Tamarindus indica, Zizyphus jujube, Randia dumetorium*

   d) **Rhizomes**

   *Anachorphous companulatum, Cyreus rotundus, Bamboos*

   e) **Fungi**

   *Agaricus compestris, Morchella esculenta, Volvaria terastius, Collybia albuminosa*

5. **Grasses**

   a) **Used for making thatchets**

   *Eulopsis binnata, Saccharum munj., S. spontaneum, Vateveriazizonoides, Ipomea cylindrical*

   b) **Fodder grasses**

   *Andropogon* spp, *Heteropogon contortus, Panicum antitodale, P. maximum, P. ripens, Cynadon dactylon, Typha elephantia, Chloris gayana*

Important Books for Forestry and related to Forestry

| Name of Book | Authors |
|---|---|
| Principle and Practices of Silviculture | L. S. Khanna |
| Indian Trees | Brandis |
| Forestry in Indian 1897 | Brandis |
| Forestry in Indian | Brandis |
| Indian Silviculture | AB Lal |
| Manual of Indian Timber | Gamble |
| Manual of Forestry | Schlich |
| Forestry in British India | Ribbentrop |
| Forest Management | Ram Prakash |
| Systematic Botany for Foresters | S. Dasgupta |
| A Guide on Forest Entomology | A Regupathy |
| A Hand Book of Systematic Botany | M. P. Shiva |
| A Preliminary Survey of Forest Type of India | H. G. Champion and S. K. Seth |
| Biosphere Reserve in India | S. S. Negi |
| Flora of India | Hooker |
| Forest Ecology | J. B. Lal |
| General Silviculture of India | H. G. Champion and S. K. Seth |
| Tropical Forestry in India | D. N. Tiwari |
| Plantation forestry in India | R. K. Luna |
| Taxonomy of vernacular plants | George and H. M. Lawrence |
| Forest menstruation | A N Chaturvedi and K. S. Khanna |
| Origin of Species | Charles Darwin |
| Forest Pocket Book | S. H. Howard |
| Indian Forest Ecology | G. S. Puri |
| The Forests of India (1921) | E. P. Stebbing |
| Tree Improvement | Zobal |
| Methods and approaches in forest history :IUFRO 3 | M. Agnoletti |
| Forest : the non - wood resources | Dwivedi A.P |
| Modelling forest systems | A. Amaro and D. Reed |
| Forest biotechnology in India | S. A. Ansari, C. Narayanan and A. K. Mandal |
| Sustainable management of forest – India | A. Arunachalam |
| Tropical forest ecosystem soil fauna in sub tropics | V.K, Bahuguna |
| Joint Forest management for biodiversity enhancement | Balaji, S |

| | |
|---|---|
| Forest vegetation and Soil | S.K Banerjee |
| Forest management and planning | Bettinger, P |
| The forest flora of North West And central India | Dietrich Brandis |
| Social forestry and forest management | Ghosh, S.K and R. Singh |
| Forest nursery and tree husbandry | Gopakumar, K |

National and international Journal of Forestry and related to Forestry

| Name of Journal | Publisher/Country |
|---|---|
| The Indian Forester | ICFRE, Dehra Dun |
| Annals of Forestry | Dehra Dun |
| Indian Journal of Forestry | Dehra Dun |
| Ecologist | Mumbai |
| Journal of Bombay Natural History Society | Mumbai |
| Journal of Tree Science | Y. S. Parmar University of Hort& For, Solan |
| My Forest | Bangalore |
| Tropical Ecology | BHU, Varanasi |
| Journal of Tropical Biodiversity | TFRI, Jabalpur |
| Journal of Plant Physiology | New Delhi |
| Indian Journal of Agroforestry | NRCAF, Jhansi, UP |
| Indian Journal of Range Management and Agroforestry | IFGRI, Jhansi, UP |
| Indian Journal of Traditional Knowledge | New Delhi |
| Journal of Bamboo and Rattan | KFRI |
| Sanctuary Asia | Mumbai |
| Cheetal | Dehra Dun |
| Environment and People | Hyderabad |
| Evergreen | KFRI, Peechi, Kerala |
| Environment and Ecology | West Bengal |
| Journal of Tropical Forest Science | Kuala Lumpur, Malaysia |
| Journal of Forestry Research | China |
| Agroforestry Today | Kenya |
| Forestry Abstracts | London |
| Forests, Tree and People | Sweden |
| Journal of Forestry | USA |
| Journal of Mountain Science | China |
| Environment, Development and Sustainability | China |

| | |
|---|---|
| Sustainable Forestry | China |
| Plant Ecology and Diversity | Taylore and Fransis |
| Canadian Journal of Forest Research | Canada |
| New Zealand Journal of Forestry | New Zealand |
| Forestry Reviews | Commanwealth Forestry Association |
| Journal of Forest and Environmental science | Kangwon National University (Korea) |
| Ecosystem | USA |
| Oecologia | Springer |
| Forest Ecology and Management | Elsevier |
| Tree Physiology | Oxford University Press |
| New Forests | Springer |
| Scandinavian Journal of Forest Research | Springer |
| Forestry Chronicle | Canada |
| Northern Journal of Applied Forestry | USA |
| Western Journal of Applied Forestry | USA |
| Southern Journal of Applied Forestry | USA |
| Agricultural and Forest Meteorology | Elsevier |
| Journal of Forest Research | Japan |

List of ICAR Institutes

| S.No | Name of Institute | Name of Institute (Acronym) | Address | State |
|---|---|---|---|---|
| 1 | National Bureau of Plant Genetic Resources | NBPGR | Pusa Campus, New Delhi | Delhi |
| 2 | Regional Station,NBPGR (Akola) | NBPGR , RS | Opposite,P K V Guest House,Dr.PDKV Campus, Akola | Maharashtra |
| 3 | Regional Station,NBPGR (Nainital) | NBPGR , RS | Bhowali, Nainital | Uttaranchal |
| 4 | Regional Station,NBPGR (Trichur) | NBPGR,RS | Vellanikkara, Trichur | Kerala |
| 5 | Regional Station,NBPGR (Shillong) | NBPGR,RS | New Kanch's Trace,Bishnupur,East Khasi Hills, Shillong | Meghalaya |
| 6 | Regional Station,NBPGR (Shimla) | NBPGR,RS | Phagli, Shimla | Himachal Pradesh |
| 7 | Regional Station,NBPGR, Exploration Base Center(Cuttack) | NBPGR,RS | C/o CRRI Campus | Orissa |
| 8 | Regional Station,NBPGR, Plant Quarantine Station(Hyderabad) | NBPGR,RS | ARI Campus, Rajendra Nagar | Andhra Pradesh |
| 9 | Regional Station,NBPGR, Exploration Base Center(Ranchi) | NBPGR,RS | Ches Campus, P.O.Rkandld | Bihar |
| 10 | Regional Station,NBPGR Satellite Center(Amravati) | NBPGR,RS | Mendse appa Garden Road | Maharashtra |
| 11 | Regional Station,NBPGR (Jodhpur) | NBPGR,RS | C/o CAZRI | Rajasthan |
| 12 | Regional Station,NBPGR(Srinagar) | NBPGR,RS | C/o CITH , PO- Sanat Nagar | Jammu & Kashmir |
| 13 | National Bureau for Agriculturally Important Insects | NBAII | Kushmaur, P.B. No. 6, Kaithauli, Mau Nath Bhajan - 275101 | Uttar Pradesh |

| 14 | National Bureau of Soil Survey and Land Use planning | NBSSLUP | Amravati Road, Nagpur - 440010 | Maharashtra |
|---|---|---|---|---|
| 15 | Regional Station,NBSSLUP(Banglore) | NBSSLUP,RS | Hebbal Agricultural Farm,P.B.NO 24 | Karnataka |
| 16 | Regional Station,NBSSLUP(Calcutta) | NBSSLUP,RS | Salt Lake City,D K Block,Sector II,Bidhan Nagar | West Bengal |
| 17 | Regional Station,NBSSLUP(New Delhi) | NBSSLUP,RS | NTC Building ,IARI Campus, New Delhi -110012 | Delhi |
| 18 | Regional Station,NBSSLUP(Jorhat) | NBSSLUP,RS | NER Center,Jamujuri Road, Rawriah - 785004 | Assam |
| 19 | Regional Station,NBSSLUP(Udaipur) | NBSSLUP,RS | Bohra Ganeshji Road, University Campus - 313001 | Rajasthan |
| 20 | National Bureau of Agricultural Important Microorganisms | NBAIMO | Kusmaur, Post Bag No 6 | Uttar Pradesh |
| 21 | National Bureau of Animal Genetics Resources | NBAGR | Makarmpur Campus, G.T. Road Bypass P.O. Box No.129 , Karnal | Haryana |
| 22 | National Bureau of Fish Genetics Resources | NBFGR | Canal Ring Road, P.O.Dilkusha, Telibagh | Uttar Pradesh |
| 23 | National Research Centre for Banana | NRCB | Thogamalai Road , Thayanur PostTiruchirapalli - 620 102 | Tamilnadu |
| 24 | National Research Centre for Citrus | NRCCITRUS | P.B. No. 464, Shankar Nagar P.O., Amravati Road | Maharashtra |
| 25 | National Research Centre for Grapes | NRCGRAPES | Post Box No. 3, Manjri Farm P.O., Solapur Road | Maharashtra |
| 26 | National Research Centre for Agroforestry | NRCAF | Gwalior Road, Near Pahuj Dam | Uttar Pradesh |
| 27 | National Reseaech Centre on Camel | NRCCAMEL | Jorbeer, P.B. No.7 , Jodhpur Bypass | Rajasthan |
| 28 | National Research Centre on Mithun | NRCMITHUN | NH39, Jharnapani, Medziphema | Nagaland |

| | | | | |
|---|---|---|---|---|
| 29 | National Research Center on Seed Spices | NRCSS | NA | Rajasthan |
| 30 | National Reseach Centre on Yak | NRCYAK | Dirang | Arunachal Pradesh |
| 31 | National Centre for Integrated Pest Management | NCIPM | Lal Bahadur Shastri Building, Pusa Campus, New Delhi | Delhi |
| 32 | National Research Centre for Pomegranate | NRCPom | Shelagi, Bypass, N.H.-9 Pune – Hyderabad Highway (M.S.) | Maharashtra |
| 33 | National Research Centre for Litchi | NRCL | Mushahari Farm PO Mushahari Distt. Muzaffarpur, Bihar | Bihar |
| 34 | National Research Centre on Equines | NRCEQUINE | Sirsa Road, Hisar-125 001 | Haryana |
| 35 | Regional Station, NRCE, Equine Production SubCampus (Bikaner) | NRCE,RS | Post Box No.80, Shivbari, Jorbeer, Bikaner-334 001 | Rajasthan |
| 36 | National Research Centre for Orchids | NRCO | Pakyong - 737106 | Sikkim |
| 37 | National Centre for Agricultural Economics and Policy Research | NCAP | PO Box 11305, Dev Prakash Marg, Pusa, New Delhi | Delhi |
| 38 | National Reserach Center on Plant Biotechnology | NRCPB | Pusa Campus , New Delhi | Delhi |
| 39 | National Research Centre on Meat | NRCM | P.B. No. 19, Boduppal (PO), Chengicherla | Andhra Pradesh |
| 40 | National Research Centre on Pig | NRCP | Rani (Near) Air Port | Assam |
| 41 | Indian Council of Agricultural Research New Delhi | ICAR | Krishi Bhavan | Delhi |
| 42 | Regional Station.CICR,( Coimbatore) | CICR,RS | CICR,Regional Station | Tamilnadu |
| 43 | Regional Station CICR,(Sirsa) | CICR,RS | CICR,Regional Station,P.O.Box 57 | Haryana |
| 44 | Indian Council of Agricultural Research New Delhi | ICAR | Krishi Bhavan | Delhi |

| | | | | |
|---|---|---|---|---|
| 45 | Vivekananda Parvatiya Krishi Anusandhan Sansthan | VPKAS | Almorra | Uttranchal |
| 46 | Central Institute of Temperate Horticulture | CITH | K.D.Farm Old Airfield Rangreth P/O Sanatnagar | Jammu & Kashmir |
| 47 | Regional Station,CITH(Mukteshwar) | CITH,RS | Regional Station ,Mukteswar | Uttranchal |
| 48 | Central Potato Research Institute | CPRI | Shimla | Himachal Pradesh |
| 49 | Regional Station,CPRI (Shillong) | CPRI ,RS | Shillong | Meghalaya |
| 50 | Regional Station,CPRI (Jalandhar) | CPRI,RS | P O Model Town p B No.4 | Punjab |
| 51 | Regional Station,CPRI (Meerut) | CPRI, RS | Modipuram | Uttar Pradesh |
| 52 | Regional Station,CPRI (Gwalior) | CPRI, RS | P B No.4 Morar | Madhya Pradesh |
| 53 | Regional Station,CPRI (Patna) | CPRI, RS | P O Sahaynagar | Bihar |
| 54 | Regional Station,CPRI (Nilgiri) | CPRI ,RS | Muthorai,Nilgiri distt. | Tamilnadu |
| 55 | Regional Station,CPRI (Shimla) | CPRI, RS | Kufri,Shimla | Himachal Pradesh |
| 56 | Regional Station,CPRI(Rajgurunagar) | CPRI,RS | CPRI,Rajgurunagar | Chandigarh |
| 57 | Indian Institute of Soil Science | IISS | Nabibagh, Berasia Road | Madhya Pradesh |
| 58 | Central Institute of Agricultural Engineering | CIAE | Nabibagh, Berasia Road | Madhya Pradesh |
| 59 | Regional Station,CIAE (Coimbratore) | CIAE,RS | Lawley Road, TNAU Campus,Coimbratore | Tamilnadu |
| 60 | Central Institute of Post-harvest Engineering and Technology | CIPHET | PAU Campus | Punjab |
| 61 | Regional Station, CIPHET,(Abohar) | CIPHET,RS | Malout Hanumangarh Bye-Pass Road, Abohar | Punjab |
| 62 | National Institute of Research on Jute and Allied Fibre Technology | NIRJAFT | 12, Regent Park | West Bengal |

| 63 | Regional Station,NIRJAFT, (Cuttack) | NIRJAFT,RS | Bldg.NO.C-2.<br><br>(Beside IDCO),Cuttack | Orissa |
|---|---|---|---|---|
| 64 | Central Institute for Research on Buffaloes | CIRB | Sirsa Road | Haryana |
| 65 | Regional Station,CIRB (Nabha) | CIRB,RS | Birdosangh | Punjab |
| 66 | Central Sheep & Wool Research Institute | CSWRI | Tehsil Malpura,Distt. Tonk | Rajasthan |
| 67 | Regional Station,CSWRI(Bikaner) | CSWRI, RS | Post R.C.P Colony | Rajasthan |
| 68 | Regional Station,CSWRI(Kullu) | CSWRI, RS | Dist.Kullu Via Bhuntar | Himachal Pradesh |
| 69 | Regional Station,CSWRI(Mannavanur) | CSWRI, RS | Kodaikanal Mannavanur ,P.O Kodai Kanal | Tamilnadu |
| 70 | Central Inland Fisheries Research Institute | CIFRI | Monirampur (Post) ,Barrackpore, Kolkata - 700 120 | West Bengal |
| 71 | Regional Station, CICFRI, (Calcutta) | CICFRI,RS | Kolkata Centre of CIFRI,<br>CGO Complex, (2nd floor, C-Wing), DF Block, Salt Lake, Kolkata - 700 064 | West Bengal |
| 72 | Regional Station, CICFRI, (Coimbatore) | CICFRI,RS | 68 , Raja Naidu Road , Coimbatore - 641 012, | Tamilnadu |
| 73 | Regional Station,CICFRI (Alappuzha) | CICFRI,RS | Moncompu Thekkekara P.O. Distt. Alappuzha – 688503 | Kerala |
| 74 | Regional Station,CICFRI (Kakdwip) | CICFRI,RS | South 24 Parganas , Kakdwip-743 347 | West Bengal |
| 75 | Regional Station,CICFRI , (Vadodara) | CICFRI,RS | B-12, Hans Society, Harney Road, Vadodara-390 022, | Gujarat |
| 76 | Regional Station, CIFRI (Malda) | CICFRI,RS | Malda | West Bengal |
| 77 | Regional Station, CICFRI (Alahabad) | CICFRI,RS | 24 Pannalal Road, Allahabad - 211002, | Uttar Pradesh |

| | | | | |
|---|---|---|---|---|
| 78 | Regional Station,CICFRI (Guwahati) | CICFRI,RS | Housefed Complex, Central Building,4th Floor, Beltola Basistha Road, Dispur, Guwahati 781006, | Assam |
| 79 | Regional Station, CICFRI, (Karnal) | CICFRI,RS | House Marg, Karnal - 132 001 | Haryana |
| 80 | Regional Station,CICFRI, (Bangalore) | CICFRI,RS | Hessarghatta Lake Post, Bangalore-560 089 | Karnataka |
| 81 | Regional Station,CICFRI,(Eluru) | CICFRI, RS | Eluru | Andhra Pradesh |
| 82 | Regional Station, CICFRI, (Hoshangabad) | CICFRI,RS | Hoshangabad | Madhya Pradesh |
| 83 | Central Institute of Brackishwater Aquaculture | CIBA | No.75, Santhome High Road, Raja Annamalai Puram, | Tamilnadu |
| 84 | Regional Station, CIBA (Kakdwip) | CIBA, RS | Lower Sunderbans, Kakdwip-743 347 | West Bengal |
| 85 | Regional Station, CIBA (Puri) | CIBA,RS | 15 B.S Nagar, Talabania | Orissa |
| 86 | Regional Station, CIBA , (Muttukadu) | CIBA,RS | Kovalam Post, Muttukadu, Chennai-613112 | Tamil Nadu |
| 87 | Central Institute of Freshwater Aquaculture | CIFA | Kausalyanga, Bhubaneswar-751002 | Odisha |
| 88 | Regional Station,CIFA (Akola) | CIFA,RS | Panjabrao Krishi Vidyapeeth, Krishi Nagar | Maharashtra |
| 89 | Regional Station, CIFA(Ludhiana) | CIFA,RS | Punjab Agricultural University, Department Of Fishries | Punjab |
| 90 | Regional Station,CIFA(Banglore) | CIFA,RS | 170,8th Cross L 7th Main Road ,Matswaram | Karnataka |
| 91 | Regional Station,CIFA(Rahara) | CIFA,RS | Rahara, Kolkatta-700 118 | West Bengal |
| 92 | Regional Station, CIFA (Anand) | CIFA,RS | ATIC, Anand Agriculture University, Anand, -388001 | Gujarat |

| | | | | |
|---|---|---|---|---|
| 93 | Regional Station,CIFA (East Kalyani) | CIFA,RS | A-5,Phase-III, Santal Para Kalyani, Nadia | West Bengal |
| 94 | Central Marine Fisheries Research Institute | CMFRI | CMFRI, P.B.No.1603, Emakulam North(P.O) | Kerala |
| 95 | Regional Station,CMFRI (Mandapam) | CMFRI,RS | Mandapam Marine Fishries, P O Camp | Tamilnadu |
| 96 | Regional Station,CMFRI,(Visakhapatnam) | CMFRI,RS | Andhra Univ. P.O., Panduranga Puram | Andhra Pradesh |
| 97 | Vizhinjam Research Centre of CMFRI | CMFRI,RS | P.B.No. 9, Vizhinjam | Kerala |
| 98 | Calicut Research Centre of CMFRI | CMFRI,RS | West Hill P O | Kerala |
| 99 | Research Centre,CMFRI(Mangalore) | CMFRI,RS | P.Box No 244, Bolar, | Karnataka |
| 100 | Karwar Research Centre of CMFRI | CMFRI,RS | P.B No. 5, Karwar, Uttar Kannada | Karnataka |
| 101 | Regional Station,CMFRI(Mumbai) | CMFRI,RS | 2nd Floor, C.I.F.E. Old Campus, Fisheries University Road, Versova | Maharashtra |
| 102 | Veraval Regional Centre of CMFRI | CMFRI,RS | Matsya Bhavan, Bidia Plot, PB No. 17 | Gujarat |
| 103 | Regional Station,CMFRI(Minicoy),Lakshadweep | CMFRI,RS | Minicoy | Lakshdeep |
| 104 | Regional Station CMFRI (Kakinada) | CMFRI,RS | Kakinada | Andhra Pradesh |
| 105 | Regional Station. CMFRI (Mandapam) | CMFRI,RS | Mandapam | Tamilnadu |
| 106 | Tuticorin Research Centre of CMFRI | CMFRI,RS | South Beach Road | Tamilnadu |
| 107 | Regional Station,CMRI,Madras | CMFRI,RS | 75, santhome High Road, Raja Annamalaipuram, Chennai | Tamilnadu |
| 108 | Regional Station,CMFRI,KVK(Narakkal) | CMFRI,RS | Narakkal, Kochi | Kerala |
| 109 | Central Research Institute For Jute and Allied Fibres | CRIJAF | 24 parganas | West Bengal |
| 110 | Regional Station,CRIJAF(Partapgarh) | CRIJAF,RS | Sunnhemp Research Stations | Uttar Pradesh |

| 111 | Regional Station,CRIJAF(Bamra) | CRIJAF,RS | Sisal Research Station | Orissa |
|---|---|---|---|---|
| 112 | Regional Station,CRIJAF(Barpeta) | CRIJAF,RS | Ramie Research Station,P.O Sorbhog | Assam |
| 113 | Regional Station,CRIJAF(Burdwan) | CRIJAF,RS | P.O BudBud | West Bengal |
| 114 | Central Institute of Fisheries Education | CIFE | Yari Road, Off Paanch Marg, Versova, Andheri(W) | Maharashtra |
| 115 | Regional Station,CIFE(Calcutta) | CIFE,RS | 32 GN Block,SectorV,Salt Lake City | West Bengal |
| 116 | Regional Station,CIFE(Kakinada) | CIFE,RS | CIFE Center,Kakinada, Near Old Burma Shell, Beach Road | Andhra Pradesh |
| 117 | Regional Station,CIFE(Lucknow) | CIFE,RS | CIFE Center,Chinhat, Kathola Tal, Chinhat | Uttar Pradesh |
| 118 | Regional Station,CIFE(Balbhadrapuram) | CIFE,RS | Officer Incharge,Balbhadrapuram | Andhra Pradesh |
| 119 | Regional Station,CIFE(Hoshangabad) | CIFE,RS | Freshwater Fish Farm of CIFE, Powarkheda | Madhya Pradesh |
| 120 | Regional Station,CIFE(Rohtak) | CIFE,RS | CIFE Center, Rohtak, Lahti, via Anawal | Haryana |
| 121 | Central Institute of Fisheries Technology | CIFT | Matsypuri,P.O. | Kerala |
| 122 | Regional Station,CIFT(Veraval) | CIFT,RS | Matsya Bhavan,bhidia Plot,veraval | Gujarat |
| 123 | Regional Station,CIFT (Visakhapatnam) | CIFT,RS | Pandurangapuram Andhra University P.O | Andhra Pradesh |
| 124 | Regional Station,CIFT (Hoshangabad) | CIFT,RS | Anand Nagar | Madhya Pradesh |
| 125 | Regional Station,CIFT(Mumbai) | CIFT,RS | CIDCO Administrative Bldg.(Ground Floor),Sector-1,Vashi400703 | Maharashtra |
| 126 | Regional Station,CIFT (Calicut) | CIFT,RS | Beach Of Road,West Hill | Kerala |
| 127 | Regional Station,CIFT(Burla) | CIFT,RS | Burla | Orissa |
| 128 | Central Rice Research Institute | CRRI | Cuttack | Orissa |
| 129 | Regional Station,CRRI(Hazaribagh) | CRRI, RS | PB NO. 48 | Bihar |
| 130 | Regional Station,CRRI(Kharagpur) | CRRI,RS | I.I.T campus | West Bengal |

| | | | | |
|---|---|---|---|---|
| 131 | Regional Station,CRRI(Kamrup) | CRRI, RS | Gerua, Hajo District | Assam |
| 132 | Central Tobacco Research Institute | CTRI | Bhaskar Magar, Rajahmundry, East Godavari Dist., | Andhra Pradesh |
| 133 | Regional Station,CTRI (Pusa) | CTRI,RS | Pusa | Bihar |
| 134 | Regional Station,CTRI (Vedasandur) | CTRI,RS | Vadasandur | Tamilnadu |
| 135 | Regional Station,CTRI (Jeelugumillii) | CTRI,RS | Jeelugumilli | Andhra Pradesh |
| 136 | Regional Station,CTRI (Kandukuru) | CTRI, RS | Kandukur | Andhra Pradesh |
| 137 | Regional Station,CTRI(Dinhata) | CTRI,RS | Dinhata | West Bengal |
| 138 | Regional Station,CTRI (Hunsur) | CTRI,RS | CTRI Research Station | Karnataka |
| 139 | Regional Station,CTRI(Rajahmundry) | CTRI,RS | CTRI,Bhaskera nagar | Andhra Pradesh |
| 140 | Regional Station,CTRI (Guntur) | CTRI,RS | CTRI Res. Station | Andhra Pradesh |
| 141 | Regional Station,CTRI(KVK) | CTRI,KVK | KVK | Andhra Pradesh |
| 142 | Indian Agricultural Research Institute | IARI | Pusa, | Delhi |
| 143 | Water Technology Centre | IARI,RS | Water Technology Center ,IARI Campus | Delhi |
| 144 | Regional Station,IARI (Pune) | IARI ,RS | Shivaji Nagar,Pune | Maharashtra |
| 145 | Regional Station.IARI (Pusa) | IARI,RS | Pusa | Bihar |
| 146 | Regional Station IARI (Dharwad) | IARI,RS | Gayathri Road No.2 Malmaddi | Karnataka |
| 147 | Regional Station.IARI (Katrain) | IARI, RS | Katrain | Himachal Pradesh |
| 148 | Regional Station.IARI (Shimla) | IARI, RS | Tutikandi | Himachal Pradesh |
| 149 | Regional Station,IARI (Karnal) | IARI, RS | Karnal | Haryana |
| 150 | Regional Station,IARI (Indore) | IARI, RS | Old Schone Road | Madhya Pradesh |
| 151 | Regional Station,IARI (Wellington) | IARI, RS | Wellington | Tamilnadu |
| 152 | Regional Station,IARI (Darjeeling) | IARI, RS | Kalimpong | West Bengal |
| 153 | Bioinformatics Centre | IARI,RS | Bioinformatics Centre , IARI Campus | Delhi |

| | | | | |
|---|---|---|---|---|
| 154 | Regional Station,IARI,National Facility for<br>Blue-Green Algae(New Delhi) | IARI,RS | National Facility for Blue-green Algae, IARI Campus | Delhi |
| 155 | Indian Grassland and Fodder Research Institute | IGFRI | Gwalior Road, Near Pahuj Dam | Uttar Pradesh |
| 156 | Regional Station, IGFRI(Avikanagar) | IGFRI,RS | IGFRI Western Regional Research Station,<br>Avikanagar (Malpura) via Jaipur, Tonk – 304501 | Rajasthan |
| 157 | Regional Station,IGFRI(Palampur) | IGFRI,RS | IGFRI Regional Research Station, Ch. Sarwan Kumar<br>Himachal Pradesh Krishi Vishwa Vidhyalaya Campus | Himachal Pradesh |
| 158 | Regional Station,IGFRI (Dharwad) | IGFRI,RS | Opposite U.A.S Campus | Karnataka |
| 159 | Regional Station IGFRI(Mansabal) | IGFRI,RS | IGFRI , Manasbal | Jammu & Kashmir |
| 160 | Indian Institute of Pulses Reseach | IIPR | G.T. Road, Kalyanpur | Uttar Pradesh |
| 161 | Indian Institute of Sugarcane Research | IISUGR | P.O.Dilkusha | Uttar Pradesh |
| 162 | All India Coordinated Research Project on Sugarcane | IISUGR,RS | Raibareli Road, PO Dilkusha | Uttar Pradesh |
| 163 | Regional Station,IISugR (Motipur) | IISugR, RS | Zamindari Building | Bihar |
| 164 | Sugarcane Breeding Institute | SBI | Coimbatore | Tamilnadu |
| 165 | Regional Station,SBI(Karnal) | SBI, RS | P.B.NO.52 ,Kunjpura Road | Haryana |
| 166 | Reseach Center,SBI(Kannur) | SBI, RS | Cilvil Station P.O | Kerala |
| 167 | Regional Station,SBI (Chagallu) | SBI, RS | 15-3-21,babuji Nagar | Andhra Pradesh |
| 168 | Regional Station,SBI (Jamkhandi) | SBI, RS | ADC,Farm, Girish Nagar,P.O.Bijapur Distt. | Karnataka |

| 169 | Central Institute for Subtropical Horticulture | CISH | RehmanKhera, PO Kakori | Uttar Pradesh |
|---|---|---|---|---|
| 170 | Central Plantation Crops Research Institute | CPCRI | Kasaragod | Kerala |
| 171 | CPCRI Regional Station,Kayamkulam | CPCRI,RS | P O Krishnapuram,Alapuzha Distt. | Kerala |
| 172 | Regional Station,CPCRI(Vittal) | CPCRI,RS,Vittal | Vittal Regional Station | Karnataka |
| 173 | Regional Station,CPCRI (Minicoy) | CPCRI,RS | Research Center | Lakshdeep |
| 174 | Research Center,CPCRI(Kahikuchi) | CPCRI,RS | Kamrup Distt. | Assam |
| 175 | Research Center,CPCRI(Mohitnagar) | CPCRI,RS | Mohit Nagar | West Bengal |
| 176 | Research Center,CPCRI(Kidu) | CPCRI,RC,Kidu | CPCRI,Puttur Taluk | Karnataka |
| 177 | Central Tuber Crops Research Institute | CTCRI | Sreekariyam | Kerala |
| 178 | Regional Station,CTCRI(Bhubaneswar) | CTCRI,RS | Housing Board | Orissa |
| 179 | ICAR Research Complex for Goa | ICARGOA | Ela | Goa |
| 180 | Indian Institute of Horticultural Research | IIHR | Hessarghata Lake Post | Karnataka |
| 181 | Regional Station IIHR-CHES(Hirehalli) | IIHR,RS | Post Hirehalli, distt.Tumkur | Karnataka |
| 182 | Regional Station,IIHR - CHES(Chettali),Coorg | IIHR,RS | Centra Horticultural Experimental Station, Chettalli | Karnataka |
| 183 | Regional Station,IIHR-CHES(Bhubaneswer) | IIHR,RS | AIGINIA, NH_5, ALUGODAM | Orissa |
| 184 | Regional Station,IIHR-KVKGonikoppal) | IIHR,RS | krishi Vigyan Kendra, Gonikoppal | Karnataka |
| 185 | Indian Institute of Spices Research | IISR | P.B. No.1701, Marikunnu P.O | Kerala |
| 186 | Regional Station,IISR (Kodagu) | IISR,RS | Appangala Hervanad P.O Madikeri | Karnataka |
| 187 | Indian Institute of Vegetable Research | IIVR | P.O. Jakhini (Shahanshahpur) | Uttar Pradesh |
| 188 | Central Agricultural Research Institute | CARI(CS) | P.B. No. 181 | Andaman & Nicobar |
| 189 | Central Arid Zone Research Institute | CAZRI | Near I.T.I, Jodhpur - 342 003 | Rajasthan |

| | | | | |
|---|---|---|---|---|
| 190 | Regional Station,CAZRI(Jaisalmer) | CAZRI ,RS | Regional Research Station, Jaisalmer | Rajasthan |
| 191 | Regional Station,CAZRI(Bikaner) | CAZRI ,RS | Banglanagar | Rajasthan |
| 192 | Regional Station,CAZRI(Pali) | CAZRI,RS | Regional Research Institute, Pali,(Raj.) | Rajasthan |
| 193 | Regional Station,CAZRI(Bhuj) | CAZRI,RS | Kukma | Gujarat |
| 194 | Central Research Institute for Dryland Agriculture | CRIDA | Santoshnagar | Andhra Pradesh |
| 195 | Central Soil and Water Conservation Research & Training Institute | CSWCRTI | 218, kaulagarh Road | Uttranchal |
| 196 | Regional Station,CSWCR (Agra) | CSWCR, RS | P.O Chhalesar | Uttar Pradesh |
| 197 | Regional Station,CSWCR (Chandigarh) | CSWCR, RS | Sector 27 A | Chandigarh |
| 198 | Regional Station,CSWCR (Bellary) | CSWCR, RS | Bellary | Karnataka |
| 199 | Regional Station,CSWCR (Datia) | CSWCR, RS | Gwalior-Jhansi Road, Datia-475 661 | Madhya Pradesh |
| 200 | Regional Station,CSWCR (Kota) | CSWCR, RS | Kota | Rajasthan |
| 201 | Regional Station,CSWCR (Koraput) | CSWCR, RS | Semiliguda, P.B.No.12, Sunabeda | Orissa |
| 202 | Regional Station,CSWCR (Udhagamandalam) | CSWCR, RS | Farm Hill P.O. | Tamilnadu |
| 203 | Regional Station,CSWCR (Vasad) | CSWCR, RS | Vasad | Gujarat |
| 204 | Central Soil Salinity Research institute | CSSRI | Zarifa Farm, Kachhwa Road | Haryana |
| 205 | Regional Station,CSSRI(Canning Town) | CSSRI, RS | South 24 Parganas | West Bengal |
| 206 | Regional Station,CSSRI(Bharauch) | CSSRI, RS | 3 Swami Narain Society Anand | Gujarat |
| 207 | Regional Station,CSSRI(Lucknow) | CSSRI,RS | CSSRI, Regional Station, Lucknow | Uttar Pradesh |
| 208 | ICAR Research Complex for Eastern Region | ICARRCER | ICAR Parisar, P.O.-Bihar Veterinary College | Bihar |

| | | | | |
|---|---|---|---|---|
| 209 | Regional Station,ICAR-RCER(Ranchi) | ICAR-RCER,RS | Horticulture and Agroforestry Research Programme, Namkum, Plandu, Tata Road | Bihar |
| 210 | Regional Station,ICAR-RCER(Darbhanga) | ICAR-RCER,RS | Centre for Makhana, Europian Guest House, L.N.M.U. Campus | Bihar |
| 211 | ICAR Research Complex for NEH Region | ICARNEH | Umroi Road | Meghalaya |
| 212 | Regional Station,ICAR Complex For NEH(Agartala) | ICARNEH,RS | Tripura Center,Lembucherra | Tripura |
| 213 | Regional Station,ICAR Complex For NEH(Basar) | ICARNEH,RS | Arunachal Pradesh center,P.O Basar | Arunachal Pradesh |
| 214 | Regional Station,ICAR Complex For NEH(Imphal) | ICARNEH,RS | Manipur Center , Lamphelpat | Manipur |
| 215 | Regional Station,ICAR Complex For NEH(Gangtok) | ICARNEH,RS | Tadong | Sikkim |
| 216 | Regional Station,ICAR Complex For NEH(Kolisib) | ICARNEH,RS | Mizoram Center | Mizoram |
| 217 | Regional Station ICAR Complex For NEH(Jharnapani) | ICARNEH,RS | Nagaland, Center Medziphema | Nagaland |
| 218 | Central Institute for Research on Cotton Technology | CIRCOT | Adenwala Road Matunga | Maharashtra |
| 219 | Regional Station,CIRCOT(Dahrwad) | CIRCOT,RS | Agricultural Research Station ,Dahrwad Farm ,BPO | Karnataka |
| 220 | Regional Station,CIRCOT(Coimbatore) | CIRCOT,RS | Tamilnadu Agricultural University,Lawley Road PO | Tamilnadu |
| 221 | Regional Station,CIRCOT(Guntur) | CIRCOT,RS | C/O Sr.Scientist(Cotton) ,Agricultural Research Station ,Lam Farm | Andhra Pradesh |

| | | | | |
|---|---|---|---|---|
| 222 | Regional Station,CIRCOT(Nagpur) | CIRCOT,RS | Amravati Road,Wadi PO | Maharashtra |
| 223 | Regional Station,CIRCOT(Surat) | CIRCOT,RS | Agricultural Farm,Athwa | Gujarat |
| 224 | Regional Station,CIRCOT(Sirsa) | CIRCOT,RS | C/O CICR Regional Station | Haryana |
| 225 | Indian Institute of Natural Resins and Gums | IINRG | Namkum | Jharkhand |
| 226 | Regional Station,ILRI(Raigarh) | ILRI,RS | PO Dharamjaigarh,Diat.Raigarh | Madhya Pradesh |
| 227 | Regional Station,ILRI(Mayurbhanj) | ILRI,RS | PO Jasipur(Baripada) Dist.Mayurbhanj | Orissa |
| 228 | Regional Station,ILRI(Purulia) | ILRI,RS | PO Bakrampur | West Bengal |
| 229 | Central Avian Research Institute | CARI(AS) | Izatnagar | Uttar Pradesh |
| 230 | Regional Station,CARI (Bhubaneshwar) | CARI(AS),RS | CARI Regional Centre Opp. Kalinga Studio, Khandgiri Road, Jokalundi | Orissa |
| 231 | Central Institute for Research on Goats | CIRG | Makhdoom, P.O. Farah | Uttar Pradesh |
| 232 | Regional Station,CIRG,WRRC(Avikanagar) | CIRG,RS | W.R.R.C | Rajasthan |
| 233 | Indian Veterinary Research Institute | IVRI | Izatnagar | Uttar Pradesh |
| 234 | Regional Station,IVRI (Kumaon) | IVRI,RS | Mukteswar,Dist Nainital | Uttranchal |
| 235 | Regional Station,IVRI(Calcutta) | IVRI,ERS | 37, Belgachia Road | West Bengal |
| 236 | Regional Station,IVRI (Rawalpura) | IVRI,RS | Srinagar, J &K | Jammu & Kashmir |
| 237 | Regional Station,IVRI (Palampur) | IVRI,RS | Palampur | Himachal Pradesh |
| 238 | HSADL, Regional Station,IVRI (Bhopal) | HSADL, IVRI,RS | Anand Nagar, Kokta | Madhya Pradesh |
| 239 | Regional Station,IVRI(Hebbal) | IVRI,RS | Hebbal | Karnataka |
| 240 | National Dairy Research Institute | NDRI | NDRI, Karnal | Haryana |
| 241 | Regional Station,NDRI(Adugodi) | NDRI,RS | Adugodi | Karnataka |
| 242 | Regional Station,NDRI(Kalyani) | NDRI,RS | Kalyani | West Bengal |

| | | | | |
|---|---|---|---|---|
| 243 | National Institute of Animal Nutrition and Physiology | NIANP | Hosur Road, Adugodi, Bangalore, | Karnataka |
| 244 | Indian Agricultural Statistics Research Institute | IASRI | Library Avenue, Pusa Campus, New Delhi | Delhi |
| 245 | National Academy of Agricultural Reseach Management | NAARM | Rajendranagar, Hyderabad - 500 030 | Andhra Pradesh |
| 246 | Central Institute for Cotton Research | CICR | P.Box No.2, Shankar Nagar, Post Office | Maharashtra |
| 247 | Regional Station,CICR,( Coimbatore) | CICR,RS | CICR,Regional Station | Tamilnadu |
| 248 | Regional Station,CICR,(Sirsa) | CICR,RS | CICR,Regional Station,P.O.Box 57 | Haryana |
| 249 | Central Institute for Arid Horticulture | CIAH | Ganganagar Road , Beechwal, NH-15, Bikaner - 334 006 | Rajasthan |
| 250 | Regional Station, Central Horticultura Experiment Station | CIAH, RS | Godhra-Baroda, Highway, Vejalpur-389340 | Gujarat |
| 251 | National Institute of Abiotic Stress Management | NIASM | Baramati, Pune - 413 115 | Maharashtra |
| 252 | Project Directorate for Farming Systems Research | PDFSR | Modipuram, Meerut – 250110 | Uttar Pradesh |
| 253 | Project Directorate on Cattle | PDCATTLE | Grass Farm Road | Uttar Pradesh |
| 254 | Project Directorate On Poultry | PDPOULTRY | Rajendranagar,Distt Ranga Reddy | Andhra Pradesh |
| 255 | Directorate of Coldwater Fisheries Research | DCFR | Industrial Area, Bhimtal | Uttranchal |
| 256 | Directorate of Maize Research | DMR | Library Avenue, Pusa Campus, New Delhi | Delhi |
| 257 | DMR,RS | DMR | Directorate of Maize Research,Regional Maize Research & SeedProduction Unit , Begusarai | Kushmohut |

| | | | | |
|---|---|---|---|---|
| 258 | DMR,RS | DMR | Regional Station,DMR(Hyderabad) | Amberpete Farm |
| 259 | Directorate of Oilseeds Research | DOR | Rajendranagar | Andhra Pradesh |
| 260 | Directorate of Rice Research | DRR | Rajendra nagar | Andhra Pradesh |
| 261 | Directorate of Wheat Research | DWR | P.B. No. 158, Kunjpura Road | Haryana |
| 262 | DWR,RS | DWR | Regional Station,DWR(Shimla) | Post Box No.2,Shimla |
| 263 | DWR,RS | DWR | Regional Station,DWR(Lahul Valley) | Dalang Maidan,P.O Keylong |
| 264 | Directorate of Groundnut Research | DGR | Ivnagar Road,P.B. No.5 | Gujarat |
| 265 | Directorate of Sorghum Research | DSR | Rajendra Nagar | Andhra Pradesh |
| 266 | DSR,CRS | DSR | Regional Station,DSR(Solapur) | C/O agricultural School |
| 267 | Directorate of Soybean Research | NRCS | Khandwa Road | Madhya Pradesh |
| 268 | NRCS,RS | NRCS | Regional Station,NRCS(Warangal) | C/O Agricultural Research Station(APAU) |
| 269 | Directorate of Rapeseed-Mustard Research | DRMR | Directorate of Rapeseed-Mustard Research, Sewar,Bharatpur( Rajasthan)-321303 | Rajasthan |
| 270 | Directorate of Cashew Resaerch | DCR | Indira Nagar | Karnataka |
| 271 | Directorate of Mushroom Research | DMR | DMR, Chambaghat | Himachal Pradesh |
| 272 | Directorate of Medicinal and Aromatic Plants Research | DMAPR | Boriavi | Gujarat |
| 273 | Directorate of Oil Palm Research | DOPR | Near Jawahar Navodaya Vidyalaya | Andhra Pradesh |
| 274 | National Research Centre on Oil Palm | NRCOP | Godavari | Andhra Pradesh |
| 275 | NRCOP, RS | NRCOP | Regional Station, NRCOP | Palode, Pacha P.O. 695562 |

| | | | | |
|---|---|---|---|---|
| 276 | Directorate on Onion & Garlic Research | NRCONION | Rajgurunagar | Maharashtra |
| 277 | Directorate of Weed Science Research | DWSR | Maharajpur, Adhartal | Madhya Pradesh |
| 278 | Directorate of Water Management | DWM | Chandrasekharpur, | Orissa |
| 279 | Directorate of Research on Women in Agriculture | DRWA | OPP Kalinga Studio, Baramunda Post | Orissa |
| 280 | Directorate of Floricultural Research | DFR | Pusa | Delhi |
| 281 | Project Directorate on Foot and Mouth Disease | PDFMD | IVRI Campus, Mukteswar | Uttranchal |
| 282 | Directorate of Knowledge Management in Agriculture | DKMA | 5th Floor, Krishi Anusandhan Bhawan-1, Pusa | Delhi |
| 283 | Directorate of Seed Research | DSR | Post bag no: 11, Vil-Kushmaur, Post-Kaithauli | Uttar Pradesh |
| 284 | Project Directorate on Animal Disease Monitoring and Surveillance | PDADMS | PD-ADMAS, IVRI Campus, Bellary Road, Hebbal | Karnataka |
| 285 | Zonal Project Directorate - Zone-VII | ZPD-VII | Jawaharlal Nehru Krishi Viswavidyalaya, Krishi Nagar, Adhartal, Jabalpur | Madhya Pradesh |
| 286 | Zonal Project Directorate, Zone-III | ZPD-III | Zonal Project Directorate, Zone-III, ICAR Research Complex for NEH Region | Meghalaya |
| 287 | Zonal Coordinator –IV | ZC-IV | Zonal Project Directorate, Zone-IV, ICAR, G.T. Road, Rawatpur (Near Vikas Bhawan) | Uttar Pradesh |
| 288 | Zonal Coordinator –VI | ZC-VI | Zonal Coordinating Unit VI, Indian Council of Agricultural Research CAZRI Campus | Rajasthan |

| 289 | Zonal Project Directorate –VIII | ZPD-VIII | ICAR, Zonal Project Directorate, MRS, HA Farm Post, Bhoopasandra Main Road, Hebbal | Karnataka |
|---|---|---|---|---|
| 290 | Zonal Project Directorate, Zone-I | ZPD-I | PAU Campus, Ludhiana | Punjab |
| 291 | Zonal Coordinator –II | ZC-II | Bhumi Vihar Complex, Salt Lake City, Sector III, Block – GB | West Bengal |
| 292 | Zonal Project Directorate, Zone-V | ZC-V | Zonal Project Directorate, Zone V, CRIDA Campus, Santoshnagar | Andhra Pradesh |

Days we have celebrated as:

| Sl No. | Day | Date/Month |
|---|---|---|
| 1. | Day of Silence | 3rd January |
| 2. | NRI Day | 9th January |
| 3. | National Youth Day | 12th January |
| 4. | Indian Republic Day | 26th January |
| 5. | National Science Day | 28th February |
| 6. | World Water Day | 22nd March |
| 7. | World Heritage Day | 18th April |
| 8. | World Forestry Day | 21st March |
| 9. | Earth Day | 22nd April |
| 10. | National Technology Day | 11th May |
| 11. | International Day for Biological Diversity | 22nd May |
| 12. | Commonwealth Day | 24th May |
| 13. | World Environment Day | 5th June |
| 14. | Indian Independence Day | 15th August |
| 15. | Teacher's Day | 5th September |
| 16. | International Day of the Preservation of the Ozone Layer | 16th September |
| 17. | World Tourism Day | 27th September |
| 18. | World Animal Welfare Day | 4th October |
| 19. | World Food Day | 16th October |
| 20. | United Nation's Day | 24th October |
| 21. | Farmer's Day (Kishan Divas) | 23rd December |

List of Some ImportantTree Species

| S.No | Scientific Name | Common Name | Family |
|---|---|---|---|
| 1. | *Abies Pindrow* | Fir, Silver fir, Tosh | Coniferae |
| 2. | *Acacia auriculiformis* | Australian Wattle | Leguminosae |
| 3. | *Acacia mangium* | Australian Teak | Leguminosae |
| 4. | *Adina cordifolia* | Haldu | Rubiaceae |
| 5. | *Ailanthus grandis* | Gokul | Simarubaceae |
| 6. | *Albizia lebbeck* | Siris | Leguminosae |
| 7. | *Albizia oderatissima* | Kala Siris | Leguminosae |
| 8. | *Albizia procera* | Safed Siris | Leguminosae |
| 9. | *Alstonia scholaris* | Devils Tree, Shaitan Wood, Satpatti | Apocynaceae |
| 10. | *Amoora wallichi* | Amari, Lanchini | Meliaceae |
| 11. | *Anthocephalus chinensis* | Kadam | Rubiaceae |

| | | | |
|---|---|---|---|
| 12. | *Artocarpus heterophyllus* | Kathal, Jackfruit | Moraceae |
| 13. | *Azadirachta indica* | Neem | Meliaceae |
| 14. | *Bamboo spp.* | Bans | Poaceae |
| 15 | *Bauhinia malabarica* | Amli, Malabar Mountain Ebony | Leguminosae |
| 16 | *Bauhinia purpurea* | La Kachnar, Pink Bauhinia | Leguminosae |
| 17 | *Bauhinia racemosa* | Kanchal, Gurial | Leguminosae |
| 18 | *Bauhinia vahli* | Camels Foot Climber, Fallur | Leguminosae |
| 19 | *Bauhinia variegate* | Kachnar | Leguminosae |
| 20 | *Bixa orellana* | Jafran | Bombacaceae |
| 21 | *Bombax ceiba* | Semul, Silk Cotton Tree, Cotton Wood | Bombacaceae |
| 22 | *Callophylhum innophy-lum* | Polang | Guttiferae |
| 23 | *Cassia fistula* | Amaltas | Leguminosae |
| 24 | *Cassia siamea* | Ironwood Tree | Leguminosae |
| 25 | *Casurina equisetifolia* | Jhau | Casuarinaceae |
| 26 | *Cedrus deodara* | Deodara, Devdar, Himalayan Cedar | Coniferae |
| 27 | *Ceiba pentandra* | Kapok, White Silk Cotton Tree | Bombacaceae |
| 28 | *Chukrasia velutina* | Chittagong Redwood, Chikrasy | Meliaceae |
| 29 | *Cinnamomum zeylancum* | Dalchini | Lauraceae |
| 30 | *Cryptomera japonica* | Sugi, Japanese Cedar | Taxodiaceae |
| 31 | *Dalbergia sissoo* | Shisham, Sissoo | Leguminosae |
| 32 | *Delonix regia* | Gulmohar | Leguminosae |
| 33 | *Dillenia indica* | Elephant apple | Delleniaceae |
| 34 | *Emblica officinalis* | Amla, Aonla | Euphorbiaceae |
| 35 | *Erythrina variegate* | Mandar, Indian Corel Tree | Leguminosae |
| 36 | *Eucalyptus camaldulensis* | River Red Gum | Myrtaceae |
| 37 | *Eucalyptus globulus* | Blue gum | Myrtaceae |
| 38 | *Gliricidia sepium* | Gliricidia | Leguminosae |
| 39 | *Gmelina arborea* | Gamari, Gamhar | Verbenaceae |
| 40 | *Grevillea pteridifolia* | Pteridifolia | Proteaceae |
| 41 | *Grevillea robusta* | Silver Oak | Proteaceae |
| 42 | *Indigofera taysmanii* | Assam Shade Tree | Leguminosae |
| 43 | *Lagerstoemia* | Benteak, Lendi | Lythraceae |
| 44 | *Lagerstoemia speciosa* | Jarul, Queens Flower | Lythraceae |
| 45 | *Jacaranda mimosaefolia* | Jacaranda, The Mimosa-Leaved Jacaranda | Bignoniaceae |
| 46 | *Lagerstoemia flosreginae* | Sidha | Lythraceae |

| | | | |
|---|---|---|---|
| 47 | *Leucacena diversifolia* | Diversifolia | Leguminosae |
| 48 | *Leucacena leucocephala* | Subabul | Leguminosae |
| 49 | *Machilus edulis* | Lepeha Phul | Lauraceae |
| 50 | *Mangifera indica* | Mango | Anacardiaceae |
| 51 | *Melia azedarach* | Bakain, Mahaneem | Meliaceae |
| 52 | *Michelia champaca* | Champa, Champak | Magnoliaceae |
| 53 | *Mimosopus elengii* | Bakul, Mausari | Sapotaceae |
| 54 | *Morianga oleifera* | Drumstick, Sajan | Moringaceae |
| 55 | *Oroxyllum indicum* | Susimala | Bignoniaceae |
| 56 | *Picea smithiana* | Spruce, Himalayan Spruce, Rai | Coniferae |
| 57 | *Pinus roxburghii* | Chir pine | Coniferae |
| 58 | *Pinus wallichiana* | Blue pine | Coniferae |
| 59 | *Polyalthia longifolia* | Debdaru, Ashok | Annonaceae |
| 60 | *Populous celiata* | Himalayan Poplar | Salicaceae |
| 61 | *Populous deltoids* | Eastern Cottonwood | Salicaceae |
| 62 | *Salix alba* | White Willow | Salicaceae |
| 63 | *Samanea saman* | Rain Tree | Leguminosae |
| 64 | *Pterocarpus marsupium* | Bijasal | Leguminosae |
| 65 | *Sapindus mukorossi* | Ritha, Soapnut Tree of Northern India | Sapindaceae |
| 66 | *Sesbania grandiflora* | Agathi, Sesban | Leguminosae |
| 67 | *Shorea robusta* | Sal | Dipterocarpaceae |
| 68 | *Streculia urens* | Katira , Gulu | Sterculiaceae |
| 69 | *Swetenia mahogani* | Mahagani, Small-leaved Mahogony | Meliaceac |
| 70 | *Syzigium cumini* | Jamun | Myrtaceae |
| 71 | *Tamarindus indica* | Imli | Leguminosae |
| 72 | *Tectona grandis* | Teak | Verbenaceae |
| 73 | *Tephorosia candida* | Tephphrosia | Leguminosae |
| 74 | *Terminalia alata* | Laurel | Combretaceae |
| 75 | *Terminalia arjuna* | Arjun | Combretaceae |
| 76 | *Terminalia bellerica* | Bahera | Combretaceae |
| 77 | *Terminalia catappa* | Indian Almond Wood | Combretaceae |
| 78 | *Terminalia chebula* | Chebulic Myrobalan | Combretaceae |
| 79 | *Terminalia myriocarpa* | Hollock | Combretaceae |
| 80 | *Terminalia tomentosa* | Pakasaj | Combretaceae |
| 81 | *Toona ciliate* | Toon, Red Cedar | Meliaceae |
| 82 | *Zizyphus mauritiana* | Ber | Rhamnaceae |

# Annexure 2

## Status of Wildlife Conservations & Procted Area

**India**

| | | |
|---|---|---|
| Geographical Area of India | = | 32,87,590 km$^2$ |
| Forest cover of India (FSI, 2013) | = | 6,97,898 km$^2$ |
| Percentage Area under Forest cover | = | 21.23 % of Geographical Area of India |

**Protected Areas of India (as on 09 February, 2016)**

| Protected Area | No. | Area (km$^2$) | % of Geographical Area of India (%) |
|---|---|---|---|
| National Parks (NPs) | 103 | 40500.13 | 1.23 |
| Wildlife Sanctuaries (WLSs) | 535 | 118004.92 | 3.59 |
| Conservation Reserves (CRs) | 66 | 2344.53 | 0.07 |
| Community Reserves | 26 | 46.93 | 0.001 |
| Protected Areas (PAs) | 730 | 160896.51 | 4.88 |

**Protected Areas of India from 2000 to 2015 (as on 09 February, 2016)**

| Year | No. of National Parks | Area under National Parks | No. of wildlife Sanctuaries | Area under wildlife Sanctuaries | No. of ommunity Reserves | Area under Community Reserves | No. of onsevation Reserves | Area under onsevation Reserves | No. of Protected Areas | Area under Protected Areas |
|---|---|---|---|---|---|---|---|---|---|---|
| 2000 | 89 | 37593.94 | 489 | 117881.68 | - | - | - | - | 578 | 155475.63 |
| 2006 | 96 | 38183.01 | 506 | 120244.39 | - | - | 4 | 42.87 | 606 | 158470.27 |
| 2007 | 98 | 38219.72 | 510 | 120543.95 | 4 | 20.69 | 7 | 94.82 | 619 | 158879.19 |
| 2008 | 99 | 39232.58 | 513 | 122138.33 | 4 | 20.69 | 45 | 1259.84 | 661 | 162651.45 |
| 2009 | 99 | 39232.58 | 513 | 122138.33 | 4 | 20.69 | 45 | 1259.84 | 661 | 162651.45 |
| 2010 | 102 | 40074.46 | 516 | 122585.56 | 4 | 20.69 | 47 | 1382.28 | 669 | 164062.99 |
| 2011 | 102 | 40074.46 | 517 | 122615.94 | 4 | 20.69 | 52 | 1801.29 | 675 | 164512..37 |
| 2012 | 102 | 40074.46 | 524 | 123548.33 | 4 | 20.69 | 56 | 1998.15 | 686 | 165641.62 |
| 2013 | 102 | 40074.46 | 526 | 124234.52 | 4 | 20.69 | 57 | 2017.94 | 689 | 166347.6 |
| 2014 | 103 | 40332.89 | 525 | 116254.36 | 4 | 20.69 | 60 | 2037.11 | 692 | 158645.05 |
| 2015 | 103 | 40500.13 | 531 | 117607.62 | 26 | 46.93 | 66 | 2344.53 | 726 | 160499.31 |
| 2016 | 103 | 40500.13 | 535 | 118004.92 | 26 | 46.93 | 66 | 2344.53 | 730 | 160896.51 |

Tiger Reserves of India (as on 17 March, 2016)

*Source*: National Wildlife Database Cell, Wildlife Institute of India

*Note: All areas are in km²*

Community Reserves have been established in India from 2007 onwards and Conservation Reserves from 2005 onwards. Hence these values are zero.

| S No | Name of Tiger Reserve | State | Area of the core / critical tiger habitat (Sq. Kms.) | Area of the buffer / peripheral ( Sq. Kms.) | Total area (Sq. Kms.) |
|---|---|---|---|---|---|
| 1 | Nagarjunsagar Srisailam (part)* | Andhra Pradesh | 2595.72* | 700.59* | 3296.31* |
| 2 | Namdapha | Arunachal Pradesh | 1807.82 | 245 | 2052.82 |
| 3 | Pakke | Arunachal Pradesh | 683.45 | 515 | 1198.45 |
| 4 | Manas | Assam | 840.04 | 2310.88 | 3150.92 |
| 5 | Nameri | Assam | 200 | 144 | 344 |
| 6 | Orang Tiger Reserve | Assam | 79.28 | 413.18 | 492.46 |
| 7 | Kaziranga | Assam | 625.58 | 548 | 1173.58 |
| 8 | Valmiki | Bihar | 598.45 | 300.93 | 899.38 |
| 9 | Udanti-Sitanadi | Chhattisgarh | 851.09 | 991.45 | 1842.54 |
| 10 | Achanakmar | Chattisgarh | 626.195 | 287.822 | 914.017 |
| 11 | Indravati | Chhattisgarh | 1258.37 | 1540.7 | 2799.07 |
| 12 | Palamau | Jharkhand | 414.08 | 715.85 | 1129.93 |
| 13 | Bandipur | Karnataka | 872.24 | 584.06 | 1456.3 |
| 14 | Bhadra | Karnataka | 492.46 | 571.83 | 1064.29 |
| 15 | Dandeli-Anshi | Karnataka | 814.884 | 282.63 | 1097.51 |
| 16 | Nagarahole | Karnataka | 643.35 | 562.41 | 1205.76 |
| 17 | Biligiri Ranganatha Temple | Karnataka | 359.1 | 215.72 | 574.82 |
| 18 | Periyar | Kerala | 881 | 44 | 925 |
| 19 | Parambikulam | Kerala | 390.89 | 252.772 | 643.662 |
| 20 | Kanha | Madhya Pradesh | 917.43 | 1134.361 | 2051.791 |
| 21 | Pench | Madhya Pradesh | 411.33 | 768.30225 | 1179.63225 |
| 22 | Bandhavgarh | Madhya Pradesh | 716.903 | 820.03509 | 1598.1 |
| 23 | Panna | Madhya Pradesh | 576.13 | 1021.97 | 1578.55 |
| 24 | Satpura | Madhya Pradesh | 1339.264 | 794.04397 | 2133.30797 |
| 25 | Sanjay-Dubri | Madhya Pradesh | 812.571 | 861.931 | 1674.502 |
| 26 | Melghat | Maharashtra | 1500.49 | 1268.03 | 2768.52 |
| 27 | Tadoba-Andhari | Maharashtra | 625.82 | 1101.7711 | 1727.5911 |
| 28 | Pench | Maharashtra | 257.26 | 483.96 | 741.22 |
| 29 | Sahyadri | Maharashtra | 600.12 | 565.45 | 1165.57 |

| 30 | Nawegaon-Nagzira | Maharashtra | 653.674 | - | 653.674 |
|---|---|---|---|---|---|
| 31 | Bor | Maharashtra | 138.12 | - | 138.12 |
| 32 | Dampa | Mizoram | 500 | 488 | 988 |
| 33 | Similipal | Odisha | 1194.75 | 1555.25 | 2750 |
| 34 | Satkosia | Odisha | 523.61 | 440.26 | 963.87 |
| 35 | Ranthambore | Rajasthan | 1113.364 | 297.9265 | 1411.291 |
| 36 | Sariska | Rajasthan | 881.1124 | 332.23 | 1213.342 |
| 37 | Mukandra Hills | Rajasthan | 417.17 | 342.82 | 759.99 |
| 38 | Kalakad-Mundan-thurai | Tamil Nadu | 895 | 706.542 | 1601.542 |
| 39 | Anamalai | Tamil Nadu | 958.59 | 521.28 | 1479.87 |
| 40 | Mudumalai | Tamil Nadu | 321 | 367.59 | 688.59 |
| 41 | Sathyamangalam | Tamil Nadu | 793.49 | 614.91 | 1408.4 |
| 42 | Kawal | Telangana | 893.23 | 1125.89 | 2019.12 |
| 43 | Amrabad | Telangana | 2166.37* | 445.02* | 2611.39* |
| 44 | Dudhwa | Uttar Pradesh | 1093.79 | 1107.9848 | 2201.7748 |
| 45 | Pilibhit | Uttar Pradesh | 602.798 | 127.4518 | 730.2498 |
| 46 | Amangarh (buffer of Corbett TR) | Uttar Pradesh | - | 80.6 | 80.6 |
| | Corbett | Uttarakhand | 821.99 | 466.32 | 1288.31 |
| 47 | Rajaji TR | Uttarakhand | 255.63 | 819.54 | 1075.17 |
| 48 | Sunderbans | West Bengal | 1699.62 | 885.27 | 2584.89 |
| 49 | Buxa | West Bengal | 390.5813 | 367.3225 | 757.9038 |
| | **TOTAL** | | **39669.12** | **30574.98** | **70244.10** |

*Source: Project Tiger *Combined with Andhra Pradesh*

**Elephant (Elephas maximus) population estimates for 2007 and 2012**

| Sl. No | States | Elephant Population | |
|---|---|---|---|
| | | 2007 | 2012 |
| 1 | Arunachal Pradesh | 1690 | 1690 |
| 2 | Assam | 5281 | 5281 |
| 3 | Meghalaya | 1811 | 1811 |
| 4 | Nagaland | 152 | 212 |
| 5 | Tripura | 59 | 59 |
| 6 | West Bengal | 325-350 | 325-350 |
| 7 | Jharkhand | 624 | 688 |

| | | | |
|---|---|---|---|
| 8 | Odisha | 1862 | 1930 |
| 9 | Chattisgarh | 122 | 215 |
| 10 | Uttarakhand | 1346 | 1346 |
| 11 | Uttar Pradesh | 380 | 380 |
| 12 | Tamil Nadu | 3867 | 3726 |
| 13 | Karnataka | 4035 | 3900-7458 |
| 14 | Kerela | 6068 | 6177 |
| 15 | Andhra Pradesh | 28 | 41 |
| 16 | Maharshtra | 7 | 4 |
| | | 27657-27682 | 27785-31368 |

(*Source*: MoEF, 2013)

**RAMSAR WETLANDS SITES**

| Sl. No | Name of Site | State Location | Date of Declaration | Area (km$^2$) |
|---|---|---|---|---|
| 1. | Asthamudi Wetland | Kerala | 19.8.2002 | 1860 |
| 2 | Bhitarkanika Mangroves | Orissa | 19.8.2002 | 525 |
| 3 | Bhoj Wetlands | Madhya Pradesh | 19.8.2002 | 31 |
| 4 | Chandertal Wetland | Himachal Pradesh | 8.11.2005 | 38.56 |
| 5 | Chilka Lake | Orissa | 1.10.1981 | 1140 |
| 6 | Deepor Beel | Assam | 19.8.2002 | 4.14 |
| 7 | East Calcutta Wetlands | West Bengal | 19.8.2002 | 378 |
| 8 | Harike Lake | Punjab | 23.3.1990 | 86 |
| 9 | Hokera Wetland | Jammu and Kashmir | 8.11.2005 | 13.75 |
| 10 | Kanjli Lake | Punjab | 22.1.2002 | 14.84 |
| 11 | Keoladeo Ghana NP | Rajasthan | 1.10.1981 | 28.73 |
| 12 | Kolleru Lake | Andhra Pradesh | 19.8.2002 | 673 |
| 13 | Loktak Lake | Manipur | 23.3.1990 | 945 |
| 14 | Nalsarovar Bird Sanctuary | Gujarat | 24/09/12 | 120 |
| 15 | Point Calimere | Tamil Nadu | 19.8.2002 | 17.26 |
| 16 | Pong Dam Lake | Himachal Pradesh | 19.8.2002 | 307.29 |
| 17 | Renuka Wetland | Himachal Pradesh | 8.11.2005 | Not Available |
| 18 | Ropar Lake | Punjab | 22.1.2002 | 41.36 |
| 19 | Rudrasagar Lake | Tripura | 8.11.2005 | 2.40 |
| 20 | Sambhar Lake | Rajasthan | 23.3.1990 | 736 |

| | | | | |
|---|---|---|---|---|
| 21 | Sasthamkotta Lake | Kerala | 19.8.2002 | 11.3 |
| 22 | Surinsar-Mansar Lakes | Jammu and Kashmir | 8.11.2005 | 3.50 |
| 23 | Tsomoriri Lake | Jammu and Kashmir | 19.8.2002 | 120 |
| 24 | Vembanad Kol Wetland | Kerala | 19.8.2002 | 4583 |
| 25 | Upper Ganga River (Brijghat to Narora Stretch) | Uttar Pradesh | 8.11.2005 | 265.90 |
| 26 | Wular Lake | Jammu & Kashmir | 23.3.1990 | 173 |

*Source*: Ministry of Environment & Forests, Government of India

**Biosphere Reserves in India (as on Dec, 2014)**

| Sl. No | Name | Date of Notification | Area ($Km_2$) | Location (Site) |
|---|---|---|---|---|
| 1 | Nilgiri | 01.09.1986 | 5520<br>(Core 1240 & Buffer 4280) | Part of Wayanad, Nagarhole, Bandipur and Madumalai, Nilambur, Silent Valley and Siruvani hills (Tamil Nadu, Kerala and Karnataka). |
| 2 | Nanda Devi | 18.01.1988 | 5860.69<br>(Core 712.12, Buffer 5,148.570) & T. 546.34) | Part of Chamoli, Pithoragarh, and Bageshwar districts (Uttarakhand). |
| 3 | Nokrek | 01.09.1988 | 820<br>(Core 47.48 & Buffer 227.92, Transition Zone 544.60) | Part of Garo hills (Meghalaya). |
| 4 | Great Nicobar | 06.01.1989 | 885 (Core 705 & Buffer 180) | Southern most islands of Andaman And Nicobar (A&N Islands). |
| 5 | Gulf of Mannar | 18.02.1989 | 10,500 km2<br>Total Gulf area<br>(area of Islands 5.55 km2) | Indian part of Gulf of Mannar between India and Sri Lanka (Tamil Nadu). |
| 6 | Manas | 14.03.1989 | 2837<br>(Core 391 & Buffer 2,446) | Part of Kokrajhar, Bongaigaon, Barpeta, Nalbari, Kamprup and Darang districts (Assam) |
| 7 | Sunderbans | 29.03.1989 | 9630<br>(Core 1700 & Buffer 7900) | Part of delta of Ganges and Brahamaputra river system , (West Bengal). |
| 8 | Simlipal | 21.06.1994 | 4374<br>(Core 845, Buffer 2129 & Transition 1400 | Part of Mayurbhanj district (Orissa). |

| | | | | |
|---|---|---|---|---|
| 9 | Dibru-Saik-howa | 28.07.1997 | 765 (Core 340 & Buffer 425) | Part of Dibrugarh and Tinsukia Districts (Assam) |
| 10 | Dehang-Dibang | 02.09.1998 | 5111.50 (Core 4094.80 &Buffer 1016.70) | Part of Siang and Dibang Valley in Arunachal Pradesh. |
| 11 | Pachmarhi | 03.03.1999 | 4926 | Parts of Betul, Hoshangabad and Chindwara districts of Madhya Pradesh. |
| 12 | Khangchend-zonga | 07.02.2000 | 2619.92 (Core 1819.34 & Buffer 835.92) | Parts of Khangchendzonga hills and Sikkim. |
| 13 | Agasthyamalai | 12.11.2001 | 1828 | Neyyar, Peppara and Shendurney Wildlife Sanctuaries and their adjoining areas in Kerala. |
| 14 | Achanakamar - Amarkantak | 30.3.2005 | 3835.51 (Core 551.55 & Buffer 3283.86) | Covers parts of Anupur and Dindori districts of M.P. and parts of Bilaspur districts of Chhattishgarh State. |
| 15 | Kachchh | 29.01.2008 | 12,454 km2 | Part of Kachchh, Rajkot, Surendra Nagar and Patan Civil Districts of Gujarat State |
| 16 | Cold Desert | 28.08.2009 | 7770 | Pin Valley National Park and surroundings; Chandratal and Sarchu&Kibber Wildlife Sancturary in Himachal Pradesh |
| 17 | Seshachalam Hills | 20.09.2010 | 4755.997 | Seshachalam Hill Ranges covering parts of Chittoor and Kadapa districts of Andhra Pradesh |
| 18 | Panna | 25.08.2011 | 29980.98 | Part of Panna and Chhattarpur districts in Madhya Pradesh |

*Source*: Wildlife Institute of India

**State-wise break up of National Parks (July, 2015)**

| S. No. | Name of State / Protected Area | Year of Establishment | Area (km$^2$) | District(s) |
|---|---|---|---|---|
| **Andaman & Nicobar Islands** | | | | |
| 1 | Campbell Bay NP | 1992 | 426.23 | Nicobar |
| 2 | Galathea Bay NP | 1992 | 110.00 | Nicobar |
| 3 | Mahatama Gandhi Marine (Wandoor) NP | 1983 | 281.50 | Andaman |
| 4 | Middle Button Island NP | 1987 | 0.44 | Andaman |
| 5 | Mount Harriett NP | 1987 | 46.62 | Andaman |
| 6 | North Button Island NP | 1987 | 0.44 | Andaman |
| 7 | Rani Jhansi Marine NP | 1996 | 256.14 | Andaman |
| 8 | Saddle Peak NP | 1987 | 32.54 | Andaman |
| 9 | South Button Island NP | 1987 | 0.03 | Andaman |
| **Andhra Pradesh** | | | | |
| 1 | Papikonda NP | 2008 | 1012.86 | East & West Godavari |
| 2 | Rajiv Gandhi (Rameswaram) NP | 2005 | 2.40 | Kadapa |
| 3 | Sri Venkateswara NP | 1989 | 353.62 | Chittoor & Cuddapah |
| **Arunachal Pradesh** | | | | |
| 1 | Mouling NP | 1986 | 483.00 | Upper Siang |
| 2 | Namdapha NP | 1983 | 1807.82 | Changlang |
| **Assam** | | | | |
| 1 | Dibru-Saikhowa NP | 1999 | 340.00 | Tinsukia & Dibrugarh |
| 2 | Kaziranga NP | 1974 | 858.98 | Golaghat, Nagaon & Sonitpur |
| 3 | Manas NP | 1990 | 500.00 | Barpeta & Bongaigaon |
| 4 | Nameri NP | 1998 | 200.00 | Sonitpur |
| 5 | Rajiv Gandhi Orang NP | 1999 | 78.81 | Darrang & Sonitpur |
| **Bihar** | | | | |
| 1 | Valmiki NP | 1989 | 335.65 | West Champaran |
| **Chhattisgarh** | | | | |
| 1 | Guru Ghasidas (Sanjay) NP | 1981 | 1440.71 | Surguja & Koria |
| 2 | Indravati (Kutru) NP | 1982 | 1258.37 | Dantewada |
| 3 | Kanger Valley NP | 1982 | 200.00 | Bastar |
| **Goa** | | | | |
| 1 | Mollem NP | 1992 | 107.00 | North Goa |

| Gujarat | | | | |
|---|---|---|---|---|
| 1 | Vansda NP | 1979 | 23.99 | Navasari |
| 2 | Blackbuck (Velavadar) NP | 1976 | 34.53 | Bhavnagar |
| 3 | Gir NP | 1975 | 258.71 | Junagadh |
| 4 | Marine (Gulf of Kachchh) NP | 1982 | 162.89 | Jamnagar |
| **Haryana** | | | | |
| 1 | Kalesar NP | 2003 | 46.82 | Yamuna Nagar |
| 2 | Sultanpur NP | 1989 | 1.43 | Gurgaon |
| **Himachal Pradesh** | | | | |
| 1 | Great Himalayan NP | 1984 | 754.40 | Kullu |
| 2 | Inderkilla NP | 2010 | 104.00 | Kullu |
| 3 | Khirganga NP | 2010 | 710.00 | Kullu |
| 4 | Pin Valley NP | 1987 | 675.00 | Lahul & Spiti |
| 5 | Simbalbara NP | 2010 | 27.88 | Sirmaur |
| **Jammu & Kashmir** | | | | |
| 1 | City Forest (Salim Ali) NP | 1992 | 9.00 | Srinagar |
| 2 | Dachigam NP | 1981 | 141.00 | Srinagar & Pulwama |
| 3 | Hemis NP | 1981 | 3350.00 | Leh |
| 4 | Kishtwar NP | 1981 | 425.00 | Kishtwar & Doda |
| **Jharkhand** | | | | |
| 1 | Betla NP | 1986 | 226.33 | Latehar |
| **Karnataka** | | | | |
| 1 | Anshi NP | 1987 | 417.34 | Uttara Kannada |
| 2 | Bandipur NP | 1974 | 874.20 | Mysore & Chamarajanagar |
| 3 | Bannerghatta NP | 1974 | 260.51 | Bangalore |
| 4 | Kudremukh NP | 1987 | 600.32 | Dakshin Kannada, Udipi & Chikmagalur |
| 5 | Nagarahole (Rajiv Gandhi) NP | 1988 | 643.39 | Kodagu & Mysore |
| **Kerala** | | | | |
| 1 | Anamudi Shola NP | 2003 | 7.50 | Idukki |
| 2 | Eravikulam NP | 1978 | 97.00 | Idukki |
| 3 | Mathikettan Shola NP | 2003 | 12.82 | Idukki |
| 4 | Pambadum Shola NP | 2003 | 1.32 | Idukki |

| | | | | |
|---|---|---|---|---|
| 5 | Periyar NP | 1982 | 350.00 | Idukki & Quilon |
| 6 | Silent Valley NP | 1984 | 89.52 | Palakkad |
| **Madhya Pradesh** | | | | |
| 1 | Bandhavgarh NP | 1968 | 448.85 | Umaria & Katni |
| 2 | Fossil NP | 1983 | 0.27 | Mandla |
| 6 | Indira Priyadarshini Pench NP | 1975 | 292.85 | Seoni & Chhindwara |
| 3 | Kanha NP | 1955 | 940.00 | Mandla, Balaghat & Dindori |
| 4 | Madhav NP | 1959 | 375.22 | Shivpuri |
| 5 | Panna NP | 1981 | 542.67 | Panna & Chhatarpur |
| 7 | Sanjay NP | 1981 | 466.88 | Sidhi |
| 8 | Satpura NP | 1981 | 585.17 | Hoshangabad |
| 9 | Van Vihar NP | 1979 | 4.45 | Bhopal |
| **Maharashtra** | | | | |
| 1 | Chandoli NP | 2004 | 317.67 | Sangli, Satara, Kolhapur, Ratnagiri |
| 2 | Gugamal NP | 1975 | 361.28 | Amravati |
| 3 | Nawegaon NP | 1975 | 133.88 | Bhandara (Gondia) |
| 4 | Pench (Jawaharlal Nehru) NP | 1975 | 257.26 | Nagpur |
| 5 | Sanjay Gandhi (Borivilli) NP | 1983 | 86.96 | Thane & Mumbai |
| 6 | Tadoba NP | 1955 | 116.55 | Chandrapur |
| **Manipur** | | | | |
| 1 | Keibul-Lamjao NP | 1977 | 40.00 | Bishnupur |
| **Meghalaya** | | | | |
| 1 | Balphakram NP | 1985 | 220.00 | South Garo Hills |
| 2 | Nokrek Ridge NP | 1986 | 47.48 | East Garo Hills |
| **Mizoram** | | | | |
| 1 | Murlen NP | 1991 | 100.00 | Champhai |
| 2 | Phawngpui Blue Mountain NP | 1992 | 50.00 | Lawngtlai |
| **Nagaland** | | | | |
| 1 | Intanki NP | 1993 | 202.02 | Dimapur |
| **Odisha** | | | | |
| 1 | Bhitarkanika NP | 1988 | 145.00 | Kendrapara |
| 2 | Simlipal NP | 1980 | 845.70 | Mayurbhanj |

| **Rajasthan** | | | | |
|---|---|---|---|---|
| 1 | Mukundra Hills NP | 2006 | 200.54 | Kota & Chittourgarh |
| 2 | Desert NP | 1992 | 3162.00 | Barmer & Jaisalmer |
| 3 | Keoladeo Ghana NP | 1981 | 28.73 | Bharatpur |
| 4 | Ranthambhore NP | 1980 | 282.00 | Sawai Madhopur |
| 5 | Sariska NP | 1992 | 273.80 | Alwar |
| **Sikkim** | | | | |
| 1 | Khangchendzonga NP | 1977 | 1784.00 | North Sikkim |
| **Tamil Nadu** | | | | |
| 1 | Guindy NP | 1976 | 2.82 | Chennai |
| 2 | Gulf of Mannar Marine NP | 1980 | 6.23 | Ramanathpuram & Tuticorin |
| 3 | Indira Gandhi (Annamalai) NP | 1989 | 117.10 | Coimbatore |
| 4 | Mudumalai NP | 1990 | 103.23 | Nilgiris |
| 5 | Mukurthi NP | 1990 | 78.46 | Nilgiris |
| **Telangana** | | | | |
| 1 | Kasu Brahmananda Reddy NP | 1994 | 1.43 | Hyderabad |
| 2 | Mahaveer Harina Vanasthali NP | 1994 | 14.59 | Ranga Reddy |
| 3 | Mrugavani NP | 1994 | 3.60 | Ranga Reddy |
| **Tripura** | | | | |
| 1 | Clouded Leopard NP | 2007 | 5.08 | West Tripura |
| 2 | Bison (Rajbari) NP | 2007 | 31.63 | South Tripura |
| **Uttar Pradesh** | | | | |
| 1 | Dudhwa NP | 1977 | 490.00 | Lakhimpur-Kheri |
| **Uttarakhand** | | | | |
| 1 | Corbett NP | 1936 | 520.82 | Nainital & Pauri Garhwal |
| 2 | Gangotri NP | 1989 | 2390.02 | Uttarkashi |
| 3 | Govind NP | 1990 | 472.08 | Uttarkashi |
| 4 | Nanda Devi NP | 1982 | 624.60 | Chamoli |
| 5 | Rajaji NP | 1983 | 820.00 | Dehradun, Pauri Garhwal & Haridwar |
| 6 | Valley of Flowers NP | 1982 | 87.50 | Chamoli |
| **West Bengal** | | | | |

| | | | | |
|---|---|---|---|---|
| 1 | Buxa NP | 1992 | 117.10 | Jalpaiguri |
| 2 | Gorumara NP | 1992 | 79.45 | Jalpaiguri |
| 3 | Jaldapara NP | 2014 | 216.51 | Jalpaiguri |
| 4 | Neora Valley NP | 1986 | 159.89 | Darjeeling |
| 5 | Singalila NP | 1986 | 78.60 | Darjeeling |
| 6 | Sunderban NP | 1984 | 1330.10 | North & South 24-Paraganas |

*Source*: Wildlife Institute of India

**State-wise break up of Wildlife Sanctuaries (As on February, 2016)**

| S. No. | Name of State/ Protected Area | Year of Establishment | Area (km$^2$) | District (s) |
|---|---|---|---|---|
| **Andaman & Nicobar Islands** | | | | |
| 1 | Arial Island WLS | 1987 | 0.05 | Andaman |
| 2 | Bamboo Island WLS | 1987 | 0.05 | Andaman |
| 3 | Barren Island WLS | 1987 | 8.10 | Andaman |
| 4 | Battimalv Island WLS | 1987 | 2.23 | Nicobar |
| 5 | Belle Island WLS | 1987 | 0.08 | Andaman |
| 6 | Benett Island WLS | 1987 | 3.46 | Andaman |
| 7 | Bingham Island WLS | 1987 | 0.08 | Andaman |
| 8 | Blister Island WLS | 1987 | 0.26 | Andaman |
| 9 | Bluff Island WLS | 1987 | 1.14 | Andaman |
| 10 | Bondoville Island WLS | 1987 | 2.55 | Andaman |
| 11 | Brush Island WLS | 1987 | 0.23 | Andaman |
| 12 | Buchanan Island WLS | 1987 | 9.33 | Andaman |
| 13 | Chanel Island WLS | 1987 | 0.13 | Andaman |
| 14 | Cinque Islands WLS | 1987 | 9.51 | Andaman |
| 15 | Clyde Island WLS | 1987 | 0.54 | Andaman |
| 16 | Cone Island WLS | 1987 | 0.65 | Andaman |
| 17 | Curlew (B.P.) Island WLS | 1987 | 0.16 | Andaman |
| 18 | Curlew Island WLS | 1987 | 0.03 | Andaman |
| 19 | Cuthbert Bay WLS | 1997 | 5.82 | Andaman |
| 20 | Defence Island WLS | 1987 | 10.49 | Andaman |
| 21 | Dot Island WLS | 1987 | 0.13 | Andaman |
| 22 | Dottrell Island WLS | 1987 | 0.13 | Andaman |
| 23 | Duncan Island WLS | 1987 | 0.73 | Andaman |
| 24 | East Island WLS | 1987 | 6.11 | Andaman |

| | | | | |
|---|---|---|---|---|
| 25 | East of Inglis Island WLS | 1987 | 3.55 | Andaman |
| 26 | Egg Island WLS | 1987 | 0.05 | Andaman |
| 27 | Elat Island WLS | 1987 | 9.36 | Andaman |
| 28 | Entrance Island WLS | 1987 | 0.96 | Andaman |
| 29 | Gander Island WLS | 1987 | 0.05 | Andaman |
| 30 | Galathea Bay WLS | 1997 | 11.44 | Nicobar |
| 31 | Girjan Island WLS | 1987 | 0.16 | Andaman |
| 32 | Goose Island WLS | 1987 | 0.01 | Andaman |
| 33 | Hump Island WLS | 1987 | 0.47 | Andaman |
| 34 | Interview Island WLS | 1987 | 133.87 | Andaman |
| 35 | James Island WLS | 1987 | 2.10 | Andaman |
| 36 | Jungle Island WLS | 1987 | 0.52 | Andaman |
| 37 | Kwangtung Island WLS | 1987 | 0.57 | Andaman |
| 38 | Kyd Island WLS | 1987 | 8.00 | Andaman |
| 39 | Landfall Island WLS | 1987 | 29.48 | Andaman |
| 40 | Latouche Island WLS | 1987 | 0.96 | Andaman |
| 41 | Lohabarrack (Saltwater Crocodile) WLS | 1987 | 22.21 | Andaman |
| 42 | Mangrove Island WLS | 1987 | 0.39 | Andaman |
| 43 | Mask Island WLS | 1987 | 0.78 | Andaman |
| 44 | Mayo Island WLS | 1987 | 0.10 | Andaman |
| 45 | Megapode Island WLS | 1987 | 0.12 | Nicobar |
| 46 | Montogemery Island WLS | 1987 | 0.21 | Andaman |
| 47 | Narcondam Island WLS | 1987 | 6.81 | Andaman |
| 48 | North Brother Island WLS | 1987 | 0.75 | Andaman |
| 49 | North Island WLS | 1987 | 0.49 | Andaman |
| 50 | North Reef Island WLS | 1987 | 3.48 | Andaman |
| 51 | Oliver Island WLS | 1987 | 0.16 | Andaman |
| 52 | Orchid Island WLS | 1987 | 0.10 | Andaman |
| 53 | Ox Island WLS | 1987 | 0.13 | Andaman |
| 54 | Oyster Island-I WLS | 1987 | 0.08 | Andaman |
| 55 | Oyster Island-II WLS | 1987 | 0.21 | Andaman |
| 56 | Paget Island WLS | 1987 | 7.36 | Andaman |
| 57 | Parkinson Island WLS | 1987 | 0.34 | Andaman |
| 58 | Passage Island WLS | 1987 | 0.62 | Andaman |
| 59 | Patric Island WLS | 1987 | 0.13 | Andaman |
| 60 | Peacock Island WLS | 1987 | 0.62 | Andaman |

| | | | | |
|---|---|---|---|---|
| 61 | Pitman Island WLS | 1987 | 1.37 | Andaman |
| 62 | Point Island WLS | 1987 | 3.07 | Andaman |
| 63 | Potanma Islands WLS | 1987 | 0.16 | Andaman |
| 64 | Ranger Island WLS | 1987 | 4.26 | Andaman |
| 65 | Reef Island WLS | 1987 | 1.74 | Andaman |
| 66 | Roper Island WLS | 1987 | 1.46 | Andaman |
| 67 | Ross Island WLS | 1987 | 1.01 | Andaman |
| 68 | Rowe Island WLS | 1987 | 0.01 | Andaman |
| 69 | Sandy Island WLS | 1987 | 1.58 | Andaman |
| 70 | Sea Serpent Island WLS | 1987 | 0.78 | Andaman |
| 71 | Shark Island WLS | 1987 | 0.60 | Andaman |
| 72 | Shearme Island WLS | 1987 | 7.85 | Andaman |
| 73 | Sir Hugh Rose Island WLS | 1987 | 1.06 | Andaman |
| 74 | Sisters Island WLS | 1987 | 0.36 | Andaman |
| 75 | Snake Island-I WLS | 1987 | 0.73 | Andaman |
| 76 | Snake Island-II WLS | 1987 | 0.03 | Andaman |
| 77 | South Brother Island WLS | 1987 | 1.24 | Andaman |
| 78 | South Reef Island WLS | 1987 | 1.17 | Andaman |
| 79 | South Sentinel Island WLS | 1987 | 1.61 | Andaman |
| 80 | Spike Island-I WLS | 1987 | 0.42 | Andaman |
| 81 | Spike Island-II WLS | 1987 | 11.70 | Andaman |
| 82 | Stoat Island WLS | 1987 | 0.44 | Andaman |
| 83 | Surat Island WLS | 1987 | 0.31 | Andaman |
| 84 | Swamp Island WLS | 1987 | 4.09 | Andaman |
| 85 | Table (Delgarno) Island WLS | 1987 | 2.29 | Andaman |
| 86 | Table (Excelsior) Island WLS | 1987 | 1.69 | Andaman |
| 87 | Talabaicha Island WLS | 1987 | 3.21 | Andaman |
| 88 | Temple Island WLS | 1987 | 1.04 | Andaman |
| 89 | Tillongchang Island WLS | 1985 | 16.83 | Nicobar |
| 90 | Tree Island WLS | 1987 | 0.03 | Andaman |
| 91 | Trilby Island WLS | 1987 | 0.96 | Andaman |
| 92 | Tuft Island WLS | 1987 | 0.29 | Andaman |
| 93 | Turtle Islands WLS | 1987 | 0.39 | Andaman |
| 94 | West Island WLS | 1987 | 6.40 | Andaman |
| 95 | Wharf Island WLS | 1987 | 0.11 | Andaman |

| 96 | White Cliff Island WLS | 1987 | 0.47 | Andaman |
|---|---|---|---|---|
| **Andhra Pradesh** | | | | |
| 1 | Coringa WLS | 1978 | 235.70 | East Godavari |
| 2 | Gundla Brahmeswaram WLS | 1990 | 1194.00 | Kurnool & Prakasam |
| 3 | Kambalakonda WLS | 2002 | 71.39 | Visakhapatnam |
| 4 | Koundinya WLS | 1990 | 357.60 | Chittoor |
| 5 | Kolleru WLS | 1953 | 308.55 | West Godavari & Krishna |
| 6 | Krishna WLS | 1989 | 194.81 | Krishna & Guntur |
| 7 | Nagarjuna Sagar-Srisailam WLS | 1978 | 3568.09* | Guntur, Prakasam & Kurnool |
| 8 | Nellapattu WLS | 1976 | 4.59 | Nellore |
| 9 | Pulicat Lake WLS | 1976 | 500.00 | Nellore |
| 10 | Rollapadu WLS | 1988 | 6.14 | Kurnool |
| 11 | Sri Lankamalleswara WLS | 1988 | 464.42 | Cuddapah |
| 12 | Sri Penusila Narasimha WLS | 1997 | 1030.85 | Cuddapah & Nellore |
| 13 | Sri Venkateswara WLS | 1985 | 172.35 | Cuddapah & Chittoor |
| | *combined area with Telangana | | | |
| **Arunachal Pradesh** | | | | |
| 1 | D'Ering Memorial (Lali) WLS | 1978 | 190.00 | Upper Siang |
| 2 | Dibang WLS | 1991 | 4149.00 | Dibang Valley |
| 3 | Eagle Nest WLS | 1989 | 217.00 | West Kameng |
| 4 | Itanagar WLS | 1978 | 140.30 | Papum Pare |
| 5 | Kamlang WLS | 1989 | 783.00 | Lohit |
| 6 | Kane WLS | 1991 | 31.00 | West Siang |
| 7 | Mahao WLS | 1980 | 281.50 | Dibang Valley |
| 8 | Pakke (Pakhui) WLS | 1977 | 861.95 | East Kameng |
| 9 | Sessa Orchid WLS | 1989 | 100.00 | West Kameng |
| 10 | Tale WLS | 1995 | 337.00 | Lower Subansiri |
| 11 | Yordi Rabe Supse WLS | 1996 | 397.00 | West Siang |
| **Assam** | | | | |

| | | | | |
|---|---|---|---|---|
| 1 | Amchang WLS | 2004 | 78.64 | Kamrup |
| 2 | Barail WLS | 2004 | 326.24 | Cachar Karimgang |
| 3 | Barnadi WLS | 1980 | 26.22 | Udalguri (Darrang) |
| 4 | Bherjan-Borajan-Padumoni WLS | 1999 | 7.22 | Tinsukia |
| 5 | Burachapari WLS | 1995 | 44.06 | Sonitpur |
| 6 | Chakrasila WLS | 1994 | 45.57 | Dhubri |
| 7 | Deepor Beel WLS | | 4.14 | Guwahati |
| 8 | Dihing Patkai WLS | 2004 | 111.19 | Dibrugarh & Tinsukia |
| 9 | East Karbi Anglong WLS | 2000 | 221.81 | Karbi-Anglong |
| 10 | Garampani WLS | 1952 | 6.05 | Karbi-Anglong |
| 11 | Hollongapar Gibbon WLS | 1997 | 20.98 | Jorhat |
| 12 | Lawkhowa WLS | 1972 | 70.13 | Nagaon |
| 13 | Marat Longri WLS | 2003 | 451.00 | Karbi-Anglong |
| 14 | Nambor WLS | 2000 | 37.00 | Karbi-Anglong |
| 15 | Nambor-Doigrung WLS | 2003 | 97.15 | Karbi-Anglong |
| 16 | Pabitora WLS | 1987 | 38.81 | Marigaon |
| 17 | Pani-Dihing Bird WLS | 1995 | 33.93 | Sibsagar |
| 18 | Sonai Rupai WLS | 1998 | 220.00 | Sonitpur |
| **Bihar** | | | | |
| 1 | Barela Jheel Salim Ali Bird WLS | 1997 | 1.96 | Vaishali |
| 2 | Bhimbandh WLS | 1976 | 681.99 | Munger |
| 3 | Gautam Budha WLS | 1976 | 138.34 | Gaya |
| 4 | Kaimur WLS | 1982 | 1342.00 | Rohtas |
| 5 | Kanwarjheel WLS | 1989 | 63.11 | Begusarai |
| 6 | Kusheshwar Asthan Bird WLS | 1994 | 29.17 | Darbhnaga |
| 7 | Nagi Dam WLS | 1987 | 1.92 | Jamui |
| 8 | Nakti Dam WLS | 1987 | 3.33 | Jamui |
| 9 | Pant (Rajgir) WLS | 1978 | 35.84 | Nalanda |
| 10 | Udaipur WLS | 1978 | 8.87 | Pashchim Champaran |
| 11 | Valmiki WLS | 1978 | 545.15 | Pashchim Champaran |

| | | | | |
|---|---|---|---|---|
| 12 | Vikramshila Gangetic Dolphin WLS | 1990 | 50.00 | Bhagalpur |
| **Chandigarh (UT)** | | | | |
| 1 | City Bird WLS | 1998 | 0.03 | Chandigarh |
| 2 | Sukhna Lake WLS | 1986 | 25.98 | Chandigarh |
| **Chhattisgarh** | | | | |
| 1 | Achanakmar WLS | 1975 | 551.55 | Bilaspur |
| 2 | Badalkhol WLS | 1975 | 104.45 | Jashpur |
| 3 | Barnawapara WLS | 1976 | 244.66 | Raipur |
| 4 | Bhairamgarh WLS | 1983 | 138.95 | Dantewada |
| 5 | Bhoramdev WLS | 2001 | 351.24 | Kawardha |
| 6 | Sarangarh-Gomardha WLS | 1975 | 277.82 | Raigarh |
| 7 | Pamed Wild Buffalo WLS | 1985 | 262.12 | Dantewada |
| 8 | Semarsot WLS | 1978 | 430.35 | Surguja |
| 9 | Sitanadi WLS | 1974 | 553.36 | Dhamtari |
| 10 | Tamor Pingla WLS | 1978 | 608.51 | Surguja |
| 11 | Udanti Wild Buffalo WLS | 1985 | 237.27 | Raipur |
| **Dadra & Nagar Haveli (UT)** | | | | |
| 1 | Dadra & Nagar Haveli WLS | 2000 | 92.16 | Dadra & Nagar Haveli |
| **Daman & Diu (UT)** | | | | |
| 1 | Fudam WLS | 1991 | 2.18 | Diu |
| **Delhi** | | | | |
| 1 | Asola Bhati (Indira Priyadarshini) WLS | 1992 | 27.82 | South Delhi |
| | **Goa** | | | |
| 1 | Bondla WLS | 1969 | 7.95 | North Goa |
| 2 | Dr. Salim Ali Bird (Chorao) WLS | 1988 | 1.78 | North Goa |
| 3 | Cotigaon WLS | 1968 | 85.65 | South Goa |
| 4 | Madei WLS | 1999 | 208.48 | North Goa |
| 5 | Bhagwan Mahavir WLS | 1967 | 133.00 | North Goa |
| 6 | Netravali WLS | 1999 | 211.05 | South Goa |
| **Gujarat** | | | | |
| 1 | Balaram Ambaji WLS | 1989 | 542.08 | Banas Kantha |
| 2 | Barda WLS | 1979 | 192.31 | Jamnagar & Porbandar |

| | | | | |
|---|---|---|---|---|
| 3 | Gaga (Great Indian Bustard) WLS | 1988 | 3.33 | Jamnagar |
| 4 | Gir WLS | 1965 | 1153.42 | Junagadh & Amreli |
| 5 | Girnar WLS | 2008 | 178.80 | Junagadh |
| 6 | Hingolgadh WLS | 1980 | 6.54 | Rajkot |
| 7 | Jambughoda WLS | 1990 | 130.38 | Panchmahal |
| 8 | Jessore Sloth Bear WLS | 1978 | 180.66 | Banas Kantha |
| 9 | Kachchh (Lala) Great Indian Bustard WLS | 1995 | 2.03 | Kachchh |
| 10 | Kachchh Desert WLS | 1986 | 7506.22 | Kachchh |
| 11 | Khijadiya Bird WLS | 1981 | 6.05 | Jamnagar |
| 12 | Marine (Gulf of Kachchh) WLS | 1980 | 295.03 | Jamnagar |
| 13 | Mitiyala WLS | 2004 | 18.22 | Amreli |
| 14 | Nal Sarovar Bird WLS | 1969 | 120.82 | Ahmadabad & Surendrnagar |
| 15 | Narayan Sarovar Chinkara WLS | 1995 | 442.91 | Kachchh |
| 16 | Paniya WLS | 1989 | 39.63 | Amreli |
| 17 | Porbandar Bird WLS | 1988 | 0.09 | Porbander |
| 18 | Purna WLS | 1990 | 160.84 | Dangs |
| 19 | Rampara Vidi WLS | 1988 | 15.01 | Rajkot |
| 20 | Ratanmahal Sloth Bear WLS | 1982 | 55.65 | Dahod |
| 21 | Shoolpaneswar (Dhumkhal) WLS | 1982 | 607.70 | Bharuch |
| 22 | Thol Lake WLS | 1988 | 6.99 | Mahesana |
| 23 | Wild Ass WLS | 1973 | 4953.71 | Kachchh, Rajkot, Mahesana & Banas Kantha |
| **Haryana** | | | | |
| 1 | Abubshehar WLS | 1987 | 115.30 | Sirsa |
| 2 | Bhindawas Lake WLS | 1986 | 4.12 | Rohtak |
| 3 | Bir Shikargarh WLS | 1987 | 7.67 | Panchkula |
| 4 | Chhilchhila Lake WLS | 1986 | 0.29 | Kaithal |
| 5 | Kalesar WLS | 1996 | 54.06 | Yamuna Nagar |
| 6 | Khaparwas WLS | 1991 | 0.83 | Jhajjar |

| 7 | Morni Hills (Khol-Hi-Rai-tan) WLS | 2004 | 48.83 | Panchkula |
|---|---|---|---|---|
| 8 | Nahar WLS | 1987 | 2.11 | Rewari |
| **Himachal Pradesh** | | | | |
| 1 | Bandli WLS | 1962 | 32.11 | Mandi |
| 2 | Chail WLS | 1976 | 16.00 | Solan & Shimla |
| 3 | Chandratal WLS | 2007 | 38.56 | Lahul & Spiti |
| 4 | Churdhar WLS | 1985 | 55.52 | Sirmaur & Shimla |
| 5 | Daranghati WLS | 1962 | 171.50 | Shimla |
| 6 | Dhauladhar WLS | 1994 | 982.86 | Kangra |
| 7 | Gamgul Siyabehi WLS | 1962 | 108.40 | Chamba |
| 8 | Kais WLS | 1954 | 12.61 | Kullu |
| 9 | Kalatop-Khajjiar WLS | 1958 | 17.17 | Chamba |
| 10 | Kanawar WLS | 1954 | 107.29 | Kullu |
| 11 | Khokhan WLS | 1954 | 14.94 | Kullu |
| 12 | Kibber WLS | 1992 | 2220.12 | Lahaul & Spiti |
| 13 | Kugti WLS | 1962 | 405.49 | Chamba |
| 14 | Lippa Asrang WLS | 1962 | 31.00 | Kinnaur |
| 15 | Majathal WLS | 1954 | 30.86 | Solan |
| 16 | Manali WLS | 1954 | 29.00 | Kullu |
| 17 | Nargu WLS | 1962 | 132.3731 | Kullu |
| 18 | Pong Dam Lake WLS | 1982 | 207.59 | Kangra |
| 19 | Renuka WLS | 2013 | 4.00 | Sirmaur |
| 20 | Rupi Bhaba WLS | 1982 | 503.00 | Kinnaur |
| 21 | Sainj WLS | 1994 | 90.00 | Kullu |
| 22 | Rakchham Chitkul (Sangla Valley) WLS | 1989 | 304.00 | Kinnaur |
| 23 | Sech Tuan Nala WLS | 1962 | 390.29 | Chamba |
| 24 | Shikari Devi WLS | 1962 | 29.94 | Mandi |
| 25 | Shimla Water Catchment WLS | 1958 | 10.00 | Shimla |
| 26 | Talra WLS | 1962 | 16.18 | Shimla |
| 27 | Tirthan WLS | 1992 | 61.00 | Kullu |
| 28 | Tundah WLS | 1962 | 64.00 | Chamba |
| **Jammu & Kashmir** | | | | |
| 1 | Baltal-Thajwas WLS | 1987 | 210.50 | Ganderbal |
| 2 | Changthang WLS | 1987 | 4000.00 | Leh |

| | | | | |
|---|---|---|---|---|
| 3 | Gulmarg WLS | 1987 | 180.00 | Baramulla |
| 4 | Hirapora WLS | 1987 | 110.00 | Shopian |
| 5 | Hokersar WLS | 1992 | 13.75 | Srinagar |
| 6 | Jasrota WLS | 1987 | 25.75 | Kathua |
| 7 | Karakoram (Nubra Shyok) WLS | 1987 | 5000.00 | Leh |
| 8 | Lachipora WLS | 1987 | 80.00 | Baramulla |
| 9 | Limber WLS | 1987 | 26.00 | Baramulla |
| 10 | Nandni WLS | 1981 | 33.34 | Jammu |
| 11 | Overa-Aru WLS | 1987 | 425.00 | Anantnag |
| 12 | Rajparian (Daksum) WLS | 2002 | 20.00 | Anantnag |
| 13 | Ramnagar Rakha WLS | 1981 | 31.50 | Jammu |
| 14 | Surinsar Mansar WLS | 1981 | 55.50 | Udhampur, Samba & Jammu |
| 15 | Trikuta WLS | 1981 | 31.77 | Udhampur |
| **Jharkhand** | | | | |
| 1 | Dalma WLS | 1976 | 193.22 | East Singhbhum & Saraikela |
| 2 | Gautam Budha | 1976 | 121.14 | Koderma & Hazaribagh |
| 3 | Hazaribagh WLS | 1976 | 186.25 | Hazaribagh |
| 4 | Kodarma WLS | 1985 | 177.35 | Koderma |
| 5 | Lawalong WLS | 1978 | 211.03 | Chatra |
| 6 | Mahuadanr Wolf WLS | 1976 | 63.26 | Latehar |
| 7 | Palamau WLS | 1976 | 752.94 | Latehar |
| 8 | Palkot WLS | 1990 | 182.83 | Gumla & Simdega |
| 9 | Parasnath WLS | 1984 | 49.33 | Giridih |
| 10 | Topchanchi WLS | 1978 | 12.82 | Dhanbad |
| 11 | Udhwa Lake Bird WLS | 1991 | 5.65 | Sahebganj |
| **Karnataka** | | | | |
| 1 | Adichunchunagiri Peacock WLS | 1981 | 0.84 | Mandya |
| 2 | Arabithittu WLS | 1985 | 13.50 | Mysore |
| 3 | Attiveri Bird WLS | 1994 | 2.22 | Uttara Kannada |
| 4 | Bhadra WLS | 1974 | 492.46 | Chikmagalur & Shimoga |

| | | | | |
|---|---|---|---|---|
| 5 | Bhimgad WLS | 2010 | 190.42 | Belgaum |
| 6 | Biligiri Rangaswamy Temple (B.R.T.) WLS | 1987 | 539.52 | Chamarajanagar |
| 7 | Brahmagiri WLS | 1974 | 181.29 | Kodagu |
| 8 | Cauvery WLS | 1987 | 1027.53 | Mysore, Bangalore & Mandya |
| 9 | Chincholi WLS | 2012 | 134.88 | Gulbarga & Yadgir |
| 10 | Dandeli WLS | 1987 | 886.41 | Uttara Kannada |
| 11 | Daroji Bear WLS | 1992 | 82.72 | Bellary |
| 12 | Ghataprabha Bird WLS | 1974 | 29.79 | Belgaum |
| 13 | Gudavi Bird WLS | 1989 | 0.73 | Shimoga |
| 14 | Gudekote Sloth Bear WLS | 2013 | 38.48 | Bellary |
| 15 | Malai Mahadeshwara WLS | 2013 | 906.19 | Chamarajanagar |
| 16 | Melkote Temple WLS | 1974 | 49.82 | Mandya |
| 17 | Mookambika WLS | 1974 | 370.37 | Udipi |
| 18 | Nugu WLS | 1974 | 30.32 | Mysore |
| 19 | Pushpagiri WLS | 1987 | 102.96 | Kodagu & Dakshina Kannada |
| 20 | Ranebennur Black Buck WLS | 1974 | 119.00 | Dharwad |
| 21 | Ranganathittu Bird WLS | 1940 | 0.67 | Mysore |
| 22 | Ramadevara Betta Vulture WLS | 2012 | 3.46 | Ramanagara |
| 23 | Rangayyanadurga Four-horned antelope | 2011 | 77.24 | Davangere |
| 24 | Sharavathi Valley WLS | 1974 | 431.23 | Shimoga |
| 25 | Shettihalli WLS | 1974 | 395.60 | Shimoga |
| 26 | Someshwara WLS | 1974 | 314.25 | Udipi |
| 27 | Talakaveri WLS | 1987 | 105.01 | Kodagu |
| **Kerala** | | | | |
| 1 | Aralam WLS | 1984 | 55.00 | Kannur |
| 2 | Chimmony WLS | 1984 | 85.00 | Thrissur |
| 3 | Chinnar WLS | 1984 | 90.44 | Idukki |
| 4 | Chulannur Peafowl WLS | 2007 | 3.42 | Thrissur & Palakkad |
| 5 | Idukki WLS | 1976 | 70.00 | Idukki |

| | | | | |
|---|---|---|---|---|
| 6 | Kottiyoor WLS | 2011 | 30.38 | Kannur |
| 7 | Kurinjimala WLS | 2006 | 32.00 | Idukki |
| 8 | Malabar WLS | 2010 | 74.22 | Kozhikode |
| 9 | Mangalavanam Bird WLS | 2004 | 0.03 | Ernakulam |
| 10 | Neyyar WLS | 1958 | 128.00 | Thiruvanantha-puram |
| 11 | Parambikulam WLS | 1973 | 285.00 | Palakkad |
| 12 | Peechi-Vazhani WLS | 1958 | 125.00 | Thrissur |
| 13 | Peppara WLS | 1983 | 53.00 | Thiruvanantha-puram |
| 14 | Periyar WLS | 1950 | 427.00 | Idukki |
| 15 | Shendurney WLS | 1984 | 100.32 | Ouilon |
| 16 | Thattekad Bird WLS | 1983 | 25.00 | Idukki |
| 17 | Wayanad WLS | 1973 | 344.44 | Wayanad |
| **Lakshadweep (UT)** | | | | |
| 1 | Pitti (Bird Island) WLS | 1995 | 0.01 | Lakshadweep |
| **Madhya Pradesh** | | | | |
| 1 | Bagdara WLS | 1978 | 478.00 | Sidhi |
| 2 | Bori WLS | 1977 | 485.72 | Hoshangabad |
| 3 | Gandhi Sagar WLS | 1981 | 368.62 | Mandsaur & Neemuch |
| 4 | Ghatigaon WLS | 1981 | 511.00 | Gwalior |
| 5 | Karera WLS | 1981 | 202.21 | Shivpuri |
| 6 | Ken Gharial WLS | 1981 | 45.20 | Panna & Chha-tarpur |
| 7 | Kheoni WLS | 1982 | 122.70 | Dewas & Sehore |
| 8 | Narsighgarh WLS | 1978 | 59.19 | Raigarh |
| 9 | National Chambal WLS | 1978 | 435.00 | Morena & Bhind |
| 10 | Noradehi WLS | 1984 | 1194.67 | Damoh, Sagar & Narsimhapur |
| 11 | Orcha WLS | 1994 | 44.91 | Tikamgarh |
| 12 | Pachmarhi WLS | 1977 | 417.78 | Hoshngabad |
| 13 | Kuno WLS | 1981 | 344.68 | Morena |
| 14 | Panna (Gangau) WLS | 1979 | 68.14 | Panna |
| 15 | Panpatha WLS | 1983 | 245.84 | Umaria |
| 16 | Pench WLS | 1975 | 118.47 | Seoni & Ch-hindwara |

| | | | | |
|---|---|---|---|---|
| 17 | Phen WLS | 1983 | 110.74 | Mandla |
| 18 | Ralamandal WLS | 1989 | 2.35 | Indore |
| 19 | Ratapani WLS | 1978 | 823.84 | Raisen |
| 20 | Sailana WLS | 1983 | 12.96 | Ratlam |
| 21 | Sanjay Dubari WLS | 1975 | 364.59 | Sidhi |
| 22 | Sardarpur WLS | 1983 | 348.12 | Dhar |
| 23 | Singhori WLS | 1976 | 287.91 | Raisen |
| 24 | Son Gharial WLS | 1981 | 41.80 | Sidhi, Shahdol & Satna |
| 25 | Veerangna Durgavati WLS | 1997 | 23.97 | Damoh |
| **Maharashtra** | | | | |
| 1 | Amba Barwa WLS | 1997 | 127.11 | Buldhana |
| 2 | Andhari WLS | 1986 | 509.27 | Chandrapur |
| 3 | Aner Dam WLS | 1986 | 82.94 | Dhule |
| 4 | Bhamragarh WLS | 1997 | 104.38 | Gadchiroli |
| 5 | Bhimashankar WLS | 1985 | 130.78 | Pune & Thane |
| 6 | Bor WLS | 1970 | 61.10 | Wardha & Nagpur |
| 7 | Chaprala WLS | 1986 | 134.78 | Gadchiroli |
| 8 | Deulgaon-Rehekuri WLS | 1980 | 2.17 | Ahmednagar |
| 9 | Dhyanganga WLS | 1997 | 205.23 | Buldhana |
| 10 | Gautala-Autramghat WLS | 1986 | 260.61 | Aurangabad & Jalgaon |
| 11 | Great Indian Bustard WLS | 1979 | 1222.61 | Solapur & Ahmednagar |
| 12 | Jaikwadi WLS | 1986 | 341.05 | Aurangabad & Ahmednagar |
| 13 | Kalsubai Harishchandragad WLS | 1986 | 361.71 | Ahmednagar |
| 14 | Karnala Fort WLS | 1968 | 4.48 | Raigad |
| 15 | Karanja Sohal Blackbuck WLS | 2000 | 18.32 | Akola |
| 16 | Katepurna WLS | 1988 | 73.63 | Akola & Washim |
| 17 | Koyana WLS | 1985 | 423.55 | Satara |
| 18 | Lonar WLS | 2000 | 1.17 | Buldhana |
| 19 | Malvan Marine WLS | 1987 | 29.12 | Sindhudurg |
| 20 | Mansingdeo WLS | 2010 | 182.59 | Nagpur |
| 21 | Mayureswar Supe WLS | 1997 | 5.15 | Pune |

| | | | | |
|---|---|---|---|---|
| 22 | Melghat WLS | 1985 | 778.75 | Amravati |
| 23 | Nagzira WLS | 1970 | 152.81 | Gondia, Bhandara |
| 24 | Naigaon Peacock WLS | 1994 | 29.89 | Beed |
| 25 | Nandur Madhameshwar WLS | 1986 | 100.12 | Nashik |
| 26 | Narnala Bird WLS | 1997 | 12.35 | Akola |
| 27 | Nawegaon WLS | 2012 | 122.76 | Gondia |
| 28 | New Bor WLS | 2012 | 60.70 | Nagpur-Wardha |
| 29 | New Nagzira WLS | 2012 | 151.33 | Gondia |
| 30 | Painganga WLS | 1986 | 324.62 | Yeotmal & Nanded |
| 31 | Phansad WLS | 1986 | 69.79 | Raigad |
| 32 | Radhanagari WLS | 1958 | 351.16 | Kolhapur |
| 33 | Sagareshwar WLS | 1985 | 10.87 | Sangali |
| 34 | Tansa WLS | 1970 | 304.81 | Thane |
| 35 | Thane Creek Flamingo WLS | 2015 | 16.905 | Mumbai Suburban |
| 36 | Tipeshwar WLS | 1997 | 148.63 | Yeotmal |
| 37 | Tungareshwar WLS | 2003 | 85.00 | Thane |
| 38 | Yawal WLS | 1969 | 177.52 | Jalgaon |
| 39 | Yedsi Ramlin Ghat WLS | 1997 | 22.38 | Aurangabad (Osmanabad) |
| 40 | Umred-Kharngla WLS | 2012 | 189.30 | Nagpur & Bhandara |
| 41 | Wan WLS | 1997 | 211.00 | Amravati |
| **Manipur** | | | | |
| 1 | Yangoupokpi Lokchao WLS | 1989 | 184.40 | Chandel |
| **Meghalaya** | | | | |
| 1 | Baghmara Pitcher Plant WLS | 1984 | 0.02 | South Garo Hills |
| 2 | Nongkhyllem WLS | 1981 | 29.00 | Ri-Bhoi (North Khasi Hills) |
| 3 | Siju WLS | 1979 | 5.18 | South Garo Hills |
| **Mizoram** | | | | |
| 1 | Dampa WLS | 1985 | 500.00 | Mamit |
| 2 | Khawnglung WLS | 1992 | 35.00 | Serchhip |

| 3 | Lengteng WLS | 1999 | 60.00 | Champhai |
|---|---|---|---|---|
| 4 | Ngengpui WLS | 1991 | 110.00 | Lawngtlai |
| 5 | Pualreng WLS | 2004 | 50.00 | Kolasib |
| 6 | Tawi WLS | 1978 | 35.75 | Aizawl |
| 7 | Thorangtlang WLS | 2002 | 50.00 | Serchhip |
| 8 | Tokalo WLS | 2007 | 250.00 | Saiha |
| **Nagaland** | | | | |
| 1 | Fakim WLS | 1980 | 6.41 | Tuensang |
| 2 | Puliebadze WLS | 1980 | 9.23 | Kohima |
| 3 | Rangapahar WLS | 1986 | 4.70 | Dimapur |
| **Odisha** | | | | |
| 1 | Badrama WLS | 1962 | 304.03 | Sambalpur |
| 2 | Baisipalli WLS | 1981 | 168.35 | Nayagarh |
| 3 | Balukhand Konark WLS | 1984 | 71.72 | Puri |
| 4 | Bhitarkanika WLS | 1975 | 525.00 | Kendrapara |
| 5 | Chandaka Dampara WLS | 1982 | 175.79 | Khurda & Cuttack |
| 6 | Chilika (Nalaban) WLS | 1987 | 15.53 | Khurda, Puri & Ganjam |
| 7 | Debrigarh WLS | 1985 | 346.91 | Sambalpur |
| 8 | Gahirmatha (Marine) WLS | 1997 | 1435.00 | Kendrapara |
| 9 | Hadgarh WLS | 1978 | 191.06 | Keonjhar & Mayurbhanj |
| 10 | Karlapat WLS | 1992 | 147.66 | Kalahandi |
| 11 | Khalasuni WLS | 1982 | 116.00 | Sambalpur |
| 12 | Kothagarh WLS | 1981 | 399.50 | Phulbani |
| 13 | Kuldiha WLS | 1984 | 272.75 | Balasore |
| 14 | Lakhari Valley WLS | 1985 | 185.87 | Gajapati |
| 15 | Nandankanan WLS | 1979 | 14.16 | Khurda |
| 16 | Satkosia Gorge WLS | 1976 | 745.52 | Angul, Boudh & Cuttack |
| 17 | Simlipal WLS | 1979 | 1354.30 | Mayurbhanj |
| 18 | Sunabeda WLS | 1988 | 500.00 | Nuapada |
| **Puducherry (UT)** | | | | |
| 1 | Oussudu WLS | 2008 | 3.90 | Pondicherry |
| **Punjab** | | | | |
| 1 | Abohar WLS | 1988 | 186.50 | Firozpur |

| | | | | |
|---|---|---|---|---|
| 2 | Bir Aishvan WLS | 1952 | 2.64 | Sangrur |
| 3 | Bir Bhadson WLS | 1952 | 10.23 | Patiala |
| 4 | Bir Bunerheri WLS | 1952 | 6.62 | Patiala |
| 5 | Bir Dosanjh WLS | 1952 | 5.18 | Patiala |
| 6 | Bir Gurdialpura WLS | 1977 | 6.20 | Patiala |
| 7 | Bir Mehaswala WLS | 1952 | 1.23 | Patiala |
| 8 | Bir Motibagh WLS | 1952 | 6.54 | Patiala |
| 9 | Harike Lake WLS | 1982 | 86.00 | Firozpur |
| 10 | Jhajjar Bacholi WLS | 1998 | 1.16 | Ropar |
| 11 | Kathlaur Kushlian WLS | 2007 | 7.58 | Gurdaspur |
| 12 | Takhni-Rehampur WLS | 1992 | 3.82 | Hoshiarpur |
| 13 | Nangal WLS | 2009 | 2.90 | Rupnagar |
| **Rajasthan** | | | | |
| 1 | Bandh Baratha WLS | 1985 | 199.50 | Bharatpur |
| 2 | Bassi WLS | 1988 | 138.69 | Chittaurgarh |
| 3 | Bhensrodgarh WLS | 1983 | 229.14 | Chittaurgarh |
| 4 | Darrah WLS | 1955 | 80.75 | Kota & Jhal-awar |
| 5 | Jaisamand WLS | 1955 | 52.00 | Udaipur (Rajs-amand) |
| 6 | Jamwa Ramgarh WLS | 1982 | 300.00 | Jaipur |
| 7 | Jawahar Sagar WLS | 1975 | 153.41 | Kota, Bundi & Chittaurgarh |
| 8 | Kailadevi WLS | 1983 | 676.38 | Karouli (Sawai Madhopur) |
| 9 | Kesarbagh WLS | 1955 | 14.76 | Dholpur |
| 10 | Kumbhalgarh WLS | 1971 | 608.58 | Pali, Rajsa-mand, Udaipur |
| 11 | Mount Abu WLS | 1960 | 326.10 | Sirohi |
| 12 | Nahargarh WLS | 1980 | 50.00 | Jaipur |
| 13 | National Chambal WLS | 1979 | 274.75 | Kota, Bundi, Sawai Madho-pur, Dholpur & Karouli |
| 14 | Phulwari Ki Nal WLS | 1983 | 692.68 | Udaipur & Pali |
| 15 | Ramgarh Vishdhari WLS | 1982 | 252.79 | Bundi |
| 16 | Ramsagar WLS | 1955 | 34.40 | Dholpur |
| 17 | Sajjangarh WLS | 1987 | 5.19 | Udaipur |
| 18 | Sariska WLS | 1955 | 219.00 | Alwar |

| | | | | |
|---|---|---|---|---|
| 19 | Sawaimadhopur WLS | 1955 | 131.30 | Sawai Madhopur |
| 20 | Sawai Man Singh WLS | 1984 | 103.25 | Sawai Madhopur |
| 21 | Shergarh WLS | 1983 | 98.71 | Kota (Baran) |
| 22 | Sitamata WLS | 1979 | 422.94 | Chittaurgarh & Udaipur |
| 23 | Tal Chhapar WLS | 1971 | 7.19 | Churu |
| 24 | Todgarh Raoli WLS | 1983 | 495.27 | Ajmer, Pali & Rajsamand |
| 25 | Van Vihar WLS | 1955 | 25.60 | Dholpur |
| **Sikkim** | | | | |
| 1 | Barsey Rhododendron WLS | 1998 | 104.00 | West Sikkim |
| 2 | Fambong Lho WLS | 1984 | 51.76 | East Sikkim |
| 3 | Kitam Bird WLS | 2005 | 6.00 | South Sikkim |
| 4 | Kyongnosla Alpine WLS | 1977 | 31.00 | East Sikkim |
| 5 | Maenam WLS | 1987 | 35.34 | South Sikkim |
| 6 | Pangolakha WLS | 2002 | 128.00 | East Sikkim |
| 7 | Shingba Rhododendron WLS | 1984 | 43.00 | North Sikkim |
| **Tamil Nadu** | | | | |
| 1 | Cauvery North WLS | 2014 | 504.33 | Kishnagiri & Dharmapuri |
| 2 | Chitrangudi Bird WLS | 1989 | 0.48 | Ramanathpuram |
| 3 | Gangaikondam Spotted Dear WLS | 2013 | 2.88 | Tirunelveli |
| 4 | Indira Gandhi (Annamalai) WLS | 1976 | 841.49 | Coimbatore |
| 5 | Kalakad WLS | 1976 | 223.58 | Tirunelveli |
| 6 | Kanjirankulam Bird WLS | 1989 | 1.04 | Ramanathpuram |
| 7 | Kanyakumari WLS | 2002 | 457.78 | Kanyakumari |
| 8 | Karaivetti Bird WLS | 1999 | 4.54 | Perambalur |
| 9 | Karikilli Birds WLS | 1989 | 0.61 | Kanchipuram |
| 10 | Kodaikanal WLS | 2013 | 608.95 | Dindigul & Theni |
| 11 | Koonthankulam-Kadankulam WLS | 1994 | 1.29 | Tirunelveli |

| | | | | |
|---|---|---|---|---|
| 12 | Megamalai | 2016 | 269.11 | Theni |
| 13 | Melaselvanoor-Keelaselva-noor WLS | 1998 | 5.93 | Ramanathpu-ram |
| 14 | Mudumalai WLS | 1942 | 217.76 | Nilgiris |
| 15 | Mundanthurai WLS | 1977 | 567.38 | Tirunelveli |
| 16 | Nellai WLS | 2015 | 356.73 | Tirunelveli |
| 17 | Oussudu Lake Bird Sanc-tuary | 2015 | 3.32 | Villupuram |
| 18 | Point Calimere WLS | 1967 | 17.26 | Nagapattinam |
| 19 | Pulicat Lake Bird WLS | 1980 | 153.67 | Tiruvellore |
| 20 | Sathyamangalam WS | 2008, 2011 | 1411.61 | Erode |
| 21 | Srivilliputhur Grizzled Squirrel WLS | 1988 | 485.20 | Virudhunagar |
| 22 | Theerthangal | 2016 | 0.29 | Ramanathpu-ram |
| 23 | Sakkarakottai | 2016 | 2.30 | Ramanathpu-ram |
| 24 | Udayamarthandapuram Lake WLS | 1991 | 0.45 | Thiruvarur |
| 25 | Vaduvoor Birds WLS | 1991 | 1.28 | Thiruvarur |
| 26 | Vedanthangal Lake Birds WLS | 1936 | 0.30 | Chengalpet |
| 27 | Vellanadu Blackbuck WLS | 1987 | 16.41 | Tuticorin |
| 28 | Vellode Birds WLS | 1997 | 0.77 | Erode |
| 29 | Vettangudi Birds WLS | 1977 | 0.38 | Sivagangai |
| **Telangana** | | | | |
| 1 | Nagarjuna Sagar-Srisailam WLS | 1978 | 3568.09* | Nalgonda & Mahaboob-nagar |
| 2 | Eturnagaram WLS | 1953 | 806.15 | Warangal |
| 3 | Kawal WLS | 1965 | 892.23 | Adilabad |
| 4 | Kinnersani WLS | 1977 | 635.41 | Khammam |
| 5 | Lanja Madugu Siwaram WLS | 1978 | 29.81 | Adilabad & Karimnagar |
| 6 | Manjeera Crocodile WLS | 1978 | 20.00 | Medak |
| 7 | Pakhal WLS | 1952 | 860.00 | Warangal |
| 8 | Pocharam WLS | 1952 | 130.00 | Medak |
| 9 | Pranahita WLS | 1980 | 136.03 | Adilabad |
| | *combined area with Andhra Pradesh | | | |

| Tripura | | | | |
|---|---|---|---|---|
| 1 | Gumti WLS | 1988 | 389.54 | South Tripura |
| 2 | Rowa WLS | 1988 | 0.86 | North Tripura |
| 3 | Sepahijala WLS | 1987 | 13.45 | West Tripura |
| 4 | Trishna WLS | 1988 | 163.08 | South Tripura |
| **Uttar Pradesh** | | | | |
| 1 | Bakhira WLS | 1990 | 28.94 | Sant Kabir Nagar |
| 2 | Chandraprabha WLS | 1957 | 78.00 | Chandauli |
| 3 | Dr. Bhimrao Ambedkar Bird WLS | 2003 | 4.27 | Pratapgarh |
| 4 | Hastinapur WLS | 1986 | 2073.00 | Muzzafar Nagar, Meerut, Muradabad, Ghaziabad, Bijnore & Jyotibhaphuley Nagar |
| 5 | Kaimur WLS | 1982 | 500.73 | Mirzapur & Sonbhadra |
| 6 | Katerniaghat WLS | 1976 | 400.09 | Bahraich |
| 7 | Kishanpur WLS | 1972 | 227.00 | Lakhim-pur-Kheri & Shahjahanpur |
| 8 | Lakh Bahosi Bird WLS | 1988 | 80.24 | Farrukhabad |
| 9 | Mahavir Swami WLS | 1977 | 5.41 | Lalitpur |
| 10 | National Chambal WLS | 1979 | 635.00 | Agra & Etawah |
| 11 | Nawabganj Bird WLS | 1984 | 2.25 | Unnao |
| 12 | Okhala Bird WLS | 1990 | 4.00 | Gautam Budha Nagar (Ghaziabad) |
| 13 | Parvati Aranga WLS | 1990 | 10.84 | Gonda |
| 14 | Patna WLS | 1990 | 1.09 | Etah |
| 15 | Ranipur WLS | 1977 | 230.31 | Banda & Chitrakoot |
| 16 | Saman Bird WLS | 1990 | 5.26 | Mainpuri |
| 17 | Samaspur Bird WLS | 1987 | 7.99 | Rae Bareli |
| 18 | Sandi Birds WLS | 1990 | 3.09 | Hardoi |
| 19 | Sohagibarwa WLS | 1987 | 428.20 | Maharajganj |
| 20 | Sohelwa WLS | 1988 | 452.47 | Gonda, Shravasti & Balrampur |

| | | | | |
|---|---|---|---|---|
| 21 | Sur Sarovar Bird WLS | 1991 | 4.03 | Agra |
| 22 | Jai Prakash Narayan (Surhatal) Bird WLS | 1991 | 34.32 | Ballia |
| 23 | Turtle WLS | 1989 | 7.00 | Varanasi |
| 24 | Vijai Sagar WLS | 1990 | 2.62 | Mahoba |
| **Uttarakhand** | | | | |
| 1 | Askot WLS | 1986 | 600.00 | Pithoragarh |
| 2 | Binsar WLS | 1988 | 47.07 | Almora |
| 3 | Govind Pashu Vihar WLS | 1955 | 485.89 | Uttarkashi |
| 4 | Kedarnath WLS | 1972 | 975.20 | Chamoli & Rudraprayag |
| 5 | Mussoorie WLS | 1993 | 10.82 | Dehradun |
| 6 | Nandhaur WLS | 2012 | 269.96 | Nainital & Champawat |
| 7 | Sonanadi WLS | 1987 | 301.18 | Pauri Garhwal |
| **West Bengal** | | | | |
| 1 | Ballavpur WLS | 1977 | 2.02 | Birbhum |
| 2 | Bethuadahari WLS | 1980 | 0.67 | Nadia |
| 3 | Bibhuti Bhusan WLS | 1980 | 0.64 | North 24-Paraganas |
| 4 | Buxa WLS | 1986 | 267.92 | Jalpaiguri |
| 5 | Chapramari WLS | 1976 | 9.60 | Jalpaiguri |
| 6 | Chintamani Kar Bird WLS | 1982 | 0.07 | South 24-Paraganas |
| 7 | Haliday Island WLS | 1976 | 5.95 | South 24-Paraganas |
| 8 | Jorepokhri Salamander WLS | 1985 | 0.04 | Darjeeling |
| 9 | Lothian Island WLS | 1976 | 38.00 | South 24-Paraganas |
| 10 | Mahananda WLS | 1976 | 158.04 | Darjeeling & Jalpaiguri |
| 11 | Raiganj WLS | 1985 | 1.30 | North Dinajpur |
| 12 | Ramnabagan WLS | 1981 | 0.14 | Burdwan |
| 13 | Sajnakhali WLS | 1976 | 362.40 | South 24-Paraganas |
| 14 | Senchal WLS | 1976 | 38.88 | Darjeeling |
| 15 | West Sunderban WLS | 2013 | 556.45 | South 24-Paraganas |

(*Source*: Wildlife Institute of India)

**State-wise break up of Conservation Reserves (As on September, 2015)**

| S No. | Name | Area (Km²) | District |
|---|---|---|---|
| **Gujarat** | | | |
| 1. | Chharidhandh Wetland | 227 | Kachchh |
| **Haryana** | | | |
| 1. | Bir Bara Ban | 4.19 | Jind |
| 2. | Saraswati | 44.53 | Kurukshetra & Kaithal |
| **Himachal Pradesh** | | | |
| 1. | Darlaghat | 0.67 | Solan |
| 2. | Shilli | 1.49 | Solan |
| 3. | Shri Naina Devi | 17.01 | Bilaspur |
| **Jammu & Kashmir** | | | |
| 1. | Ajas (WL) | 1 | Bandipora |
| 2. | Ajas | 48 | Bandipora |
| 3. | Bahu | 19.75 | Jammu |
| 4. | Boodh Karbu | 12 | Kargil |
| 5. | Brain-Nishat | 15.75 | Srinagar |
| 6. | Chatlam, Pampore (WL) | 0.25 | Pulwama |
| 7. | Gharana (WL) | 0.75 | Jammu |
| 8. | Hokera (Ramsar Site) (WL) | 13.75 | Srinagar |
| 9. | Hygam (WL) | 7.25 | Baramula |
| 10. | Jawahar Tunnel | 18 | Doda |
| 11. | Khanagund | 15 | Pulwama |
| 12. | Khimber/Dara/Sharazbal | 34 | Srinagar |
| 13. | Khiram | 15.75 | Anantnag |
| 14. | Khonmoh | 67 | Pulwama |
| 15. | Khrew | 50.25 | Pulwama |
| 16. | Kukarian (WL) | 24.25 | Jammu |
| 17. | Malgam (WL) | 4.5 | Baramula |
| 18. | Manibugh (WL) | 4.5 | Pulwama |
| 19. | Mirgund (WL) | 4 | Budgam |
| 20. | Naganari | 22.25 | Baramula |
| 21. | Nanga (WL) | 15.25 | Jammu |
| 22. | Narkara (WL) | 3.25 | Budgam |
| 23. | Norrichain (WL) | 2 | Leh |
| 24. | Panyar | 10 | Pulwama |

| | | | |
|---|---|---|---|
| 25. | Pargwal (WL) | 49.25 | Jammu |
| 26. | Sabu | 15 | Leh |
| 27. | Sangral-Asa Chak (WL) | 7 | Jammu |
| 28. | Shallabugh (WL) | 16 | Srinagar |
| 29. | Shikargah | 15.5 | Pulwama |
| 30. | Sudhmahadev | 142.25 | Udhampur |
| 31. | Thein | 19 | Kathua |
| 32. | Tsomoiri (Ramsar Site) (WL) | 120 | Leh |
| 33. | Wangat/Chatergul | 12 | Srinagar |
| 34. | Zaloora, Harwan | 25.25 | Srinagar |
| **Karnataka** | | | |
| 1. | Afghanashini | 299.52 | Uttara Kannanda |
| 2. | Bedthi | 57.3 | Uttara Kannanda |
| 3. | Bankapur Peacock | 0.56 | Haveri |
| 4. | Basur Amruth Mahal Kaval | 7.36 | Chikmagalur |
| 5. | Hornbill Con Res | 52.5 | Uttara Kannanda |
| 6. | Jayamangali Blackbuck | 3.23 | Tumkur |
| 7. | Shalmale Ripariam Bio-System | 4.89 | N.A |
| 8. | Thungabhadra Otter | 25 | Bellary & Koppal |
| **Maharashtra** | | | |
| 1. | Bhorkada (Bhorgad) | 3.49 | Nashik |
| 2. | Kolamarka | 180.72 | Gadchiroli |
| **Punjab** | | | |
| 1. | Rakh Sarai Amanat Khan | 4.95 | Taran Taran |
| **Rajasthan** | | | |
| 1. | Bisalpur | 48.31 | Tonk |
| 2. | Jor Beed Gadwala Bikaner | 56.47 | Bikaner |
| 3. | Sundha Mata | 117.49 | Jalore, Sirohi |
| 4. | Gudha Vishnoi | 2.32 | Jodhpur |
| 5. | Shakambhari | 131 | Sikar & Jhunjhunu |
| 6. | Umedganj Bird | 2.72 | Kota |
| 7. | Jawai Band Leopard | 19.79 | Pali |
| 8. | Gogelao | 3.58 | Nagaur |
| 9. | Rotu | 0.73 | Nagaur |
| 10. | Bir Jhunjhunu | 10.47 | Jhunjhunu |
| **Tamil Nadu** | | | |
| **1.** | Tiruppadaimarathur | 0.03 | Tirunelveli |

| Uttarakhand | | | |
|---|---|---|---|
| 1. | Asan Wetland | 4.444 | Dehradun |
| 2. | Jhilmi Jheel | 37.84 | Haridwar |
| 3. | Pawalgarh | 58.25 | Nanital |
| 4. | Naina Devi Himalayan Bird | 111.9 | Nanital |
| | **Total Area (sq km)** | **2369.504** | |

*Source*: Wildlife Institute of India

Existing Community Reserves in India (As on February, 2016)

| S. No. | Name | Year of Estd. | Area (Km$^2$) | District |
|---|---|---|---|---|
| **Punjab** | | | | |
| 1. | Keshopur Chhamb | 2007 | 3.40 | Gurdaspur |
| 2. | Lalwan | 2007 | 12.67 | Hoshiarpur |
| **Kerala** | | | | |
| 1. | Kadalundi | 2007 | 1.50 | Malappuram |
| **Karnataka** | | | | |
| 1. | Kokkare Bellur | 2007 | 3.12 | Mandya |
| **Meghalaya** | | | | |
| 1. | Ka Khloo Thangbru Umsymphu | 2014 | 0.196 | East Jaintia Hills |
| 2. | Ka Khloo Pohblai Mooshutia | 2014 | 0.335 | East Jaintia Hills |
| 3. | Ka Khloo Langdoh Kur Pyrtuh | 2014 | 0.154 | West Jaintia Hills |
| 4. | Nongsangu | 2014 | 1.00 | Ri-bhoi |
| 5. | Raid Nongbri | 2014 | 0.70 | Ri-bhoi |
| 6. | Lum Jusong | 2014 | 0.70 | Ri-bhoi |
| 7. | Jirang | 2014 | 2.00 | Ri-bhoi |
| 8. | Raid Nonglyngdoh/ Pdah Kyndeng | 2014 | 0.75 | Ri-bhoi |
| 9 | Phudja-ud | 2014 | 1.20 | South West Khasi Hills |
| 10. | Lawbah | 2014 | 2.10 | East Khasi Hills |
| 11. | Ryngibah | 2014 | 0.80 | East Khasi Hills |
| 12. | Mongalgre | 2014 | 0.20 | West Garo Hills |
| 13. | Dangkipara | 2014 | 0.025 | South Garo Hills |
| 14. | Aruakgre | 2014 | 1.00 | North Garo Hills |

| | | | | |
|---|---|---|---|---|
| 15. | Resu Haluapra | 2014 | 0.50 | North Garo Hills |
| 16. | Kitmadamgre | 2014 | 0.70 | North Garo Hills |
| 17. | Kpoh Eijah | 2014 | 0.17 | West Khasi Hills |
| 18. | Miewsyiar | 2014 | 0.87 | West Khasi Hills |
| 19. | Umsum Pitcher Plant | 2014 | 0.40 | South West Khasi Hills |
| 20. | Lumkohkriah | 2014 | 6.11 | South West Khasi Hills |
| 21. | Ryngud | 2014 | 5.22 | East Khasi Hills |
| 22. | Thangkharang | 2014 | 1.11 | East Khasi Hills |
| | | Total Area | 46.93 | |

*Source*: Wildlife Institute of India

## Annexure–3

## Forestry/Agroforestry Syllabus for JRF

UNIT-I: Importance of Agriculture/Forestry/Livestock in national economy. Basic principles of crop production.Important rural development programmes in India Elementary principles of economics and agri-extension.Organizational set up of Agricultural Research, education and extension in India. Major diseases andpests of crops. Elements of statistics.

UNIT-II: Forest- importance, types, classification, ecosystem, biotic and abiotic components, ecological successionand climax, nursery and planting technique, social forestry, farm forestry, urban forestry, communityforestry, forest management, silvicultural practices, forest mensuration, natural regeneration, man-madeplantations, shifting cultivation, taungya, dendrology, hardwoods, softwoods, pulp woods, fuel woods,multipurpose tree species, wasteland management. Agroforestry – importance and land use systems,forest soils, classification and conservation, watershed management, forest genetics and biotechnology and tree improvement, tree seed technology, rangelands, wildlife – importance, abuse, depletion,management, major and minor forest products including medicinal and aromatic plants, forest inventory,aerial photo interpretation and remote sensing, forest depletion and degradation – importance andimpact on environment, global warming, role of forests and trees in climate mitigation, tree diseases,wood decay and discolouration, tree pests, integrated pest and disease management, biological andchemical wood preservation, forest conservation, Indian forest policies, Indian forest act, forest engineering, forest economics, joint forest management and tribology.

## Forestry/Agroforestry syllabus for SRF and ARS/NET

### Unit 1

National Forest Policy 1894, 1952 and 1988; Indian Forest Act, 1927; Forest Conservation Act,1980 and Wildlife Protection Act, 1972; Amendments 1991, 2003 and 2006, Biological Diversity Act, 2002, The Scheduled Tribes and Other traditional forest dwellers (Recognition of Forest Rights) Act, 2006 . Forests-extent, basis for classification and distribution in India; Geographical distribution and salient features of major world forest types; Phylogeographical regions and vegetation of India; Role of forests in national economy-productive, protective and ameliorative, tribal and rural livelihoods; Forest types of India: distribution and types; Succession, climax and retrogression; Concepts of biomass, productivity, energy flow and nutrient cycling in forest ecosystem; Migration and dispersal mechanism.

## Unit 2

Concept and definition of agroforestry, social forestry, community forestry and farm forestry; Benefits and constraints of agroforestry; Historical development of agroforestry and overview of global agroforestry systems. Classification of agroforestry systems: structural, functional, socio-economic and ecological; Diagnosis and design of agroforestry system; Land capability classification and land use; Criteria of an ideal agroforestry design, productivity, sustainability and adoptability; Multipurpose tree species and their characteristics suitable for agroforestry.

## Unit 3

Plant management practices in agroforestry; Tree-crop interactions: ecological and economic; Concept of complementarity, supplementarity and competition; Productivity, nutrient cycling and light, water and nutrient competition in agroforestry; Concept of allelopathy and its impact on agroforestry; Energy plantations -choice of species and management; Lopping of top-feed species such as frequency and intensity of lopping; Organic farming; Financial analysis and economic evaluation of agroforestry systems: cost benefit analysis and land equivalent ratio; Agroforestry practices and systems in different agro -ecological zones of India. Alley cropping, home gardens, shifting cultivation, shelterbelts and windbreaks, Principles and criteria of plant selection in agroforestry –Resource use efficiency in agroforestry.

## Unit 4

Extent and causes of land denudation; Effects of deforestation on soil erosion, land degradation, environment and rural economy; Wastelands: their extent, characteristics and reclamation; Watershed management and its role in social, economic and ecological development; Biomass production for fuel wood, small timber, raw material for plant-based cottage industries, non-wood forest products such as fibres, flosses, dyes, gums, resins & tannins, medicinal plants, essential oils, edible fruits, spices, bamboo and canes; Wood quality, logging, wood seasoning and wood preservation techniques; Plywood and pulp industries.

## Unit 5

Forest mensuration-definition, object and scope; Measurement of diameter, girth, height, stem form, bark thickness, crown width and crown length; Measurement methods and their principles. Measurement and computation of volume of logs and felled/standing trees; Construction and application of volume tables; Biomass measurement; Growth and increment; Measurement of crops; Forest inventory: kinds of enumeration, sampling methods, sample plots and aerial photo interpretation; Geographic information systems and remote sensing -concept and scope.

## Unit 6

Definition, object and scope of silviculture; Site factors -climatic, edaphic, physiographic, biotic and their influence on forest vegetation; Forest regeneration: natural and artificial; Silvicultural systems -high forest and coppice systems; Silviculture of important tree species -Populus, Eucalyptus, Dalbergia, Acacia, Tectona, Shorea, Prosopis, Casurina, Pinus, Gmelina, Azadirachta, Diospyros, Pterocarpus, Anogeissus, Santalum, Quercus and Albizia bamboo, Meliadubia, Ailanthus excelsa , Simaroubaand Karanja.

## Unit 7

Seed collection, processing, storage, viability and pre-treatment; Seed dormancy and methods for breaking dormancy; Seed testing and germination tests; Seed certification and ISTA Rules; Forest nursery -need, selection and preparation of site, layout and design of nursery beds; Types of containers; Root trainers; Growing media and sowing methods; Management of nursery-shading, watering, manuring, fertilizer application, weed control, insect pest and diseases control; Planting techniques: site selection, evaluation and protection; Soil working techniques for various edaphic and climatic conditions; Planting patterns; Plant spacing, manure and fertilizer application, irrigation/moisture conservation techniques; Choice of species. Afforestation on difficult sites: saline-alkaline soils, coastal sands, lateritic soils, wetlands, ravines and sand dunes, dry and rocky areas, cold desert; Tending operations -weeding, cleaning, climber cutting, thinning -mechanical, ordinary, crown and selection thinning, improvement felling, pruning and girdling; Forest fires: causes, types, impacts and control measures; Major forest pests and weeds.

## Unit 8

Forest management: definition and scope; Concept of sustained yield and normal forest; Rotation; Estimation of growing stock, density and site quality; Management of even aged and uneven aged forest; Regulation of yield in regular and irregular forests by area, volume, increment and number of trees; land equivalent ratio; Working plan; Joint forest management; Conservation and management of natural resources including wildlife; Forest evaluation; Internal rate of return, present net worth and cost benefit analysis.

## Unit 9

Tree improvement: nature and extent of variations in natural population; Natural selection; Concept of seed source/ provenance; Selection of superior trees; Seed production areas, exotic trees, land races; Collection, evaluation and maintenance of germplasm; Provenance testing. Gene tic gains; Tree breeding: general principles, mode of pollination and floral structure; Basics of forest genetics -inheritance, Hardy weinberg Law, genetic drift; Aims and methods of tree breeding. Seed orchard: types, establishment, planning and manageme nt, progeny test and designs; Clonal forestry -merits and demerits; Techniques of vegetative propagation, tissue culture, mist chamber; Role of growth substances in vegetative propagation

## Unit 10

Forestry in bio-economic productivity of different agro-eco-systems and environmental management; Global overview and classification of agroforestry systems; Tree-crop interaction in agroforestry; Biomass production for fuel' wood, small timber, raw material for plants -based cottage industries, Principle and criteria of plant selection in agroforestry; Resource use-efficiency in agroforestry. Measurement of rangeland productivity, Ecosystem services, Population estimation in wildlife –census methods, Man-Animal conflicts and management strategies.

## Unit 11

Measurement of trees and stand –diameter, girth, height, form and crown characteristics; Measurement methods and their principles; Volume/biomass estimation, volume tables; Measurement of rangeland productivity; Forest enumeration: sampling methods, sample plots, surveys and photo interpretation; Concept and application of GIS and remote sensing; Introduction to internal rate of return, present net worth, cost benefit analysis and land equivalent ratio; Agroforestry and environmental conservation; Role of green revolution in forest conservation in India. In situ and ex situ conservation of forest genetic resources –Sacred groves; Urban forestry –Choice of species, design, development and management, Eco-tourism.

## Unit 12

Climate change: greenhouse effect, sources and sinks of greenhouse gases, major greenhouses gases; Global climate change –its history and future predictions; Impact of climate change on agriculture, forestry, wildlife, water resources, sea level; Livestock, fishery and coastal ecosystems; International conventions on climate change; Global warming: effect of enhanced CO2 on productivity; Ozone layer depletion; Disaster management, floods, droughts, earthquakes; Tsunami, cyclones and landslides; Agroforestry and carbon sequestration

## Unit 13

Statistics: definition, object and scope; Frequency distribution; Mean, median, mode and standard deviation, introduction to correlation and regression; Experimental designs: basic principles, completely randomized, randomized block, Latin square and split plot designs.